The Morality of Money

Also by the authors

Adrian Walsh
ETHICS, MONEY AND SPORT (*with Richard Giulianotti*)
A NEO-ARISTOTELIAN THEORY OF SOCIAL JUSTICE

Tony Lynch
THE POLITICAL ECOLOGIST (*with David Wells*)

The Morality of Money

An Exploration in Analytic Philosophy

Adrian Walsh and Tony Lynch
University of New England, Australia

palgrave
macmillan

First published 2008 by
PALGRAVE MACMILLAN
Houndmills, Basingstoke, Hampshire RG21 6XS and
175 Fifth Avenue, New York, N.Y. 10010
Companies and representatives throughout the world

PALGRAVE MACMILLAN is the global academic imprint of the Palgrave
Macmillan division of St. Martin's Press, LLC and of Palgrave Macmillan Ltd.
Macmillan® is a registered trademark in the United States, United Kingdom
and other countries. Palgrave is a registered trademark in the European
Union and other countries.

ISBN-13: 978–0–230–53543–5 hardback
ISBN-10: 0–230–53543–7 hardback

This book is printed on paper suitable for recycling and made from fully
managed and sustained forest sources. Logging, pulping and manufacturing
processes are expected to conform to the environmental regulations of the
country of origin.

A catalogue record for this book is available from the British Library.

Library of Congress Cataloging-in-Publication Data
Walsh, Adrian J.
    The morality of money : an exploration in analytic philosophy /
    Adrian Walsh and Tony Lynch.
        p.   cm.
    Includes bibliographical references and index.
    ISBN 0–230–53543–7 (alk. paper)
    1. Money—Moral and ethical aspects.   I. Lynch, Tony, 1960–   II. Title.
    HG220.3.W35 2008
    174—dc22   2008016328

10   9   8   7   6   5   4   3   2   1
17   16   15   14   13   12   11   10   09   08

Printed and bound in Great Britain by
CPI Antony Rowe, Chippenham and Eastbourne

So merciless is the tyranny of economic appetites, so prone to self-aggrandisement the empire of economic interests, that a doctrine which confines them to their proper sphere, as the servant, not the master, of civilisation, may reasonably be regarded as among the pregnant truisms which are a permanent element in any sane philosophy.

R.H. Tawney, Religion and the Rise of Capitalism.

Contents

Preface

This project began five years ago, when we came to the realisation that money itself had not been subject to the kind of critical philosophical examination that many other social phenomena have enjoyed. It was written primarily in an old shed on the outskirts of the village of Uralla with one of us (alternatively) at the keyboard and the other pacing up and down. The tone of the book reflects in many ways the environment in which it was written.

We would like to thank our respective colleagues in the Philosophy Discipline at the University of New England and at the Centre for Applied Philosophy and Public Ethics at the University of Melbourne for encouragement and support. We are especially grateful to Peter Forrest, Anthony Fisher, Rutger Claasen, Constant Mews, Matthew Maxwell and Graham Maddox for their helpful comments on the earlier versions of the manuscript. Any mistakes or infelicities are, of course, entirely of our own making. We are grateful to *Philosophy* and the *Australasian Journal of Philosophy* for allowing us to make use of material which was previously published in their issues. We would also like to thank the editorial staff at Palgrave Macmillan, in particular Dan Bunyard, Melanie Blair and Priyanka Pathak, for their assistance in bringing the project to realisation. Finally, we would like to thank our families and partners for their understanding and patience whilst we have been engaged in this work.

Adrian Walsh and Tony Lynch
Uralla

1
Introduction

> ... there is nothing which requires more to be illustrated by philosophy than trade does.
>
> Samuel Johnson.[1]

Money and morality in everyday life

Money raises deeply perplexing moral issues that run through the whole of our lives. Many central questions in our lives involve financial considerations: Do we have enough money to raise children? How should we earn our money? How much do we want of it? What should we do with it? To whom should we bequeath it? From birth to death we live enmeshed in the skeins of commercial exchange. However, if we cannot escape this enmeshment, we can perhaps understand it; and having done so, we may find things go better morally.

Of course, there would be no moral philosophy of money to pursue if it were the case that all of us were simply 'in it for the money', so that all we ever thought of was how to acquire it, or spend it. While we may have cynical moments in which we profess that life is a matter of who has the most money when they die, this is not how most of us think.

We might not always notice it, but moral concerns over money arise in many different spheres of our private and public lives. To illustrate the pervasiveness of money-based moral issues in our everyday lives, consider the following seven illustrative cases, some of which would clearly lead us to a rejection of money in our lives and others in which our responses are more ambivalent.

Case 1: The Dogs of War
You are a soldier in the national forces of a certain country and you are approached by representatives from another country. They offer you large sums of money if you will fight for them.

Many would be inclined to condemn you for accepting such an offer, but why? Clearly, we may have nothing against national armies and their capacity for violence in the national interest, but to fight solely for pecuniary reasons seems morally wrong. Equally, the army that refuses to fight unless (say) it is given a massive pay rise may already strike us as less than ideal.

We face all kinds of public policy decisions. How should we decide them? Should we employ money measures to determine the fundamental questions of public policy? But this too raises moral concerns.

Case 2: Deciding Everything on a Dollar Basis
You are working for a council that has to decide about whether to allow oil drilling on an environmentally sensitive and beautiful coral reef. The mayor suggests that one should simply undertake a cost–benefit analysis of the relative financial benefits of the tourism that the reef brings compared to those to be derived from oil revenues.

Is it always desirable to deploy cost–benefit techniques that demand we place a price on everything under consideration? What moral standing should we give to cost–benefit analysis? Are there reasons for using criteria other than the monetary rewards?

There might be cases where cost–benefit analysis will deliver repugnant conclusions. It might lead, for instance, to the conclusion that poorer nations are under-polluted since people there earn less than in more developed nations, so that the morbidity and mortality costs of the impact of pollution is less than in those nations which, in fact, produce the toxins? Are objections to this mere, misguided, sentimentality?

Such concerns with money-measurement reflect more general worries about the ubiquity of pricing in the ever-increasing commodification of our lives. Is it really true that everything has its price? Should we determine all our political and social decisions on the basis of cost–benefit analyses when this means assigning a dollar value to things that are 'priceless' or 'irreplaceable'? Is it true that everything can be homogenised into quantitative monetary terms, so that Beethoven's Fifth Symphony is 'worth the same' as 400 000 cartons of beer or as the lives of 3000 subsistence farmers? Surely there are goods that are sacred and so should be excluded from monetary valuation.

We find money worries also in our private celebrations and rituals. Consider the following.

Case 3: The Bridal Register
You are invited to a friend's wedding and acquainted with the Bridal Register which stipulates just what you should buy as a gift, where you should buy it and roughly what price you should pay for it.

We might well resent, even be horrified by, such a demand with its unashamed financial valuation of our prospective gifts. Is it right to feel bullied by a list of 'desired items' at 'recommended cost', and is one wrong to think that somehow the very act of giving has been debased? Consider babysitting for a friend who, on their return, insists on paying you for your time. Is it wrong to feel that somehow the fact of payment has cheapened what you have done, and so, to some degree, debased the friendship?

Consider now our fourth example.

Case 4: The Really Indecent Proposal.
You are pressed for money. Perhaps seriously so. And a proposal is made to you by a wealthy friend: 'Let me sleep with your spouse and I will give you one million dollars.'

Is this offer to be welcomed? Even considered? (Would even considering it be a case of one-thought-too-many?)

The intrusion of money into the private sphere may lead us into drawing subtle moral distinctions between kinds of money paid.

Case 5: The Honorarium
A human rights activist comes to your university to give a talk on some worthy matter, such as the progress being made in the development of legislation protecting freedom of speech. She is awarded an honorarium of $1000 by the university as an expression of gratitude and to help cover her costs.

The financial reward is not understood by the university or the activist as simply a commercial transaction. There is, on all sides, a resistance to the idea that the relationship is essentially commercial in nature.

Similar points apply to the stipend of the clergyman. Typically, the clergyman does not understand the money he is afforded as *wages*, for he does not regard his work as wage-labour. (Presumably, this is the point of calling it a 'stipend' rather than a 'wage'.) This distinction marks a different relationship to what one does at work than is usually associated with jobs, and thus the stipend (and equally the honorarium) is not to be bluntly assimilated to wage-payment; indeed it may be seen as excluding it.

This ambiguity towards the markers of commercial exchange occasionally produces some oddities. Consider the peculiar institution of the Gentleman's Club, where no money actually changes hands at the time or place that services are provided. The point is not that money payments are eliminated – the bill for account arrives in the mail – but that the face-to-face relationships between the employee/service provider and the consumer do not present themselves as of the commercial kind; a point important to the recipients, if not the providers. But given that the exchanges are, in fact, commercial, and known by all the participants to be such, for what reasons might the members of such clubs wish for such an occlusion of the cash nexus? The attempt to maintain the appearance of a money-free zone even where that is a known fiction demonstrates our ambiguity about such matters.

There might even be instances where we would welcome the advent of specifically monetary relations. In *The Philosophy of Money* the German sociologist and cultural critic Georg Simmel (1858–1918) argues that freedom came to the serf not when he lost that status, but when he could pay his tithes in money rather than being asked to provide a specific amount of a certain product (e.g. wheat, cheese).[2] When it is a question of money, the serf is no longer bound to the production of a particular product, but is free to acquire the necessary monies as he sees fit. Now money does not look so much like an insult to a valued relationship, so much as a conduit to a greater degree of personal freedom.[3]

But if there are cases of commercial exchange that we take to be morally permissible, even desirable, this does not mean that such exchanges are insulated from our moral concerns. For instance, taking out a loan might be morally unobjectionable, but are all loan practices acceptable? Consider the following.

Case 6: The Pay-Day Loan
You are rung by the Electricity Commission to inform you that if you do not pay your electricity bill within 24 hours, your power will be cut off. Pay-day is a week away and you have no money whatsoever until then. You go to a pawn-broker who will lend you the money against your next pay, but at an extremely high interest rate. Out of necessity you accept the loan.

Such pay-day loans are typically for small amounts, at high interest rates, secured against the recipient's next pay cheque. They may be required to meet necessity, but they tend to impose their own demands that may lead us further and deeper into debt. Often the necessities in question are the result of an addiction for which the loan provides the most temporary of relief while further embedding the demand and the associated self-destructive behaviours.

Case 6 concerns *consumption* loans. But would we have the same kind of worries about *investment* loans? Who could argue against levying interest on a loan oriented towards future development? But what if the level of interest charged is such that it more than swallows any investment returns, and demands further loaning at interest to fulfil the repayments? This is the case with much lending to third-world countries, and it results in chronic and seemingly irremediable debt. The debt-servitude of third-world countries tied to interest repayments and 'structural adjustments', which leaves little or nothing for national development, is surely of great concern.

Our intuitions about the morality of everyday commercial life cover the *cost* or *price* of goods themselves. We may, for example, have objections to profiteering in times of crises on the grounds that the prices charged are unjust. They are unjust because the commercial agents are taking advantage of the combination of our need, heavy demand and shortages in supply. We might also feel that there are occasions where need itself, regardless of levels of supply and demand, should set the price. Consider the following case.

Case 7: The Just Price?
You are working for a government agency in a developing nation that is ravaged by diseases that can only be treated by the use of expensive pharmaceuticals. You come across a very cheap supply of the required drugs produced in another country which ignores patent laws.

You might wonder whether the prices set by the pharmaceutical company that owns the patent are fair and whether – if they are unfair – that might justify buying the patent-free drugs. Many of us have the intuition that we should ignore the patents. But there are a range of questions here. Should prices be set by the market? Should they be subsidised so as to enable all to have access? Would selling the non-patent drugs involve injustice with respect to the resources the pharmaceutical company has invested in their development, or would it retard further research?

These seven cases are not intended to be systematic or exhaustive but illustrative. What they show is that we often have very complicated moral attitudes towards money, payment and the cash nexus. They introduce us to the range and subtlety of those moral judgements by which we may make distinctions between the appropriate and the inappropriate forms of exchange, between the appropriate and the inappropriate roles pecuniary concerns may play as we pursue our activities, and between the proper and the improper operations of pricing under conditions of scarcity and the insistent demands of need.

While there may be 'tough-minded' economists and philosophers who are prepared to condemn such attitudes as errors or delusions, and so ignore the distinctions and discriminations reflected in our everyday judgements, it is surely incumbent on moral philosophers to take a more sympathetic approach. Before one condemns something as nonsense, the first thing to do is to try and make sense of it, but it is just this effort that is generally eschewed.

Such moral intuitions about money and commercial life are remarkably resilient. As contemporary economists Bruno Frey in Switzerland and Richard Thaler in the United States have demonstrated, even an informed acquaintance with modern economic life and neoclassical economic theory is no guarantee that such attitudes will simply fall away, even though some economic theory might hold that they are simply misguided.[4] In the 1990s Frey asked 1750 households in Switzerland and Germany for their response to the following question:

> A hardware store has been selling snow shovels for 30 Swiss Francs (or 30 German Marks). The morning after a heavy snow storm, the store raises the price to CHF/DM40. How do you evaluate this rise?[5]

– He discovered that 83% of the respondents of these economically literate societies thought the opportunistic pricing of the hardware store owners was unfair.[6] Perhaps this reflects psychological or historical inertia. At the very least, it is a question that an investigation of the morality of money should leave open.

Contemporary moral philosophy and money

It is one thing to have moral intuitions when it comes to money and the kinds of relationships it establishes, crowds out or ignores; it is another thing to understand the grounds of these intuitions. If the former is simply empirical, the latter is philosophical. Now the challenge is to see if these intuitions, given our more general moral commitments, make sense to us.

Given the nature of our enquiry, one might naturally turn to contemporary moral philosophy for some answers. But for all its naturalness such a turn brings no obvious or immediate advance. For the truth is that while some contemporary analytic moral philosophers have considered various related questions, they have typically done so by focusing on *the market*. The central concern has been about the proper scope or range of the market, and while answering this question may presuppose certain moral intuitions about monetarisation, these are not the focus of attention. They are presumed, rather than explored. Indeed, given the market focus they cannot be adequately explored, for they are about money, not markets.

When we feel discomfort at a friend attempting to 'pay' us for helping them out with some chore, or when we find something repugnant about paying and receiving money for sexual relations, we are worrying about the place of money in what is going on, not anything about markets.

That philosophers have typically failed to explore our moral intuitions about money is something that needs explanation, not merely remediation. For when it comes to other morally charged issues – such as those concerned with sex, or with violence – moral philosophers have found much to say. Given the centrality of money in our lives, and the way that monetarised relationships not only underpin the formal market but extend well beyond it, it is regrettable that philosophers have not approached the morality of money with the same vigour as they have approached matters of violence and sex.

Moral philosophy's shortcomings when it comes to dealing with the morality of money sometimes lie in certain well-entrenched ideas philosophers have had about the nature of philosophy itself. After all, the man we often take to be the founder of moral philosophy – Socrates (427–347 BC) – believed that his own pursuit of philosophy should be untainted by commercial considerations. Those who pursued philosophy with financial goals in mind were 'merchants of the soul' and to be condemned as such.[7] Without that repudiation we do not have philosophy, but sophistry. This anti-commercialism was deepened and expanded by subsequent philosophers, most notably Socrates avower followers Plato (427–347 BC) and Diogenes (d. 324 BC). According to Plato the true philosopher not only refuses to dirty his hands with money-grubbing of any kind, he strives always and everywhere to transcend the material world for a life among the eternal transcendent forms, while Diogenes went even further and insisted philosophy demanded we reject not merely the commercial, but human social life altogether.

Even that most worldly of philosophers, David Hume (1711–1776) felt it important to insist that philosopher *qua* philosopher lives and thinks in a realm outside of, and separate from, 'the realm of business'.[8] And certainly Bertrand Russell, when he found he needed money to alleviate certain largely self-induced financial pressures, did not think he was actually doing philosophy when he was writing his popular works on philosophical themes. These were, as he ruefully admitted, journalistic potboilers.

To the extent that this rests on an axiomatic rejection of the 'mundane', and a commitment to the transcendent, there is nothing to say beyond the fact that while this kind of philosophy might well lead us out of the world, it throws no light at all on this world.

Such anti-monetarism would seem to rest on a *non sequitur*. For while it may be true that one cannot do philosophy, including moral philosophy, if one's animating goal is monetary reward rather than truth, it does not at all follow that one cannot think philosophically about money and the moral issues it clearly does raise in our lives. To do so would be to conflate our mentioning of the idea of money with its usage. The case is no different from that of sex or violence. Of course, one will struggle to think philosophically about either if one's basic concern in thinking about such matters is (say) to have sex or act violently, but that is not what the philosopher is aiming at.

However, what if we are wrong in thinking of money as we might think of sex or of violence. After all, while sex and violence might be seen as essential elements of the human condition, money itself has a history, and a complicated one at that. Why think that money is always one and the same thing? Might it not be related, but still quite different things in different times and circumstances? Certainly, this was something Marx (1818–1883) insisted on, distinguishing in *Capital* between 'money that is money only, and money that is capital'.[9]

If money is not one thing, but many and different things, then it follows that there cannot be a philosophy of money, for there is no specific subject matter which it might address. We do not think that this 'objection from variability' provides a serious obstacle to our project. As we shall see, those moral intuitions we might have about money and its place and role in our lives fix upon features of money which are plausibly seen as universal and invariable. In all economies, from the most primitive to the most sophisticated, the morally relevant features of money are one and the same. Money anywhere involves the commercial nexus if not markets; it involves commensurating different kinds of things and, potentially, all things; and it implies substitutability and the operations of a calculative rationality.

If the lack of philosophical concern over the morality of money may rest on the view that philosophy leads us out of the mundane world, not into it, or on the view that money is so contextually multifarious that there is no single subject matter to explore, there is a different, more radical view according to which monetarisation lies at the very heart of philosophy and so is not something that we will ever be able to see from the point of view of philosophy.

In his recent book *Money and the Early Greek Mind* the classicist Richard Seaford argues that the development of money in the Ancient Greek world produced philosophy.[10] The key idea is that monetarisation makes available the idea of the universe as an impersonal system and involves a calculative rationality. Money transformed Greek social relationships, changing what had been a world constituted by structures of personal allegiance and hostility into a world of impersonal relationships constituted around the cash nexus. It was this transformation from the personal to the impersonal that made available that view on the universe which philosophy exploited.

Such views about the generation and dependence of philosophy on the monetarised are not limited to classicists such as Seaford. They have been the common property of many on the Marxist Left. To the extent that one has a materialist view of the production of ideas, it follows at once that a system of ideas cannot comprehend the reality of things.

> What else does the history of ideas prove, than that intellectual production changes its character in proportion as material production is changed?[11]

Thus a moral philosophy of money can amount to nothing more than an *ideology* of money. Instead of comprehension and understanding we have rationalisation and reflection.

What should we make of such views? Is there really no room for a philosophy of money or, indeed, for any kind of philosophy at all? Undoubtedly there is no room for a moral philosophy of money if historical materialism is true, but then again there is no reason for thinking that it is true. And, even worse, if one does think that it is true, then this can not be because this view is the most rational or best supported by the available evidence.

What may be true is something far weaker. For it is certainly possible that money and monetarisation open up or encourage ways of viewing the world that have had an impact on philosophical theorising. It may even be true that certain styles of philosophising reflect economic interests. But all that means is that we must be as careful as we can when we reflect on money and its moral significance in our lives. We must ensure that we are not simply projecting elements of monetarised reality onto the world generally; and we should do our best to avoid the temptation to simply rationalise that which is in our economic self-interest.

Finally, there is a different view as to why there is no interesting moral philosophy of money. This view holds that markets are shaped by an 'invisible hand' which turns the pursuit of personal advantage into the unintended production of public goods. The role of money therein is simply as a medium of exchange that facilitates the efficiency of the mechanism.

We take up 'invisible hand' accounts of the market in a later chapter. For now the important thing for us is that this view – whatever its credentials – is about money-in-the-market. But money is not restricted to such markets. Nor are those intuitions we have about various kinds of exchange necessarily intuitions about markets. First off, they are intuitions about the place for money in this or that context or case. Obviously, such intuitions will have implications for how we think of markets, and of markets of this kind, but such implications are derivative, not foundational.

We do not think these arguments against the possibility of a genuine moral philosophy of money are persuasive. Further, we think it unfortunate that they seem to have had such a stultifying impact on philosophy when it comes to investigating the morality of money. After all, worries about money and monetarisation have been, and continue to be, persistent and pressing. Certainly, they have been historically significant. Consider, to take but one of many possible examples, the consequences of the criticisms of Martin Luther (1483–1546) of Papal Indulgences (through which one could purchase time out of Purgatory) and the ultimate costs of these criticisms to the Roman Catholic Church through the role his ideas played in the coming of the Reformation. Think too of the role of money-lending in shaping European society and its more recent impact, in terms of crippling debt, on lesser developed countries. Alternatively, we need only reflect for a moment on contemporary concerns with the sale of body parts, and with the 'just pricing' of needed pharmaceuticals to see the historical significance of moral concerns over money.

But if modern moral philosophers have, for various reasons, given little or no philosophical attention to the philosophy of money, this is not true of much earlier generations of philosophers. The Ancients, the Patristics and the Medievals all looked hard and closely at such matters. They gave much thought to such things as the just price and to the ethics of usury; and particular attention to the relationship – or more precisely, the antagonism – between the sacred and the monetarised.

One reason for this lacuna is sheer ignorance; another is the prevalence of the view that contemporary attempts to moralise our dealings with money and markets involve novel processes and concerns, so that any attempt to learn from earlier thinkers is simply anachronistic.[12] As we shall see, when we explore the debates on just price and the morality of commerce, learning from earlier thinkers is not anachronistic.

But if analytic philosophers have not addressed these issues – and these are issues which they should address – this is not true of the arts. In history, literature, drama and film we find numerous explorations of various ethical issues regarding money. In working through moral issues relating to money we will sometimes make use of such reflections.

The morally salient features of money

Our project then is to develop a moral philosophy of money. This requires a sensitive approach to the way that money matters in our lives as we embrace, or alternatively distance ourselves from, money concerns and the commercial life. Such an approach will try to systematise the distinctions we draw between the appropriate and the inappropriate modes of involvement in the world of money and then see whether on closer analysis these distinctions deserve our respect.

An important step is to clarify what might be the morally salient features of money. Traditionally, economists ascribe four functional roles to money in the economic life: a *unit of account* where this means it assigns a particular value to discrete commodities; a *store of abstract value* in that it can be accumulated for future use; a *means of payment* in that we use it to pay for goods purchased; and a *medium of exchange* in so far as it provides us with a means to the facilitation of commerce.[13]

It is in the final role, as a *medium of exchange*, that we find considerable discussion of the moral implications of the use of money. Beginning with Aristotle, who says that it was as a medium of exchange that money was invented, many writers pay attention to this feature of money. The twentieth-century economist Lionel Robbins (1898–1984) held that 'money *as such* is obviously merely a means – a medium of exchange'.[14] He follows David Hume, who suggested that 'Money is not, properly speaking, one of the subjects of commerce; but only the instrument which men have agreed upon to facilitate the exchange of one commodity for another.'[15] Thorstein Veblen (1857–1929) pressed this idea further towards the stronger claim that money has no moral significance beyond this: 'Money values have . . . . no significance other than that of purchasing power over consumable goods.'[16]

This stands in contrast to that tradition for which money involves more than just greasing the wheels of trade. Think here of the polemical violence of Marx in his early writings:

> Money abases all the gods of mankind and changes them into commodities. Money is the universal self-sufficient value of all things. It has, therefore, deprived the whole world, both the human world and nature, of their own proper value. Money is the alienated essence of man's work and existence; this essence dominates him and he worships it.[17]

Or think of Immanuel Kant (1724–1804), who suggested that 'everything has either a price or a dignity'.[18] For these writers money has moral significance over and above its role as a medium of exchange.

We are concerned with more than just the four functional properties of money as the economist might conceive of them; we are concerned with those features of money that impact on our understanding and conception of what has value and, particularly, what has moral value. We direct the reader's attention to four such features: the *universality* of money valuation and exchange; the *commensurating* of values that money permits; the possibilities for *unlimited acquisition* it opens up; and its role as a discriminating *distributive mechanism*. Let us take each in turn, beginning with the idea of universality.

In a barter economy, exchange takes place only if the trading parties have in their possession just those goods and services that each requires. If not, then exchange is unlikely to occur. Money, on the other hand, is *a universal substitute*. Even if parties to an exchange do not possess particular goods or services that the other requires, they can still exchange. As a universal substitute money places all commodities in relationship to one another, and in doing so is, as Aristotle (384–322 BC) says, 'our guarantor for future exchange'.[19]

Philosophers have reacted differently to this universality. Marx focuses on the negative aspect and describes money as the 'universal pander' for which all goods are substitutable and, conversely, which makes commodity goods substitutable for each and every other commodity. But, equally, there is a long tradition of viewing this in a positive light. The Medieval philosopher and theologian Albertus Magnus (c.1200–1280) suggests that it is precisely through its role as a universal pander that money opens the way 'for a flux and reflux of grateful services [which] holds the city together'.[20]

A second morally salient feature of money is its role as a *commensurating device*. Money provides a common measure of value (or 'universal comparator') and in so doing commensurates. Money allows us to rank goods in an ordering. It allows us to draw equivalences between various commodities. In the *Nicomachean Ethics*, Aristotle makes the somewhat startling observation about the relationship between three commodities, namely houses, beds and money. A house he says is worth five minae (an ancient Greek coinage) and a bed one minae, and knowing this means that we can calculate that five beds are equal to one house.[21] His point is that since money is a measure that makes things commensurable, it also equates them.

Not all philosophers have viewed this positively. Marx based much of his moral criticism of the realm of Mammon on this feature of money.[22] Since money serves as a 'universal measure of value', as soon as a commodity such as a table 'emerges as a commodity' it becomes comparable with all other goods, something he finds morally objectionable.[23] An antagonism to this capacity for universal comparison is also to be found in contemporary debates on commensurability by writers such as Elizabeth Anderson and Cass Sunstein.[24]

But, equally, positive discussions of this feature of money are also available. For instance, Plato, in *The Laws*, maintains that it is precisely this commensurating capacity of money that makes the provision of the necessities of life possible by facilitating the possibilities of rational exchange.[25]

A third morally salient feature of money concerns the opportunities for *accumulation* it opens up. Money is a store of value and one that from its own nature is subject to no upper limits of accumulation. This was a point made forcefully by the English philosopher John Locke (1632–1704).[26] Other goods, such as apples, are subject to spoliation and therefore accumulation beyond the point of individual consumption involves the wilful waste of resources. Exceeding the 'bounds of his just property' does not reside in the amount one accumulates, but 'the perishing of anything uselessly in it'.[27] However, with the advent of money, accumulation is no longer wasteful since the value does not disappear; money represents 'some lasting thing that men might keep without spoiling'.[28] For Locke, it is only with the advent of money that personal accumulation of wealth becomes morally justified. But as is the way with philosophers, this is contentious.[29] For Aristotle, it was exactly the possibilities for endless accumulation that constituted no small part of its destructive evil. Since there is no limit to the amount of money one can accumulate, the pursuit of money is an activity without an end point (without a *telos*) – regressive and circular – and without conditions for its satisfaction it cannot be a proper human activity.[30]

The last morally salient feature of money we consider involves its role as a *distributive mechanism*. Money both creates and exists within the marketplace and as such facilitates the allocation of those goods available as commodities.

The distributive mechanism provided by the commercial realm is a simple one, in which access to any good is (ideally at least) conditional solely upon the possession of economic wealth.[31] As Moll Flanders wryly notes in Daniel Defoe's novel of the same name, 'with money in the pocket one is at home anywhere'.[32]

Some like Simmel have focused on the socially progressive aspects of the use of money to allocate goods. Allocating goods according to willingness to pay can undermine oppressive traditional social structures. Indeed the sumptuary laws of the early-modern period which attempted to restrict the dress and culinary choices of those who were not born of nobility were a conservative response to this revolutionary aspect of the commercial realm. As Tim Park notes, the sumptuary laws of Medici Florence involved the following restrictions:

> No meal with more than two courses for the common classes. No more than a certain number of guests at any given meal. No clothes of more than one colour, unless you are a knight or his lady. Or a magistrate, perhaps. Or a doctor. No fine materials for children. No soft leather soles on your white linen socks. No fur collars. No buttons on women's clothes except between the wrist and elbow, and for maids, none at all. For maids, in fact, no fancy headdress and no high heels, just kerchief and clogs.[33]

Sumptuary laws constrain the commercial realm.[34] But without them, so long as one has money in one's pocket then one can buy whatever clothes one likes, regardless of one's bloodline. It is financial wealth, not personal status or individual relationships, which determines the access to commodities.[35]

At the same time, many philosophers have focused on ways in which the market does discriminate between those with economic wealth and those without it. Persons with little economic power are effectively excluded from access to many commodities. Similarly, those with wealth may be able to buy exemption from monetarised burdens, such as buying one's way out of war-service. Here our concerns over money feed directly into concerns over social justice.

It is worth noting that some of our interest will be directed more to issues of personal morality, and at other times the focus will be on issues of social justice and so on matters of public policy. We need to be careful not to conflate the two. Ordinary usage of the terms 'morality' and 'justice' is often ambiguous between the individual and the public and this is something that has afflicted moral philosophy as well. Plato, notoriously, gives an account of justice in *The Republic* which tries to explain what justice is as a personal virtue by investigating what it amounts to in the city. In developing an account of the morality of money we need to be vigilant about what sense is at issue.

Our moral philosophy of money: The approach herein

There is a widespread view according to which philosophy, and thereby moral philosophy as one of its sub-disciplines, involves the use of arcane language designed to lead us from the superficial and trivial world of 'Appearances' to that deep and important underlying reality which constitutes the 'Real World'. Philosophy is concerned with another world, another realm. This is an entirely different philosophical cast of mind to ours. Many may regard the material with which we deal – money motives, pricing, commodification, money-lending and, more generally, the morality of commercial life – as unphilosophical and mundane. We, however, do not try to go beyond the appearances but rather to *comprehend* them. In our view philosophy does not involve flight from the everyday, but demands a critical engagement with it. Indeed there is no reason to be less intellectually rigorous about the quotidian than about the structure of far-off possible worlds (indeed there may well be more). Money provides just as many opportunities for rigorous analysis as any other philosophical subject.

In order to explore this 'mundane' subject matter we employ what some might see as an equally mundane Aristotelian methodology. We hold that such enquiry should begin with our everyday intuitions, problems, difficulties, fears, reservations and concerns that arise as we deal and trade in the world of money. Everyday 'folk' views on the morality of commercial life provide us with a starting point. We take these folk views seriously (although not uncritically) and ask whether on reflection we can still endorse them or whether they should be modified or repudiated. For instance, does the idea that money corrupts make sense on closer scrutiny? The methodology is Aristotelian, in the sense of his employment of what he called *endoxa* to begin any philosophical enquiry.[36] (For Aristotle, dialectic was a method 'from which we will be able to syllogise from common beliefs about every topic proposed to us, and will say nothing conflicting when we give an account ourselves'.)[37]

Our *particular* way of making sense of those intuitions about commercial life involves what we want to call *economic casuistry*. We are neither bluntly antagonistic to commercial life nor unblushingly enamoured of it. We draw distinctions between different kinds of monetarised exchanges and different kinds of mercenary motives. Perhaps the closest parallel to the ethics of money we aim to develop is with just war theory. For just war theorists neither bluntly endorse nor condemn military violence; they are neither pacifists nor militarists. They distinguish between the legitimacy of offensive and defensive warfare, and between the motives that underpin such ventures; they distinguish between legitimate and illegitimate ways of carrying on such warfare and of ending such fighting, and the appropriate ways that various kinds of people may then be treated. In the same way we distinguish between proper and improper ways of pursuing and deploying money.

It is important that our general endorsement of commerce not be confused with a view that would approve of everything being bought and sold. The fact that we are not opposed to money and markets as such does not mean that there are not commercial acts that are beyond the pale. For the most part our economic casuistry involves placing constraints on commercial activity, rather than banning it outright. There will be some things – for instance, people – that should not be bought and sold.

One further distinctive feature of our approach is the focus on *motives*. In distinguishing between legitimate and illegitimate forms of commerce we pay particular attention to the motives that animate commercial agents in their dealings with money. (We are following a long tradition that is presently under-recognised.) In *The Politics* Aristotle famously distinguished two forms of commercial exchange, the *natural* and the *unnatural* or *chrematistic*.[38] Natural exchange involves the selling of goods originally produced for household consumption which have subsequently been found to be in excess of the household's needs. Chrematistic exchange, on the other hand, involves the sale of goods that were intentionally produced for realising a financial profit and for this reason it stands condemned. The moral distinction depends on whether monetary motives have directed the production of the good. In the

Medieval period writers such as Saint Thomas Aquinas (c.1225–1274) held that it was permissible to pursue money as a goal (and to engage in chrematistic production) so long as the money was sought as a mere means to other morally acceptable ends (such as providing for one's family or for reasons of charitable giving).

We draw a different moral distinction between money motives. On our line of thinking, the pursuit of money for its own sake is permissible *so long as we do not violate any fundamental moral norms in that pursuit.* For us it is the person who will do *anything* for money or will pursue profit whatever its source who is of real concern. Note, however, that we do not hold that questions of the morality of commerce can be entirely explained through an analysis of motives, for outcomes also matter, but we do hold that it is an important part of the story; and in many cases, the most important part of the story.

Also in our account the notion of a *moral hazard* plays a pivotal role. A moral hazard we take to be something akin to what the Medieval Schoolmen thought of as an 'occasion of sin'. The point is not that dealings with money are, in and of themselves, morally wrong – typically they are not – but that such dealings may see us confront temptations to a variety of vicious, or at least morally undesirable, actions and modes of regard. For example, they may lead us in our pursuit of filthy lucre to disregard or override important moral side-constraints, or to view other people as mere means to the accumulation of capital. The use and pursuit of money is not necessarily wrong or necessarily connected to some vice; it is simply that it has a *tendency* towards those ends.[39]

Our analysis centres on money as a moral hazard not because we wish to condemn the pecuniary in all of its manifestations, but because of the potentially adverse moral impact it has on our motives once they are incorporated into the cash nexus. There is always the danger that the pursuit of money will become all-consuming. As the Roman aesthetician Longinus (c.100 AD) noted, it is hard to see how:

> . . . if we value the possession of unlimited wealth, or, to give the truth of the matter, make a god of it, we can avoid allowing the evils that naturally attend its entry into our souls.[40]

It is the evils that follow from a pursuit of money *unconstrained by moral considerations* that are our object of study. Money and the profit-motive are necessary elements of our lives – at least as we can currently conceive of them – but we must avoid or minimise the moral hazards that commercial life places in our way. Our aim is to provide a moral typology of the various forms of the profit-motive and to delineate the logical structure of the relationship between commercial activity and non-instrumental modes of valuing so as to allow us to navigate our way around these moral hazards.

We begin with an extended exploration of the views of various philosophers in the Western tradition on the morality of commerce in general.

2
Money, Commerce and Moral Theory

Introduction

Western culture has long held a suspicion of the morally contaminating powers of money. When the father of Nausica in Homer's *Odyssey* wished to add insult to injury to the half-drowned Odysseus, he called him a merchant.[1] Think, too, of Judas Iscariot for whom the siren call of money was such that it led him to betray his God.

> Then one of the twelve, who was called Judas Iscariot, went to the priests and said 'What will you give me if I deliver him to you?' And they paid him thirty pieces of silver. And from that moment he sought an opportunity to betray him.
>
> (Matt. 26:14)[2]

Recall the legend of King Midas who, being granted one wish by the grateful God Dionysus for rescuing his drunken companion Silenus, asks that all he touches turn to gold. He narrowly avoids being the richest man ever to starve to death only by a later appeal to Dionysus, who advises him to wash in the waters of the river Paktalos so that the golden touch might be washed away.[3]

Equally, the Western philosophical tradition has a long history of reflections on commercialism that involve a suspicion, indeed repudiation of the profit-motive.[4] Perhaps this should not be so surprising when one considers the non-worldly tendencies of philosophers like Diogenes, who lived in a barrel, and for whom the asceticism of the contemplative life was seen as the highest possible calling. When asked by Alexander the Great, whose shadow was upon him, as to what he would like the Emperor of the Known World to give him, Diogenes famously asked

Alexander to move out of his light. This philosophical contempt for commerce did not have to mean a refusal to engage with the worldly things. It is said that the Greek Ionian philosopher Thales (d.c.546/5 BC) responded to slurs on his intelligence for pursuing philosophical and not commercial interests by using his philosophical knowledge to corner the market in olive presses and make a killing, thereby defending the grandeur and power of philosophy as the choice of the intellectually and socially superior person.[5]

This anti-commercialism cannot simply be explained away in terms of the idiosyncrasies of philosophers, for it reflects deeper currents in Western thinking. The philosophers merely picked out aspects of commercial life that many in their societies also saw as vicious. When Plato writes that commerce 'fills the land with wholesaling and retailing, breeds shifty and deceitful habits in a man's soul and makes citizens distrustful and hostile', he was expressing a maxim common to his audience.[6] In these following sections we explore the works of writers who saw vice as a *systematic* feature of our engagement with money, and with the commercial society that arises out of such transactions.

The Ancients

Let us begin with Plato. Plato (427–344 BC) was born in Athens to a distinguished ruling class family, and was a student of Socrates. In 388 BC he founded his famous Academy, a school that Aristotle attended. Plato wrote on many topics, metaphysics, aesthetics, politics, epistemology, but he also wrote on money and the market. Plato was particularly wary of commerce and indeed possessions in general, and saw both market-exchange and personal ownership as the province of desire, not spirit or reason, and so something essentially corrupting.

In his sketch of the perfectly just society in the *Republic*, in which there were three classes – the guardians or philosopher kings, the auxiliaries or warriors, and the artisans – the philosopher kings were to own everything in common, and to leave the provision of the material necessities of life to the artisan class (and, presumably – though he does not explicitly say so – to their slaves). Society was to be ruled by the philosophers because the direction of the state, just as, in a different field, the direction of a ship, should be in the hands of those with the necessary expertise. Such expertise meant the pursuit and discernment of that which was Good, True and Beautiful; and such pursuit required, Plato felt, a purity of attention that an enmeshment in commerce or the concerns of ownership necessarily compromises; both by distracting one from the appropriate ends, and, worse, by the threatened corruption of our sense of what is of real value.

It is true that in Book VIII of the *Republic* [554–555] Plato insists that, all things being equal, the merchant will have a *reputation* for honesty and quite rightly so. He will be more *respectable* than many people. But it would be a mistake to conclude that Plato is therefore praising the virtues of the merchant life. On the contrary, he describes the merchant as a 'shabby fellow who saves something out of everything and makes a purse for himself'; he is one who makes a 'blind god director of his chorus'.[7] To applaud the life of the merchant is to fail to recognise that the character traits it instils are those of appearance, and so not *true* virtues at all. The merchant's commitment to virtue is not to it, and its value, but is instrumental; it depends upon it being necessary for personal enrichment; and this can be shown counterfactually when the merchant is placed in a situation where vicious, and not virtuous, behaviour will be rewarded. If you wish to understand the real nature of the merchant, then, Plato tells Glaucon:

> You should see him in some position which gives him complete liberty to act dishonestly, as in the guardianship of an orphan.[8]

Then you will see that:

> in his ordinary dealings which give him a reputation for honesty he coerces his bad passions by an enforced virtue; not making them see that they are wrong, or taming them by reason, but by necessity and fear constraining them, because he trembles for his possessions...[9]

Plato holds that the merchant who trades, and the artisan who produces, for commercial reasons, is threatened with a degrading moral pathology:

> when he has made reason and spirit sit down on the ground obediently on either side of their sovereign, and made them his slaves, he compels the one to think only of how lesser sums may be turned into larger ones, and will not allow the other to worship and admire anything but riches and rich men, or to be ambitious of anything so much as the possession of wealth and the means of acquiring it.[10]

While the Guardians need to be immune to the concerns of ownership and the snares of the marketplace, the state they govern, as Plato's tripartite class division recognises, needs those who take such concerns seriously. And it would be a hard saying – and one Plato does not make – to insist that such persons *must* succumb to this pathology. For even if their virtues are not true virtues, still with sufficient strength of character the merchant and the artisan can avoid moral debasement so long as they respect the following principle for the acquisition and deployment of money and riches:

> And again in the acquisition of wealth is there not a principle of order and harmony which he will observe? He will not allow himself to be dazzled by the foolish applause of the world, and heap up riches to his own infinite harm. . . . He will look at the city which is within him, and take heed that no disorder occur in it, such as might arise either from affluence or from want; and upon this principle he will regulate his property and gain or spend according to his means.[11]

Even if the merchant does succumb to vice, Plato allows that it is better to have bad merchants than bad rulers. Cobblers who pretend to be the workmen that they are not may endanger our wallets and our feet, but they are no great danger to a state. However, guardians of laws and of the city who are not what they pretend to be destroy utterly, since they are required for good government and happiness.[12]

While the antagonism of the *Republic* might be regarded as the reaction of an aristocratic lover of the contemplative life to the distractions the grubby world of money and possessions provides, the same cannot be said of *The Laws* written late in Plato's life, which contains a swingeing attack upon commercial life in general. Plato begins with an embittered discussion of the hospitality of innkeepers – indeed, the discussion is so intemperate that one is driven to the conclusion that Plato had unfortunate dealings at such public houses – and goes on to provide a series of laws covering the nature of fraud and infamy in the marketplace.[13]

The Laws was Plato's attempt to provide a realistic outline of his ideal state, called 'Magnesia'. Magnesia was to be a neighbourless city-state, to consist of only 5040 households, and to be about 11 miles from the coast. It was to lack silver and gold, to be moderately fertile, with more hills than plains, and little in the way of good building timber.[14] The most striking thing for the reader – especially any reader who has read the *Republic* with its abstract metaphysical puzzles – is the fantastic degree of detail that is furnished. Among many other things, Plato provides laws for a variety of misdemeanours including the seduction of another's bees, adultery during the ages of child-bearing and adultery after such an age, failure to marry and innovation in songs and dances, as well as the more usual offences such as theft and homicide and much, much else besides.

Despite his antipathy towards innkeepers, Plato does not favour the prohibition of commerce altogether; a course of action which would not have been beyond his imagination for Sparta – a society he admired in many respects – had outlawed it. Indeed Lycurgus (c.800 BC), a figure whom many scholars regard as a mythical figure rather than a genuine historical leader, is said to have made trade difficult by substituting large iron bars for conventional coinage.[15] Plato, to the contrary, believes trade plays a useful role in society and so finds himself on the horns of a dilemma. For while he recognises the necessity of trade, he is certain that commerce brings in its train moral corruption and accordingly wishes to prohibit his citizens, the Magnesians, from engaging in commerce. To resolve the dilemma he introduces three measures. Trade is to be undertaken only by aliens; none of the 5040 'shall be retailers or wholesalers'[16] and if any of them do sully themselves through engaging in trade, then there are appropriate punishments. Next, the retail class should be kept as small as possible. And finally, public trade is to be heavily regulated. The regulations deal in particular with fraud and sharp practice. Plato provides a long account of the duties of the market-wardens over the practices of the marketplace. These duties are not merely procedural but concern the determination of prices. One of the duties of the Guardians of *The Laws* is to determine 'what ratio of expenditure to receipts will give the retailer a decent profit',[17] a concern which finds full expression in the work of the just price tradition. In Magnesia the just rate of profit is to be recorded in writing, put on display and imposed on traders by the market-wardens, city-wardens and country-wardens. Plato thinks that these measures will benefit the population and 'do minimum harm to those members of society who engage in it'.[18]

Interestingly, the ban on commerce for the citizens extends to their own holdings; their lots are inalienable. The citizens are not to buy and sell their holdings among themselves.[19] It is not just that buying and selling involves a failure to respect the 'upper limits of total property', the concern is a distributive one; if buying and selling occurs eventually, some will have enormous holdings and some will be propertyless. The modern North American philosopher Robert Nozick (1940–2001) makes a similar claim in his *Anarchy, State and Utopia* (1975). Nozick accepts the impossibility of maintaining any patterned distribution of holdings once bartering and sale begins, but travels in the opposite direction; such impossibility provides grounds for rejecting political projects oriented towards the establishment and maintenance of *any* patterned theories of distribution.

Plato repudiates commerce for the citizenry because of the moral corruption that commerce brings in its train. Few of us, he thinks, are able to steel ourselves to moderation. Plato's interlocutor, the Athenian, remarks that it is a rare person who is sober enough to prefer modest competence to wealth. Instead, most 'brush aside opportunities of modest gain in favour of insatiable profiteering' and this is why the various retail trades are unpopular.[20] He illustrates this with his attack upon innkeepers.

> A man goes off to some remote point on a road running through the middle of nowhere and sets up his establishment to sell provisions; he receives the weary traveller with welcome lodgings – peace and quiet for the victim of violent storms, cool refreshment for the sufferer from stifling heat – but then instead of greeting them as friends and offering them in addition to his hospitality gifts as tokens of good-will, he treats them like so many enemy prisoners that have fallen into his hands, and holds them up for ransom for a monstrously steep and iniquitous sum.[21]

What befalls the innkeeper is a corruption of natural forms of hospitality thanks to the allure of wealth and, despite the odd idea that the innkeeper should provide gifts, we are too well aware of the kinds of profiteering that goes on when a seller has a captive market. One need only think of alcohol prices in airports and sports stadia to see the point. Plato goes so far as to make such 'money-grubbing' a crime. He is also worried that the inequalities of wealth that commercial societies generate can be socially divisive and so disastrous for the good ordering of the body politic.[22] In the *Republic*, he condemns the oligarchic state where government rests 'on a valuation of property, in which the rich have power and the poor man is deprived of it' on the grounds of 'the inevitable division' that follows.[23] For 'such a State is not one, but two States, the one of poor, the other of rich men, living on the same spot and always conspiring against one another'.[24]

The roots of this tendency to immoderation arise from the potential *limitlessness* of the pursuit of money, and this is a theme that many subsequent philosophers of money pursue. Money presents a *moral hazard* because it has no limits: money begets more money – it does not spoil, and its total amount is not a fixed sum. The pursuit of profit has no natural restraints. We are led astray by the opportunities for increase.[25] For this reason, retail trade should only be carried out by aliens.

Plato never had the opportunity to put his ideas for into practice. Although he was involved on a couple of occasions as an advisor of sorts to the tyrant Dionysus of Syracuse (c.432–367 BC), there is no evidence that his advice on the restriction of commerce (or indeed upon anything else in the political realm) was ever acted upon. Indeed, on the occasion of his second attempt to advise Dionysus, Plato barely managed to escape with his life.

Aristotle (384–322 BC), a student of Plato and tutor of the young Alexander the Great, was also opposed to most commercial activities, although his arguments and approach – as in many other areas – differed significantly from that of Plato. He had a more fundamental opposition to trade and would have it restricted to the residues of domestic production, thus confining it even more than Plato. At the same time we find a deeper account of the nature of money as a medium of exchange than in Plato and, to modern minds, a deeper understanding of the dynamics of economic life.

His body of work contains some ambiguities – if not outright contradictions – regarding the role of money in the good life, some of which is a product of his separation of economic issues from the moral realm. (The latter is presumably the reason that most histories of economic thoughts begin with Aristotle rather than Plato.) In the *Nicomachean Ethics*, money is presented as a relatively benign presence. It is a morally neutral commensurating device and was invented so that people of 'different trades' could come together. It eases the strains of barter exchange and facilitates efficient circulation of goods.

On the Aristotelian model, money provides equivalences *of a kind*. Aristotle notes [N.E. 1133–1134] that money acting as a measure 'makes goods commensurate and equates them'. He does not think that things differing greatly can be made commensurate in *reality*, but for the purposes of *trading* they are so. As an example of how money functions, he discusses the commensuration of the values of a house and a bed.

> Let A be a house, B ten minae, C a bed. A is half of B, if the house is worth five minae or equal to them; the bed, C, is a tenth of B; it is plain, then, how many beds are equal to as house, viz. five. That exchange took place thus before there was money is plain; for it makes no difference whether it is five beds that exchange for a house, or the money value of five beds.[26]

Despite the odd numerical ratios (one assumes high-quality beds and poor-quality housing stock),[27] the point influenced many later discussions of money. The capacity for forging equivalences is a feature of money on which many Medieval philosophers focused, and, because of their belief in an ultimate scale of value for all (created) things, it posed them special problems.[28]

Aristotle draws a distinction between *use-value* and *exchange-value* where use-value refers to the capacity an item has to satisfy human needs and exchange-value refers to the relative value it has on the market. Any commodity, bought and sold on the market, has two aspects, both a use-value and an exchange-value. When we commodify a good we transform it from one with use-value *alone* to one with *both* use-value and exchange-value. This distinction was fundamental to discussions through the Middle Ages, right through to the eighteenth- and nineteenth-century classical economists such as Adam Smith and David Ricardo, and continues today with those influenced by Marxism.

We find in the *Nicomachean Ethics* a discussion – though aimed at the citizen rather than the merchant – of the virtues associated with the use of money. The virtue of liberality as it plays its assigned part in the moral economy of the good citizen is said to be a mean between the vices of prodigality and meanness (or the spendthrift and the miser).[29] The life dedicated to moneymaking is pursued under compulsion. Money, for Aristotle, is an element of what Marx would later call the 'realm of necessity' and for this reason could not be part of a properly flourishing life.[30]

Apart from an aristocratic bias against commerce, Aristotle raises precious few moral issues.[31] However, things are different when we turn to the *Politics* where Aristotle considers how the pursuit of exchange-value enters into people's motivations.

He draws a distinction between *natural* accumulation and *chrematistic* accumulation. Natural accumulation involves the production of goods for domestic consumption. Chrematistic exchange, on the other hand, involves the production of goods for exchange.[32] Natural accumulation, which is 'connected with the management of the household', is morally permissible, whilst the chrematistic is condemned. Aristotle allows exchange (and with it profit) when one exchanges goods initially produced for domestic use, and which, being in excess, are then sold in the market. Profit is only legitimately obtained when the goods concerned were not initially made with profit in mind. The moral status of trading depends entirely upon *the intentions* with which the traded goods are produced.[33]

What lies behind this? There are two philosophical themes here. The first concerns Aristotle's *needs-based* ethical system. The value of any productive activity depends upon its satisfying human needs. Production should therefore be oriented towards and motivated by need. Shoes produced for exchange are not in the first instance produced with the aim of satisfying needs. Here the potential exchange-value has become the dominant element in the producer's motivational set.

The second theme is not concerned with how goods should be produced, but is specific to the pursuit of money. Aristotle, developing a theme of Plato's from *The Laws*, believes that the money-seeking for its own sake is not a proper activity, for there is no limit to the end it seeks. Aristotle focuses on the lack of satisfaction conditions in 'retail acquisition'. His concern is not with *pleonexia* or greed, but with the limitlessness of the pursuit of money.[34] Proper activities have a *telos* or goal that is satisfiable, which is clearly true of needs-based activity. It is no response to contend that one has a *need* for money, since money is only a means to other ends. A need for money is elliptical for some other need and to think otherwise is unnatural and, in Aristotle's philosophical universe, morally perverse.

Aristotle corrals trade in a different way to Plato; it is to be restricted to excess domestic production. And for goods it is permissible to trade, money provides a useful medium of exchange and is a unit of account (or measuring rod). The contradiction between the various discussions of money is only apparent, but nonetheless the shift in tone is noteworthy. Given the strength of the attack in *Politics*, it is odd that money is treated so dispassionately in the *Nicomachean Ethics*.

We find similar worries when we turn to the Romans. As in so many other things, when it comes to the morality of money, the Romans tended to follow the lead of their Greek predecessors. The jurist and philosopher Cicero (106–43 BC) argued that money-lenders, retail traders and small-time merchants are to be despised. Retail traders have little to gain unless they are very dishonest and then they deserve no credit. Merchant activity was only acceptable if it was undertaken on a large scale and involved imports from all over the world. If having undertaken this activity, merchants 'become satisfied or at any rate are prepared to be content with their profits, and retire from the harbour to their country estates', then he believes such activity is entirely commendable.[35] Nonetheless, the commendable forms of commerce pale beside the proper life of agriculture:

> of all the sources of income, the life of the farmer is the best, pleasantest, most profitable and most befitting a gentleman.[36]

The stoic and slave Epictetus (c.55–135 AD) was certainly worried about morally corrosive powers of greed and avarice:

> Suppose you have once lusted after money: if reason sufficient to produce a sense of evil be applied, then the lust is checked, and the mind at once regains its original authority; whereas if you have recourse to no remedy, you can longer look for this return – on the contrary, the next time it is excited by the corresponding object, the flame of desire leaps up more quickly than before. By frequent repetition, the mind in the long run becomes callous; and thus this mental disease produces confirmed Avarice.

Who in this context could not help but be struck by Suetonius' lines (c.71–135) on Caligula:

> But when his daughter was born, complaining of his narrow means, and no longer merely of the burdens of a ruler but of those of a father as well, he took up contributions for the girl's maintenance and dowry. He also made proclamation that he would receive New Year's gifts, and on the Kalends of January took his place in the entrance to the Palace, to clutch the coins which a throng of people of all classes showered on him by handfuls and lapfuls. Finally, seized with a mania for feeling the touch of money, he would often pour out huge piles of gold pieces in some open place, walk over them barefooted, and wallow in them for a long time with his whole body.[37]

As we might expect, the Roman satirists have much to say on money. The early Roman satirist, Gaius Lucilius (180–103 BC) had perhaps the most measured view. 'Manliness', he says, 'is knowing the boundary and limit for acquiring. Manliness is the ability to pay wealth is due....'[38] Horace (65–8 BC) has more to say. 'What', he asks, 'is the key to happiness, money or moral character?' and gives his answer by specifying the proper order of rank between pecuniary and moral value.[39]

> Silver is lower than gold in value, gold than goodness.[40]

He is quite aware that this, in the popular arena, is not the standard view.

> 'Citizens, citizens, the first thing to acquire is money. Cash before conscience!' This is propounded from end to end of Janus' arcade: this is the creed recited by young and old....

But Horace admonishes us to recognise that the greedy are never satisfied; and we should fix a limit on our dreams.[41]

> while the furious itch for profit spreads around you,
> Have no mean thought, but keep your mind on higher things.[42]

If we do not do that, if we succumb to the insatiable itch, then we harm ourselves and he urges us to place a limit on the 'scramble for money'. Just this set of views is also to be found in the 10th satire of Juvenal:

> But scarce observ'd the Knowing and the Bold,
> Fall in the gen'ral massacre of Gold;
> Wide-wasting Pest! That rages unconfin'd,
> And crouds with Crimes the Records of Mankind,
> For Gold his Sword the Hireling Ruffian draws,
> For Gold the hireling Judge distorts the Laws;
> Wealth heap'd on Wealth, nor Truth nor Safety buys,
> The Dangers gather as the Treasures rise.[43]

Tertullian and the Patristic Church Fathers

Turning to the early Christian writers we find considerable hostility to the mercantile life: these writers were genuinely anti-commercial.[44] The philosophers of the early Church typically thought of commerce as a moral abomination.[45] All commercial gain was *turpe lucrum*, that is, ill-begotten or shameful gain.[46] There were two main sources to this attitude:[47] first, their conviction that a merchant must lie, deceive, cheat and commit all manners of fraud in order to sell his wares; and second, their thought the merchant was in constant 'danger of forgetting about God and his soul's health in an insane passion for wealth'.[48] Commerce was a morally perverse activity: 'No Christian should be a merchant, because no one is able to buy and sell without lying and cheating. Deceit is the very base of merchandising.'[49] Ambrose, the fourth century Bishop of Milan, pictured the merchant as one who 'laboured day and night against the principle of integrity'.[50]Although at one point in the *City of God* Augustine argues for the necessity of commerce, this was a marginal view in late Antiquity and the early Middle Ages. Tertullian (c.160–225 AD), for instance, condemned the merchant in a neatly expressed syllogism:

Trading is fit for the service of God if greed is absent.

But if the need for acquisition ceases there will no longer be any necessity for trading.

Therefore trading is not fit for the service of God.[51]

Tertullian was not alone. John of Chrysostom (347–407) suggested that no merchant can please God.[52] In the sixth century Cassiodorus (490–485) denounced traders 'who burdened their wares with lies even more than with honest prices', and in the fifth century Pope Leo the Great (d.461) summed up the general attitude: 'it is difficult for buyers and sellers not to fall into sin'.[53]

Such antagonisms derived in no small part from the merchant's control over the food supplies that could affect so decisively the survival and quality of life of urban populations during this period. But it also reflected an antagonism to private property. Many of the early Church Fathers, such as St Barnabas in the first century AD, St Justin and St Lucian in the second, Tertullian, Origen, St Cyprian in the third and Arnobius and Lactantius in the fourth, were genuine communists, insisting that among Christians all goods are held in common.[54] For such thinkers the only rational approach to economic activity is non-involvement with possessions.[55] The theological origins of this are to be found in the *Acts of the Apostles* where it is said that 'And they that believed were together and had all things in common; And sold their possessions and goods, and parted them to all men, as every man has need.'[56] Many believed that when humans were innocent they had no need for private property but when this innocence passed away, they found themselves compelled to organise society and to devise institutions which should regulate the ownership and use of the good things which they had once held in common. The institution of property thus represents the 'Fall of Man' from a state of primitive innocence. It is because of the perfidious origin of private property that the Fathers were led to believe that private property was not natural, but rather that it 'grew out of men's vicious and sinful desires'.[57]

Such communism was eventually repudiated by the Church. A Church Council in 415 AD condemned the proposition held by Pelagius that the rich cannot be saved unless they renounce their goods.[58] And many Christian writers in subsequent generations felt compelled to reject any hint of communism in Christian teaching and to defend emphatically the lawfulness of property. 'To possess riches', says Hilary of Poictiers (d.368 AD), 'is not wrongful, but rather the manner in which possession is used. It is a crime to possess wrongfully rather than simply to possess.'[59] 'Who does not understand', asks St Augustine, 'that it is not sinful to possess riches, but to love and place hope in them, and to prefer them to truth or justice?'[60] This felt need was true right into the late Middle Ages. Saint Ambrose (340–397) in his commentary on Psalm 113 [viii, 22] explains the concern by insisting that 'mercy is a part of justice and if you wish to give to the poor, this mercy is justice'. Ambrose argues that it is unjust that one should not be helped by one's neighbour; for God has wished the possession of the Earth to be common to all men, and its fruits to minister to all. However, our avarice has led to the establishment of proprietary rights. Given that such rights have been permitted, '[i]t is therefore just that if you lay claim to anything as your private property, which is really conferred in common to the whole human race, that you should dispense something to the poor, so that you may not deny nourishment to those who have the right to share with you'.[61] San Bernardino of Siena (1380–1444) was extremely careful not to revive the teaching of the *fraticelli*, a sect of the Franciscan Order, who condemned all forms of ownership, whether held in private or common and whose teachings had the taint of heresy.[62]

This communistic strand, and the hostility towards the private accumulation of resources it implied, is still strongly felt by many in the Christian community, and it played a major part in the moral appeal of later, and avowedly secular, varieties of communism and socialism. But since the work of the English philosopher John Locke in the late seventeenth century, it has enjoyed less intellectual endorsement than it previously did. In his *Second Treatise on Government*, Locke claimed to have accepted and acknowledged the legitimacy of an original and divinely established communism, but to have shown how that this did not impugn the acquisition and accumulation, indeed the unlimited acquisition and accumulation, of money.[63] The thing that struck Locke was the way that money, unlike the immutable wealth of this or that kind of property, could be accumulated without either spoiling or wastage. Thus, whereas apples and pears will rot in the private barn of the overfed farmer, the gold buried in his barnyard will not. It follows for Locke that while the former exhibits the vices of avarice, greed and a culpable indifference to the needs of his fellow creatures, this is not so for the gold burier. It is not so, because what is accumulated is not at the expense of others, nor is it essentially pointless, as Aristotle held, because of its potential endlessness. It is rather a store of value, and who can object to a man accumulating such a store in the face of the contingencies of fortune when in so doing he is neither wasting any of God's resources nor harming his fellows?[64]

The Medieval Schoolmen

We turn now to the work of the Medieval philosophers who have commonly been said to be *genuinely anti-commercial*. Consider the following passage from Robert Solomon's entry on Business Ethics in Blackwell's *A Companion to Ethics*:

> Aristotle declared such activity [trade for profit] wholly devoid of virtue and called those who engaged in such purely selfish practices 'parasites'. Aristotle's attack on the unsavoury and unproductive practice of 'usury' held force virtually until the seventeenth century. Only outsiders at the fringe of society, not respectable citizens, engaged in such practices. (Shakespeare's Shylock, in The Merchant of Venice, was an outsider and a usurer.) This, on a large historical canvas, is the history of business ethics – the wholesale attack on business and its practices. Jesus chased the money-changers from the temple, and Christian moralists from Paul to Thomas Aquinas and Martin Luther followed his example, roundly condemning most of what we today honour as 'the business world'.[65]

Solomon's views are symptomatic of a common misunderstanding of Medieval doctrine. To be sure, the early Church Fathers were anti-commercial, but this is not true of most Medieval writers. We can observe a substantial shift in attitudes towards commerce by the time Aquinas wrote his *Summa Theologica*. Eric Roll in *A History of Economic Thought* argues that we find in the works of Aquinas '... a distinct tendency to reconcile theological dogma with the existence of conditions of economic life.'[66] John Baldwin in *The Medieval Theories of Just Price* points to Augustine's earlier commentary on Psalm LXX. In it, Augustine quotes at length a conversation – one that Baldwin suspects is imaginary – between himself and a merchant. In this conversation Augustine launches a verbal assault on the merchant for his lies, deceits and scandalising of the good name of Christianity. The merchant's reply to Augustine's accusations may be divided into two parts. First, the merchant's profession involves the performance of a beneficial service; he transports goods from long distances and then sells them. If one adheres to the Christian principle that a 'labourer is worthy of his hire', then the merchant deserves a certain level of profit as compensation for his labour as well as sustenance for his living. Second, having provided a justification for his profits, the merchant then proceeded to meet the moral objection to his profession. He draws a distinction between the trader on the one hand and his trade on the other. If commerce gave rise to lies and perjuries, then these were not the fault of trade. Sins of this kind had their origins in the person, not the profession. Was it not true that shoemakers and farmers were also capable of lies, perjuries and blasphemies, and yet their profession could not be considered evil? The merchant concluded that if he lived virtuously all would go well with him, but if he lived wickedly it would not be due to his profession but due to his own moral failings. Augustine agreed with the merchant's conclusion, and thereby cleared the profession of commerce from its fundamental stain of opprobrium.[67]

But if Augustine began to open the door to commerce, for the historian John Baldwin it is the little-known twelfth-century canon lawyer, philosopher and theologian, Rufinus, who was the pivotal figure in this shift. According to Baldwin, Rufinus was the first significant Medieval philosopher to think seriously about how to set what we might call the 'moral boundaries of commercial exchange'. To understand the significance of Rufinus' work here, recall that he inhabited a moral world that was profoundly anti-commercial. Rufinus saw the conflict of such views with his experience of the world in general and analysed the merchant's function in an effort to devise a moral justification for the merchant's place in society.[68]

Rufinus examined a series of cases where profits are made by buying cheap and selling dear.[69] He divided such transactions into three general categories. First of all, there is the case of a person who buys goods for his own or for his household's use, with no intention of reselling these goods at a profit. At a later date, he is forced through circumstances of necessity or expediency to sell these goods. If he can demonstrate that his motives for resale were those of necessity and not of profit, the goods may be sold, even at a higher price than for which they were originally bought. The second category deals with artisans and craftsmen and occurs when a person buys goods cheaply and then, by changing or improving them, is able to sell them at a higher price. Here, the higher price for which the goods are sold is justified by the expenses and the labour the artisan has expended upon the goods in order to improve them. According to Rufinus, this type of business is honourable.

The final category of legitimate profit-taking is exclusive of the first two. If someone buys goods cheap with the sole motive of selling them later at a higher price for profit, without having changed the form of the goods through added expenses or labour and without being compelled to do so by necessity or expediency, then that person is conducting a commercial enterprise in the truest sense of the word. This pure merchandising, although permitted, was morally hazardous. If no labour or expenses were involved – if one made profits by observing the market and buying in times of plenty and selling in times of famine – then the enterprise was immoral. If, however, heavy expenditures had been made or if the merchant was fatigued by hard labour, then unless some other unworthy means intervened, the enterprise was an honourable one. By emphasising the factors of expense and labour, Rufinus began the Medieval redemption of the profession of the merchant.[70]

From Rufinus onwards Medieval moral thinking on the economy was, in the main, concerned to distinguish morally acceptable commercial behaviour from that which was reprehensible. There were some exceptions, the most notable being Peter Lombard (d.1160), who in a passage in the *Sentences* stated that neither soldiers nor merchants could exercise their duties without sinning.[71] But the great majority of significant moral thinking on economic issues pursued during the high and late Medieval period was not anti-commercial.

Why, then, the tendency evident in writers such as Solomon to see the Medievals as anti-commercial?[72] Perhaps the main reason is a tendency to see the views of the early Middle Ages and those of the later periods as a seamless whole. There is an all-too-eager willingness on the part of modern commentators to assimilate the views of the Medievals to those of Aristotle.[73] While Aristotle was tremendously influential in most areas of philosophical thought, Medieval thinkers did not slavishly follow his doctrines in all things. That they did not do so when it came to the analysis of trade is clear. Aristotle, unlike Aquinas and San Antonino of Florence (1389–1459), was genuinely antagonistic to trade.[74]

There are three important points if we are to understand the Medievals on the legitimacy of commerce and commercial life. First, many important scholastics argued that the sin is that of *the sinner not the trade*. For instance, Aquinas blamed the moral turpitude of trade on the sinful nature of merchants involved, rather than on mercantile practices themselves.[75] For Aquinas, moderate commercial behaviour, when oriented towards the maintenance of house and home, was morally permissible and even 'praiseworthy'.[76]

> Gain...which is the end of trading, though it does not logically involve anything honourable or necessary, does not logically involve anything sinful or contrary to virtue.[77]

Thus, *instrumental* pursuit of profit was admissible, if the end was praise-worthy, but one could never treat profit as an intrinsic end.[78] An ethically justified profit (*moderatum lucrum*) was possible so long as one's activities were not based on avaricious motives (*ex cupiditate*).

The second point is that many philosophers argued for the social necessity of merchants and their activities. Thomas Chobham (fl. c. 1220), Thomas Aquinas and Bonaventura (d.1274) all insisted on the essential utility of merchants to society; Chobham observing that merchants distributed from areas of abundance to regions of deficiency.[79]

Third, we find the emergence of the idea of profit as reward for labour. In line with the common opinion that all labour should be justly remu-nerated, the theologians came to regard commercial profits as just wages for the labour of the merchants. Thomas Aquinas termed mercantile gain a stipend for labour. They provide indispensable commodities from abroad – and so long as they do not seek gain for the sake of gain, their work was morally licit. A moderate income was permitted to remuner-ate the merchant for his services. Gratian (d.1159) preferred to maintain the condemnatory force of the term 'merchant' while yet allowing for morally acceptable forms of trading. 'Whosoever buys a thing, not that he may sell it whole and unchanged, but that it may be a material for fashioning something, he is not a merchant. But the man who buys it in order that he may gain by selling it again unchanged and as he bought it, that man is of the buyers and sellers who are cast forth from God's temple.'[80] Such nuances aside it is fair to say that William of Rennes (fl. c.1250) captured the views of the era when he wrote that:

> Although business can scarcely be conducted without sin, merchants may receive a moderate profit from their wares for the maintenance of themselves and their families. Since they work for all and perform a kind of common business by transporting merchandise back and forth between fairs, they should not be held to pay their own wages. From the merchandise itself they can accept a moderate profit, which is regulated by the judgement of a good man, because the amount of profit permitted cannot be exactly determined in shillings pounds or pennies.[81]

In this rough and ready fashion, the factors of transportation, care and risk were connected with the fundamental factors of labour and expenses as economic sources that morally justified the profit of a merchant.[82]

This less antagonistic attitude towards commerce is particularly evident in the work of San Antonino of Florence. In his *Summa Theologica*, he writes:

> The notion of business implies nothing vicious in its nature or contrary to reason. Therefore, it should be ordered to any honest and necessary purpose and is so rendered lawful, as for example, when a business man orders his moderate gain which he seeks to the end that he and his family may be decently provided for according to their condition, and that he may also assist the poor. Nor is condemnation possible when he undertakes a business as a public service lest necessary things be wanting to the state and seeks gain therefrom, not as an end, but in remuneration for his labour observing all other due considerations which we mention. But if he places his final purpose in gain, seeking only to increase wealth enormously and to keep it for himself, his attitude is to be condemned.[83]

San Antonino did not condemn the profit-motive *per se*. What was of pivotal importance is that the profit be instrumental to other, *virtuous*, goals.

Central to this shift was a more nuanced analysis of the motives of the merchant. As George O'Brien notes, what the later Medieval teaching on commerce amounted to was that, while commerce was as legitimate as any other occupation, owing to the concomitant temptations of cupidity and dishonesty, '...it must be carefully scrutinised and kept within bounds'.[84] They rejected an unqualified condemnation of the profit-motive that would have all profits from sale treated as *turpe lucrum*; rather the criterion for sale was whether it was conducted out of the motive of *cupiditas* or not. They engaged in all sorts of subtle distinction-mongering. While they condemned buying cheap so as to sell dear, doing so was permissible when one had to sell out of expediency. What mattered once again were the motives of the commercial agent.

As time went on, there were further shifts towards an acceptance of commerce. Later Medievals were more inclined to treat commerce as being in itself morally colourless rather than morally tainted, but capable of becoming evil through immoral motivations.

Interlude

While the sophisticated and nuanced approach to commercial matters developed by many later Medieval thinkers was a worthy and credible development, we must remember, as R.H. Tawney reminds us, that for these thinkers man was primarily a spiritual creature required to prudently acknowledge the role of commerce in keeping men alive. The early modern period sees this relationship alter in a crucial way. By the mid-seventeenth century the difference is manifest: for those engaged in commerce, religion has moved from the centre of man's being to something more akin to 'insurance' for the soul.

This change in emphasis helps to explain why so many of those prominent in business and industry at this period were Protestant Dissenters, for by and large the Catholic tradition continued to take the late Medieval line and in essentials this continues today. So, for instance, Pope Leo XIII, in his Encyclical of 1891, *Rerum Novarum*, writes:

> working for gain is creditable, not shameful, to a man, since it enables him to earn an honourable livelihood....

What is 'truly shameful and inhuman', he continues, is the morally unconstrained and obsessive 'pursuit of gain' which invites us to 'misuse men as though they were things'.[85]

Some Protestant thinkers were more prone to emphasise not merely that the pursuit of profit was acceptable if morally constrained in the appropriate ways, but even to make such a pursuit itself obligatory. William Penn's (1644–1718) advice to his Quaker followers was not to eschew, but to pursue riches, though to do so without allowing themselves to be ensnared by the temptations of luxury and avarice. Quakers' tastes were to be:

> plain in clothes, furniture and food, but clean and coarser the better; the rest is folly and a snare ....

And thus:

> diligence is the Way to Wealth: the diligent hand makes Rich. Frugality is a Virtue too, and not of little Use in Life, the better way to be Rich, for it has less Toil and Temptation.[86]

This celebration of a morally constrained pursuit of profit as itself a source of virtue was shared by the methodist John Wesley (1703–1791) and found expression in the thought of Benjamin Franklin (1706–1790) for whom 'Frugality & Industry, by freeing me from my remaining Debt, & producing Affluence & Independence, would make more easy the

Practice of Sincerity and Justice, &c &c.'[87] For while a Protestant thinker like Thomas Mortimer (1730–1810), in his *Elements of Commerce* (1772), could celebrate the businessman as someone who, though hardheadedly pursuing personal gain, possessed because of his faith –

> A firm attachment to the true principles of honour, a religious adherence to his word, clearness and integrity in his contracts, prudent generosity in his dealings with the industrious poor, with a becoming dignity and moral rectitude in his manners.[88]

– this was no iron-clad commitment. The displacement of man's earthly existence from the spiritual to the material plane, allied with the powerful developments, both enriching and immiserating, of emerging capitalist economic competition, and abetted by a certain 'providentialist' reading of Adam Smith's celebrated defence of the 'invisible hand' as a device by which personal self-interest could be alchemically transmuted into public good, encouraged many commercial agents to take a less subservient or respectful attitude to those moral side-constraints the late Medievals emphasised. There, thus emerged an only apparently surprising tendency to revert to the earlier Manicheanism of the Ancients and Patristic Fathers, though now with the field more evenly divided between pro- and anti-commercial attitudes. For these thinkers, as we shall now see, the status of the profit-motive and the nature of commercial society are typically presented in a sharply dichotomous manner. Either one is for profit and commerce or, as with the Ancients and Patristic Fathers, one is against it.

Fourier, Marx, and the socialist tradition

Those opposed to the pursuit of profit and commercial society, from Rousseau through Fourier to Marx – key figures in what we now think of as the socialist tradition – argue that the costs to human dignity of an enmeshment in the universe of money are morally intolerable. Three kinds of reasons are offered for this conclusion.

In the first place, and as the early Church Fathers had argued, it not merely involves but reposes upon a structure of dishonesty and deception. Further, it stunts the full development of human nature or potentiality, and, even worse, initiates in its place a spurious and alienated nature which corrupts and dehumanises. Finally, it rests on and endlessly generates exploitative relationships between the genuinely productive element of humanity and its parasitic masters. The profit-motive eats away at the humanity of the individual and of society as a cancer might eat away at its host.

That commerce is a systematic deployment of falsity and mendacity, and so is absolutely inimical to truth, is a major theme of Jean Jacques Rousseau's (1712–1778) critique of modernity. In a letter written in October 1761, he makes it clear that even the 'good merchant' who, out of enlightened self-interest, does his best to sustain a reputation for fair dealing, does something that lacks even the tincture of virtue:

> There is a sensible and tangible interest which bears solely on our material well-being, on fortune, on consideration, on the physical goods that may accrue to us from another's good opinion. Whatever one does for such an interest only produces a good of the same order, as with the good a merchant does by selling his wares on the best terms he can. If I oblige someone with a view to acquiring rights to his gratitude, I am nothing but a merchant engaged in commerce, and cheating the buyer at that. If I give alms only to rid myself of a beggar's importunacy or the sight of his misery; all actions of this kind which have some external advantage in view cannot be called good deeds, and one does not say of a merchant who has conducted his business well that he has done so virtuously.[89]

The point finds even clearer expression in the work of that erratic, occasionally brilliant, and deeply peculiar thinker, Charles Fourier (1772–1837) – a man of so singular a character and accomplishments that he deserves more than merely passing attention.

Born the son of a cloth merchant in Besancon, France, Fourier was distinguished from many other critics of commercial society by his intimate knowledge of the operations of commerce. As he said:

> I am a child of the marketplace, born and brought up in mercantile establishments. I have witnessed the infamies of commerce with my own eyes, and I shall not describe them from hearsay as our moralists do.[90]

Fourier dated his discovery that commercial life was 'a cesspool of moral filth' to his sixth year:

> From that time on I noted the opposition which prevails between commerce and truth. I was taught in catechism and at school that

one must never lie; then I was taken to the shop to be trained at an early age in the occupation of lying, *the art of selling*. Shocked by the chicanery and fraud that I saw, I proceeded to take aside the merchants who were the victims and to reveal the deception to them. One of them, in complaining, maladroitly gave me away, which cost me a thorough spanking. My parents, seeing that I had a taste for truth, cried out in a tone of reprobation, 'That child will never be worth anything in commerce.' In fact I conceived a secret aversion to commerce and at the age of seven swore the oath which Hannibal had sworn against Rome – I vowed an eternal hatred of commerce.[91]

If Fourier vowed eternal hatred of commerce, it was equally true that commerce – in the form of his father's will, which stipulated that he inherit only on condition that he assumed management of the family business – took its revenge on the occasion of Fourier's ill-fated support for the revolt of Lyon against the Republic in 1793. After assuming, then losing the business, Fourier was condemned to a life on the edge of, and all too often deep within, poverty, alleviated only by occasional menial and poorly paid work in the stores and factories he saw as the embodiment of his eternal enemy.

If the later Medievals tended to see commerce as morally hazardous, Fourier like the Patristic Fathers saw it as essentially and entirely a 'domain of falsehood and fraud' and one now 'grown to colossal dimensions by the invention of the compass and the discovery of the two Indies'.[92]

Not merely was commerce sustained by the Children of the Lie, and so an enemy of Truth in all its forms, it damaged the very souls of those who participated in its activities. Those supposed virtues celebrated by thinkers like Benjamin Franklin were, in fact, properly understood, pernicious vices. To celebrate the humanity achieved in pursuit of frugality, industry, prudence, temperance and sobriety, and so of the bourgeois family unit in which such virtues found their natural home, was for Fourier – as it was later for the Frankfurt School and the 'New Left' – to celebrate the repressive perversion of the essential human capacity for love into aggression, sadism and hostility, if not its absolute destruction.

This charge, we might notice, is a more severe one than that Oscar Wilde (1854–1900) makes in his *The Soul of Man under Socialism*. For Wilde (as too for the romantic Victorian socialist William Morris), the compulsion of the marketplace does not so much distort human nature into evil and vicious shapes as to drive it into unproductive activities which prevent it from its full realisation.

One's regret is that society should be constructed on such a basis that man has been forced into a groove in which he cannot freely develop what is wonderful, and fascinating, and delightful in him – in which, in fact, he misses the true pleasure and joy of living.[93]

Fourier's charge is harsher; it is not the way economic pressures 'force us into a groove', so much that the relationships of the commercial marketplace, and the relationship of the commercial agent to his own passionate nature, are not merely duplicitous, but loveless and *cold*. Participate enough in such relationships and, Fourier insists, the very capacity for deep and passionate commitment to others and to one's own needs and desires simply atrophies; and so atrophying we become not merely shallower and more mercenary than our pre-modern fellows, we stifle and diminish the capacity for creativity and spontaneity in diversity which, if unleashed by a favourable economic and social order, would transform human nature into a kind of super-humanity.

As for 'how . . . the champions of liberty and truth [have] been able to adopt excessive constraint in love', he points to 'the excessive falsity in commerce':[94]

There is no method more favourable to deceit than the legal system of civilized commerce and free competition, the mother of all social crimes.[95]

This excessive constraint in love spills over into, or, more accurately creates and infects, the bourgeois nuclear family. On one level, the problem is that the nuclear family provides the most limited scale for amity relationships, for each family is set in competition with every other:

Each family seeks to deceive the mass; to usurp by astuteness, larceny, and violence. The family refuses the collective solidarity that would benefit the poor branches of society, such as children, the infirm, and the unemployed.[96]

On a deeper level – and one later to figure in the 'radical psychiatry' of R.D. Laing and David Cooper[97] – the problem is that even within each egoistic and competitive unit genuine love and amity is destroyed or excluded. As the contemporary critic Mark Poster writes, for Fourier '[t]he family, the only emotionally supportive institution of civilization, has been infested by mercantile values'.[98] Fourier believed marriage contracts resembled business contracts and the arms-distance relationships of the marketplace were duplicated in the home. In marriage incompatible personalities were forced together with no possibility of escape. In the home sphere, the passions were distorted and choked, and this created the conditions for the larger misery of society. When Fourier asks –

> Could a better system have been invented to insure the languor, the venality, and the falseness which pervade our isolated families; a system more harmful to a relationship of love and pleasure?[99]

– it takes little power of discrimination to discern the bitter irony.

If all the profit-motive did was to replace truth with mendacity, and to undermine and pervert the human capacities for love and pleasure, then it might still be possible to defend it, even with these admitted defects, as in tune with the dictates of justice. After all, one might ask why should justice encompass more than distributive issues? Even in a just world – and that is, surely, the most we can hope for – there may yet remain areas of loss and suffering, and perhaps that is the case here.

Or perhaps it is not. Certainly for Fourier, as for early English socialists like Charles Hall (1745–1825), William Thompson (1775–1833) and Thomas Hodgskin (1787–1869) and, later, for Marx, to countenance such a possibility was to fail to recognise (or to deny) the essential place of injustice, of exploitation, at the very heart of commercial society.

Fourier is unclear as to whether the exploitation is of the consumer or the productive labourer, or both. Even so his views are otherwise emblematic of the socialist challenge to the profit-motive and commercial life.

> It is obvious that the science called political economy, that of free competition, has duped society in every way through the intricacy of its deceit and through the complexity and cost of unproductive middlemen, misappropriated capital, and other losses and wastes which ultimately fall back on the consumer. It is the consumer who pays for the profits and the frauds of these numerous merchants, not to mention bankruptcy from which the merchant profits at the expense of the public.[100]

And:

> rather than looking out for the profit of commerce – a true bloodsucker seeking only to pressure producers or consumers, who are a hundred times more numerous than the businessman – one should

look out for the good of the producing class and the consumers, who make up the immense majority and who pay for, in a decrease of profit and an increase of costs – the profits that the traffickers reap in distributing goods and products. This truth can be more succinctly expressed – real economy consists in favouring the services of those who increase the production of goods, and in reducing those services which add to the production cost without augmenting production … If so, by what reasoning have economists been able to persuade us that it was an advantage to triple or increase tenfold the mass of tradesmen, whose interventions, far from adding to production, introduces into the distribution of goods a horde of evil-doing criminals.[101]

Expressed in these passages is the idea that commercial society involves not merely the generation, but the enthronement, of a class of parasites who prey on either or both the consumer and the productive labourer. Fourier holds that the pursuit of commercial goals is the pursuit of injustice and deception. This is the pursuit of what Marx will later call 'surplus value', and will make the keystone of his assault on the profit-motive and commercial society.

Fourier's critique of commercial society and the predominance of the profit-motive is stigmatised by Marx as embodying a *Utopian*, rather than a *scientific*, conception of socialism. As he sees it, Fourier's critique is entirely moralistic in so far as it lacks a structural account of the systematic exploitation which characterises capitalism, and which he takes himself to have provided. We will look at the supposed need for such an account to underpin moral objections to the profit-motive and commercial society later, and at the details of Marx's scientific socialism shortly; but it is worth noting that the derogation of Fourier's analysis as Utopian does not mean that Marx eschews Utopianism, for he welcomes the coming communist society as one in which all the harms the profit-motive and commercial society inflict on humanity are transcended and, for the first time, genuinely human history begins. And if Marx thinks this is legitimated in his case because it reposes on a materialist philosophy of history, well so too Fourier's Utopian speculations are underpinned by a philosophy of history, though one might well hesitate to call materialist resting as it does on the idea that the Newtonian universe is essentially biological.[102] And if for Marx communism involves overcoming or transcending the harms of avarice and commercial life, so too with Fourier's world of Phalansteries, to which we now turn our attention.

Fourier's solution to the travails and horrors of commercial society was for individuals to come together voluntarily into communities of around 1600 people, evenly divided between male and female. Such communities were both human-sized without being stultifying small, large enough to effectively utilise the technological powers that, outside competitive commercial relationships, were easily sufficient to overcome scarcity, and – not at all incidentally for Fourier – reflected the fact that there were, as he thought, 810 different types or varieties of men and women. The basic mark of all aspects of life in the Phalanstery lay in the complete freedom of each and every person therein – a freedom that had its crucial foundation at precisely the point it was denied under the exploitative competitive relationships of the existing order. Thus work itself was to be voluntarily chosen, not the painful and depressing necessity of pressing social and economic coercion. And, of course, in such circumstances, work *would* be chosen, for human nature undistorted thrives on the creative self-expression genuinely voluntary work offers.

> Our pleasures have at present no connection with industry, and are consequently unproductive; whereas in the combined order [the Phalanstery] they will be connected with productive industry, which will itself be a succession of pleasures, when rendered attractive.[103]

And do not think that this is not true of all work, for the variety of human tastes is such that even the most 'demeaning' work can be the source of real fulfilment (so it is that 'little hordes' of children will take immense pleasure in collecting and disposing of the filth and rubbish the community generates).

In the Phalanstery lies and deception are not merely frowned upon, but are, in fact, utterly unnecessary, for here true and unqualified virtue reigns. It does so because the basis of all such deception has been eliminated, for in the Phalanstery the interdependence of each person on everyone else is not falsely denied in the service of exploitative profit for a deforming and mutilating egoism, but is everywhere and openly acknowledged, both in the voluntarism of all work and in the human scale of the community.

Equally, the self-alienation of humanity that characterises contemporary commercial society is overcome through the transparent and co-operative relationships that now exist between people. Whereas the harsh necessities of commercial society lead each to see everyone else – every other family and, worse, everyone within the family – as ultimately a mere means to cold commercial ends, the honest revelation of human community enables the emergence of a truly reciprocal love between persons as the shackles of commercial consciousness are shattered and each can now appear to every other as an end in him or herself. It is, as a consequence, an obvious truth that parasitism and exploitation are overcome, and the reign of justice inaugurated in which the free development of each is the condition for the free development of all.

Turning to the work of Karl Marx (1818–1883) a man whose career included a doctorate in philosophy, radical journalism, a long-running stint as European correspondent for the *New York Times*, exile from seven countries, charges of terrorism, awkward marital infidelity, and an absolute incapacity for the acquisition and efficient management of money, we find a writer primarily interested in commercial relations when the commodity for sale is labour power, and for whom money within the capitalist system becomes an independent phenomenon, capital, that has its own laws of motion. For Marx the pursuit of profit in capitalist society can only be achieved through the exploitation of the labouring classes, since labour power is the source of all economic value. Labour and capital are fundamentally opposed. This opposition is not simply a matter of justice, but has an eschatological dimension, since he believes the conflict between labour and capital will ultimately be resolved through a necessarily violent process whose outcome will be a society in which class conflict is over-turned and alienation overcome.

Marx's account of commercial society is developed through three main analytic devices, the first of which is the distinction between *use-value* and *exchange-value* that he takes from Aristotle. Use-value is the value of a good as it satisfies human needs. Exchange-value is the value of a good in the marketplace; that is, the proportion in which values in use of one sort are exchanged for those of another sort.[104] A commodity has both use-value and exchange-value.

The second analytic device is the *labour theory of value*. According to Marx, the exchange-value of a good is determined by the amount of labour it embodies. Here he follows Smith and Ricardo. Thus the difference between the various prices of goods is to be understood in terms of the different amounts of labour embodied therein. While the labour theory of value was orthodoxy amongst many eighteenth- and nineteenth-century economists, it is now typically believed to be mistaken, or to have what little truth there is in it captured by the impact that cost-of-production pressures may place on the price, so ultimately the provision, of a commodity. Since the 1870s, and the emergence of marginal analysis, mainstream neo-classical economists have come to explain relative prices in terms of supply and demand and the idea that labour plays any determining role is said to be disproved by empirical evidence. While the marginalists' criticisms may well be correct, it is important not to confuse the labour theory of value with the idea of value in use, as have many modern economists. Marx does not hold that the exchange-value of an item should be related to its usefulness – and neither did Smith nor Ricardo – but rather by the labour embodied.

The third element in the story is Marx's *theory of surplus value* that he employs to analyse profits. Profits for Marx are simply the surplus value which the capitalist extracts, which is the difference between the price paid to the labourer and the 'real' value of the commodity that the labourer produces, understood as the price to the consumer. The capitalist garners this surplus value. From Marx's analysis it follows that workers are exploited, and the extraction of surplus value or profit involves a kind of theft. Interestingly, there is no room in the Marxian story, as there was in the Medieval account of commerce, for the thought that the capitalist undertakes any labour in the pursuit of profit.

Marx employs these analytic devices to provide a description of capitalist society that locates it within a broad-ranging taxonomy of all hitherto societies, as well as providing a radical critique of capitalism. In capitalist society the pursuit of exchange-value becomes the primary goal of productive activity and processes of accumulation accelerate. Commodity production replaces production for the satisfaction of needs. Thus rather than the C-M-C (Commodity-Money-Commodity) circuit we find the M-C-M (Money-Commodity-Money) circuit infiltrating into all areas of human social life. Aristotle's dreaded *chrematistic* thus becomes the predominant human activity. Moreover, the logic of capitalism is such that more and more goods become produced as commodities. This process of *commodification* means that an ever-increasing array of goods are created primarily for exchange-values, not for the satisfaction of human needs.

Only that money which participates in the M-C-M circuit is *capital*. Unlike Fourier, Marx distinguishes between 'money that is money only', for it serves merely as the medium of exchange in the C-M-C circuit, and money that, in the M-C-M circuit, begins its journey in the capitalist's pocket 'which is the point to which it returns'.[105] In capitalism the circulation of money as capital is an end-in-itself.[106] It is this distinction between money as 'the appropriation of use-values, the satisfaction of wants', and money as an end-in-itself, which is a defining element of the capitalist economy, and which leads Marx to the contention that the money received as wage-labour payments plays no special or interesting role in an account of the logic of capitalism.

Capitalist society is marked by the reinvestment of capital into production. Marx thought that in Medieval societies surplus was typically employed in the pursuit of aristocratic luxury. The capitalist, on the other hand, reinvests his money in the acquisition of productive assets. Indeed he does so necessarily since there is an almost Darwinian struggle between capitalists and in this struggle those who do not reinvest fall away. The most important feature of capitalism is the division of society into two great classes, the bourgeoisie (or capitalist class) and the proletariat (or labouring class).[107] Feudal remnants are blown away; the new ruling classes are composed of merchants and industrialists, not feudal lords. And individual producers of commodities (the petty bourgeoisie) are forced to compete with large capitalist enterprises and must either expand to become fully fledged capitalists or fail and be thrown into the ranks of the proletariat.[108]

These two great classes, the bourgeoisie and the proletariat, are necessarily in conflict. The bourgeoisie own the means of production (all of the land and productive resources) while the proletariat own no productive resources and hence must sell their labour power in order to sustain themselves. The proletariat enters into the 'wage-labour contract' in which they exchange ownership of the products of their labour for wages. The products of their labour are thus alienated from them. Moreover, this is a contract the proletariat enter into under desperate circumstances, for owning no productive resources they cannot – except at a price most would regard as exorbitant – refuse to work. So the contractors do not find themselves in equal bargaining positions. But there is worse to come. Since the capitalist's profit margin is determined by the gap between the cost of the wages paid and the value of the good in the market, it is in the interests of the bourgeoisie to suppress wages to as low a rate as is possible. Moreover, not only is it in their interests, those capitalists who fail to do so will, by dint of the forces of competition, go out of business. Marx talks often of the 'logic of capital'. This logic is such that the working classes will necessarily be impoverished, a claim that later Marxists call the 'immiseration thesis'.

There is also a distinctly millennial tone to Marx's writing. The two classes each have their own distinctive historical destiny. The bourgeoisie through their relentless pursuit of profit develop our technical capacities, and, in so doing promise to free us from the realm of necessity to the realm of freedom where humans will no longer need to work to sustain themselves. It reveals a similar disgust with work as that expressed later by Philip Larkin in his poem 'Toads'.

> Why should I let the toad *work*.
> Squat on my life.
> Can't I use my wit as a pitchfork.
> And drive the brute off[109]

Marx's hope is that machine technology will provide us with the opportunity to be rid of this wretched toad. In the future we would all be free to 'hunt in morning, fish in the afternoon rear cattle in the evening, criticise after dinner'.[110] The life of the Victorian gentleman is rendered universal by the productive forces the bourgeoisie unleash. This is their historical destiny. The task of the proletariat is to liberate us from the class division that has been a feature of all human societies thus far. The immiseration of the proletariat is inevitable and provides them with a motive for overthrowing the capitalist class. However, unlike the peasants in feudal society who were also exploited, the proletariat have the necessary understanding and the appropriate collectivist mores to recognise their oppression, and to act collectively to overthrow their oppressors.

One cannot help be impressed – even if not convinced – by the sweep of Marx's history. More ambiguous is his attitude towards commerce and the profit-motive, something that is also true of his treatment of moral issues more generally. Marx presents criticism of the capitalist system as a whole and of the profit-motive, but at the same time he sees positive elements, and ultimately *morally positive* elements, in both the capitalist system and the profit-motive.

On the negative side, Marx points to the exploitation on which capitalism reposes. The capitalist, he argues, can only make profits by failing to pay the worker what his/her work is really worth. The extraction of surplus value is genuinely exploitative. He tells us in *Capital* that if money comes into the world with a congenital blood stain on one cheek 'capital comes dripping from head to foot, from every pore with blood and dirt'.[111] Moreover, the system is so constituted that the rate of exploitation must necessarily increase. The immanent laws of capitalist production are such that '[o]ne capitalist always kills many' and in so doing leads to a centralisation of capital.[112] The falling rate of profit means that any capitalist who operates on motives of mere kindliness – we do not expect benevolence or altruism here – is marking himself for oblivion. Any attempt by the well-intentioned individual to express relative virtue leads, by an inexorable logic of competition, to its elimination.

One should not think that the systemic nature of this exploitation prevents Marx's condemnation of it. In *Capital*, Vol. 1, he writes:

> within the capitalist system all methods for raising the social produc-
> tiveness of labour are brought about at the cost of the individual
> labourer; all means for the development of production transform
> themselves into means of domination over, and exploitation of, the
> producers; they mutilate the labourer into a fragment of a man,
> degrade him to the level of an appendage of a machine, destroy every
> remnant of charm in his work and turn it into a hated toil . . . they
> distort the conditions under which he works, subject him during the
> labour-process to a despotism the more hateful for its meanness; they
> transform his life-time into working-time, and drag his wife and child
> beneath the wheels of the Juggernaut of capital.[113]

Nor does it absolve the capitalist of vice. The mere fact that in order to survive one needs to engage in vicious behaviour does not *justify* the ensuing exploitation and Marx does not hesitate to condemn capitalists. So in *The Communist Manifesto* in a famous and oft-quoted passage, he writes:

> It [the bourgeoisie] has pitilessly torn asunder the motley feudal ties
> that bound man to his 'natural superiors,' and has left remaining no
> other nexus between man and man than naked self-interest, than cal-
> lous 'cash-payment.' It has drowned the most heavenly ecstasies of
> religious fervour, of chivalrous enthusiasm, of philistine sentimental-
> ism, in the icy water of egotistical calculation. It has resolved personal
> worth into exchange value, and in place of the numberless inde-
> feasible chartered freedoms, has set up that single, unconscionable
> freedom – Free Trade. In one word, for exploitation, veiled by religious
> and political illusions, it has substituted naked, shameless, direct,
> brutal exploitation.[114]

All three volumes of *Capital* are replete with passages on oppression, exploitation and shameless brutality, some having a distinctly Fourierian tone. He condemns the bastardry of commercial retailers of bread for the adulteration in which they engage.[115] In this his writing is often reminiscent of Plato's condemnation of innkeepers. In one section of

Volume One, Marx notes that the 'capitalist gets rich, not like the miser, in proportion to his personal labour and restricted consumption, but at the same rate as he squeezes out the labour-power of others, and enforces on the labourer abstinence from all life's enjoyments'.[116] And in Volume Three he writes that 'The profit made in selling the profits of labour always depend on cheating and deceit.'[117]

Marx, like Fourier, but on the basis of a deeper anthropology, had contempt for the *imaginary appetites* that capitalism generated amongst the population at large. In this he presages subsequent criticisms of the consumer culture that make play with the notion of false pleasure. Marx claims that every person 'speculates on creating a *new need* in another, so as to drive him to a fresh sacrifice, to place him in a *new dependence*' and that the extension of products and needs falls into 'contriving and ever-calculating subservience to inhuman, refined, unnatural and *imaginary appetites*'.[118]

Like Fourier he also despairs of the kind of human relations that capitalism fosters. The capitalist class has '... pitilessly torn asunder the motley feudal ties that bound man to his "natural superior", and has left no other nexus between man and man than naked self-interest, than callous "cash payment"'.[119] His writings here are reminiscent of those whom he derisively labelled 'utopian socialists'.

On the other hand, here differing from Fourier and the Utopian socialists, Marx finds positive features in capitalism and the profit-motive by virtue of the future states of affairs they are fated to realise. Marx is not, as Fourier boasted of himself, the 'eternal enemy of all commerce', since he sees capitalism as a nasty, but ultimately necessary stage in the realisation of full human value.

> [What is wealth] other than the universality of individual needs, capacities, pleasures, productive forces etc., created through universal exchange? The full development of human mastery over forces of nature, those of so-called nature as well as humanity's own nature.[120]

The pursuit of profit and the accumulation of capital allows for the development of productive resources that will free us from the realm of necessity, and so able to realise our 'species being'. It establishes the conditions of mutual interdependency on which real values and their sound appreciation depend.

The capitalist thus has a vital role to play, since being 'fanatically bent on making value expand itself, he ruthlessly forces the development of the productive powers of society' and in so doing creates those material conditions which alone can form the basis of a higher form of society '...in which the full and free development of every individual forms the ruling principle'.[121] Except in his role as personified capital, the capitalist has no historical value and it is only in this role that the capitalist is, as Marx rather quaintly puts it, 'respectable'.

This obsession with a pre-determined historical trajectory and with the necessity of fully realised capitalism had many strange consequences in subsequent Marxist philosophy and political practice. Not only did some attempt to use the falling rate of global profit to predict the exact date in which European capitalism would crumble, others used Marx's philosophy of history as grounds for stymieing proletarian resistance to capital. In Russia the Mensheviks, the Bolsheviks' Marxist rivals, put down workers' uprisings without compunction on the grounds that the time was not yet ripe.[122] As Marxists committed to the thesis that capitalism was a necessary historical stage, they believed that Russia needed to go through capitalism before socialism could be possible, and so they were obliged to help in its development and not to subvert, or retard, it. The horror of capitalism was to be fostered so as to bring about the ultimate and highest stage of human development, the future communist state. It was left to Lenin and Trotsky to reject the chain of reasoning and consign the Mensheviks to the 'dustbin of history'. Lenin and Trotsky did not believe that socialism required a prior capitalist formation; with sufficient political will it was possible to 'leapfrog' from a motley feudal order to the Socialist Utopia where the cash nexus, like the State, will wither away.[123]

Marx's ambivalence about the moral status of commerce derives in part from his intermittent antagonism to the *morality system* in general. At times Marx refers to morality, not just particular moral claims, but morality in general, as 'bourgeois right'. In *Capital*, Marx attacks Proudhon's appeal to an ideal of justice, saying that we would have little time for a chemist who, instead of studying the actual laws of molecular changes, tried to solve his theoretical problems through an appeal to eternal ideas. Equally he insists that we do not know more about usury when we say it contradicts 'eternal justice' and other like notions.[124] In the *Critique of the Gotha Programme*, he makes clear his contempt for moral vocabulary:

I have dealt more at length with...'equal right' and 'fair distribution'...in order to show what a serious crime it is to attempt.... to force our Party again, as dogmas, ideas which in a certain period of time had some meaning but have now become obsolete verbal rubbish, while again perverting... the realistic outlook, which it cost so much effort to instil into the Party but which has taken root in it, by means of ideological nonsense about right etc., so common among the democrats and French socialists.[125]

Morality is essentially corrupted by our immersion in class-based societies.

This theme raises difficulties for the obviously strong moral language of much of his criticisms of capitalism. If all morality is corrupted by class societies, then from whence does he derive grounds for criticism of current social forms or reasons for approving of as-yet unrealised forms? There has been considerable debate amongst twentieth-century Marxist philosophers about whether Marx's views on morality lead inevitably to a kind of *moral relativism* where all moral claims are to be rejected because of their sociological origins and where there can be no grounds for ethical evaluation. But as Steven Lukes argues in *Marxism and Morality*, in so far as Marxism has adopted such an approach, it has prevented itself from offering moral resistance to immoral actions taken in its name; 'despite its rich view of freedom and compelling vision of human liberation', it has been unable to offer an adequate account of justice and rights and thus an adequate response to the injustice and violations of rights in the world we in fact inhabit.[126]

Marx's difficulties with morality arose from that feature of his thought that distinguished his views from someone like Fourier. The latter's objections were moral through and through, but Marx sought to embed such moralism in a broader and deeper structural account of capitalism and economic life, as if without this such moralism would be nothing more than moralism. Marx was wrong about this necessity, just as, on the other side of the ideological divide, are those who, in defence of capitalism and commercial society, condemn the moral assessment of our participation in commercial life as either otiose or, worse, misguided in so far as it deflects us from pursuit of those self-interested goals which power the beneficent energies of the Invisible Hand as it showers – or drips – wealth on all.

We take up the question of moralism and money in our last chapter; for now, the point is that Marx's account had two important consequences for the chances of the kind of economic casuistry we champion. First, it encouraged a rejection of projects that involved the drawing of distinctions within the market and between forms of profit-seeking. Second, it fostered an intellectual climate in which it was thought that there was little to be learned from earlier moral philosophers of money. Some of this flowed directly from various intellectual tendencies within the Marxian worldview. Marx was in the end a market abolitionist who wanted us to become free to outgrow markets and money. Hence any projects aimed at drawing moral distinctions *within* the market are obviously of little interest. Equally, the tendency to treat capitalism as both a *sui generis* and a historically achieved social formation meant that there was little, antiquarian interest aside, to be learned from the musings of moral philosophers of money from earlier epochs.[127] Further, we find little interest in the role of money in our lives. If we take the distinction between capital and money, we see that money that is not capital (such as wages) plays no special or interesting role in an account of the logic of capitalism. Even worse, the identification of capital as the defining element of modern economic life encourages the view that *up until* the emergence of capitalism, money simply served the ends of facilitating the satisfaction of genuine human needs, and so possessed no moral standing outside of its beneficial role in facilitating such a process. While Tawney may have called Marx the 'last of the Schoolmen' he was no such thing if this means he was in a position to appreciate their wrestlings with money and commercial society.

Equally, Marxism's repudiation of economic casuistry had tremendous intellectual consequences because of its institutionalisation as the state ideology of a large proportion of the world. For much of the rest of the world, Marxism became the official anti-ideology against which Freedom, Money and Market were adorned in the pure light of moral virtue and golden raiment of justice. This had the effect of polarising attitudes towards money and commercial society so that one was either for it – for the free market, for profit, for money – or against it. As a corollary, it largely eliminated the possibility for the kind of casuistical reflection on these kinds of matters we saw emerging in the work of Medieval thinkers. If everything is a matter of endorsing or rejecting money and commercial society then there is no space for careful discrimination of motives or reasons for participating in, or refusing to participate in, commercial practices or the pursuit of wealth and profit; nor for critically and sensitively assessing the moral consequences, individually and collectively, of such patterns of participation and refusal. The upshot was that reflection on morality within the marketplace came to be thought irrelevant.

Modern pro-commerce traditions: Utility, virtue and freedom of exchange

The Scottish philosopher, Adam Smith (1723–1790), is typically under-stood as standing at the beginning of the modern pro-commerce tradition in just the way that A.N. Whitehead took Plato to stand not merely at the origins of philosophy, but to do so with such authority that all succeeding European philosophy consisted merely of footnotes to the master.[128] This typical understanding is, if not wrong, at least partial. But many, if not all readers, took the line of an anonymous correspondent to *The Times* who, a few weeks after Smith's death in July 1790, wrote that Smith 'had converted the chair of Moral Philosophy' at Glasgow College 'into a professorship of trade and finance'.[129] The correspondent may have intended this with a sneer, but as the economic historian Donald Winch says, today such an assimilation of ethics and economics would meet with a decided cheer. For this audience Smith stands as the exem-plary expression of the virtues of commerce and the beneficent powers of the profit-motive.

The profit-motive, Smith says, is a consequence of the intersection of two desires which are embedded in human nature. In the first place, there is 'the uniform, constant, and uninterrupted effort of every man to better his condition';[130] in the second, there is 'the propen-sity to truck, barter, and exchange one thing for another'.[131] Through commercial exchange individuals seek to advance their interests, for one only 'trucks and barters' when doing so promises to further one's private ends.

Of course, the act of exchange, as Fourier insisted, is not an act of warm co-operation, but of competitive calculation in which each aims at their own good, not that of their fellow bargainer or the good of any larger group:

> It is not from the benevolence of the butcher, the brewer, or the baker, that we expect our dinner, but from their regard to their own interest. We address ourselves not to their humanity but their self-love, and never talk to them of our necessities but of their advantages.[132]

Commercial relationships do not track any virtue more substantial than that of an individual prudence that operates on the level of mate-rial well-being; though it must also be said that, like many other eighteenth-century moralists, Smith takes such prudence to be not merely something substantial, but even constitutive, of genuine virtue.

In the steadiness of his industry and frugality, in his steadily sacrific-
ing the ease and enjoyment of the present moment for the probable
expectation of the still greater ease and enjoyment of a more dis-
tant but more lasting period of time, the prudent man is always both
supported and rewarded by the entire approbation of the impartial
spectator, and of ... the man within the breast.[133]

But for others, including Smith's teacher, Frances Hutcheson
(1694–1746), and his successor to the Chair of Moral Philosophy at Glasgow, Thomas Reid (1710–1796), it was precisely the role of prudence in
commercial activity that evacuated it of any moral content. As Reid
wrote in his *Essays on the Active Powers of Man*:

Like a cunning merchant, he [the prudential man] carries his goods to
the best market, and watches every opportunity of putting them off
to best account. He does well and wisely. But it is for himself. We owe
him nothing upon his account. Even when he does good to others,
he means only to serve himself; and therefore has no just claim to
their gratitude or affection.

This surely, if it be virtue, is not the noblest kind, but a low and
mercenary species of it. It can neither give a noble elevation to the
mind that possesses it, nor attract the esteem and love of others.[134]

The Smithian response to such charges is to argue that they arise from a
failure to situate commercial prudence within a broader framework. We
should look at more than isolated commercial acts. The pursuit of profit
and ease has *systemic consequences* which only the misanthropic could
condemn, and which the morally concerned, out of their beneficence
and charity, must endorse. Thomas Hobbes (1588–1679), anticipating
Smith, makes this kind of argument in the *Leviathan*:

and Mony (of what manner soever coyned by the Soveraign of
a Common-wealth,) is a sufficient measure of the value of all
things else [beyond gold and silver], between the Subjects of that
Common-wealth. In so much as this Concoction, is as it were the
Sanguinification of the Common-wealth; For naturall Bloud is in like
manner made of the fruits of the Earth; and circulating, nourisheth,
by the way, every Member of the Body of Man.[135]

In Smith's more familiar language, the point is that while each 'intends
only his own gain', he is, through the exercise of his prudential ends,

'led by an invisible hand to promote an end which was no part of his intention'.[136] This end is 'that universal opulence which extends itself to the lowest ranks of people'; it is the enrichment of society, and furtherance of the 'Public Interest'. On some versions, *everyone* under such a system is better off than they would be otherwise. As Samuel Johnson (1709–1784) pithily remarked:

> though the perseverance and address of the Indian excite our admiration, they nevertheless cannot procure him the conveniences which are enjoyed by the vagrant beggar of a civilised country.[137]

But on other occasions the claim was the more plausible one that by and large *most* people were better off than they would be otherwise, though certainly some individuals might be less fortunate.

> As to the rout that is made about people who are ruined by extravagance, it is no matter to the nation that some individuals suffer. When so much general productive exertion is the consequence of luxury, the nation does not care though there are debtors in gaol; nay, they would not care though their creditors were there too.[138]

It follows, on these utilitarian lines, that the Medievals' concern with the way individuals exercise their moral virtues and vices in commercial life, let alone the blanket condemnation of socialists like Fourier, is either otiose or morally perverse.[139] It is otiose insofar as the commercial realm is the realm of prudence not benevolence, and it is perverse to the extent that it means condemning those very processes that make all better off than they would otherwise be.

In a later chapter we take up these claims, in particular the moral coherence of the divide between individual and systemic virtues and vices. For now the point is that the moral credentials of commercial society lie in the material realm, everyone – or at least the vast majority – is better off. Concerns for individual virtues and vices, and concerns with the justice of 'spot commercial exchanges', reflect either an ignorance of how the system works, or a high-minded and unwarranted condemnation of those very goods and services so dear to the heart of most men.

This consequentialist justification of commercial society dominates the pro-commerce arguments today, but it would be wrong to think that Smith rests content with this, or that this line of thought exhausts the ways in which philosophers have justified the commercial realm. We turn now to two other forms of justification in Smith, which focus on virtue or character and the right to trade.

The second strand of the pro-commercial tradition concerns itself with the character or virtue that commerce fosters. Although Smith regards it as perverse or wrong to look with the eyes of morality at lone instances of exchange, he does not think it mistaken to consider the *character* of those agents who willingly participate in the activities of commercial society. Whilst these might be regarded as subsidiary arguments to his moral defence of commerce, they all flow from his contention that in a genuinely commercial society shaped by the economic determinations of the unfettered operations of the profit-motive, a system of 'natural liberty' naturally emerges.

> All systems either of preference or restraint, therefore, being thus completely taken away, the obvious and simple system of natural liberty establishes itself of its own accord. Every man, as long as he does not violate the laws of justice, is left perfectly free to pursue his own interest his own way, and to bring both his industry and capital into competition with those of any other man, or order of men. The sovereign is completely discharged from a duty, in the attempting to perform which he must always be exposed to innumerable delusions, and for the proper performance of which no human wisdom or knowledge could ever be sufficient; the duty of superintending the industry of private people, and of directing it towards the employments most suitable to the interest of the society.[140]

From this Smith drew the following points, all of which can be, and have been, taken by others as sufficient for the moral justification of commercial life and society. First, commercial society ascendant stands against systems of despotism and arbitrary government. In doing this it removes the need for rulers to engage in necessarily injurious and unjust activities. Thus it both facilitates the rulers' pursuit of virtue and allows for and protects the sphere of individual initiative and freedom in which everyone else must pursue and find virtue. Second, and because of this circumscription of power, it allows for individuals to develop their freedom into a morally valuable autonomy in which they develop virtues which are admirable in themselves, and which aid them in becoming masters of their own destiny, self-reliant and able, fittingly, to take responsibility for the choices they make and the direction their lives take.

This is the point at which the second pro-commerce argument takes off. In *The Wealth of Nations*, Smith noted that the Dutch being the most commercial are the most punctual, and John Wesley, the Founder of the Methodist religion, thought commercial society encouraged a just frugality and calculation. This increase in moral virtue was thought to be a direct consequence of immersion in commercial relations. John Lalor (1814–1856), a nineteenth-century Unitarian economist writes in *Money and Morals: A Book for Our Times* (1852):[141]

> Mercantile morals are indeed not the highest, but they are high, and perhaps mark as high a point as has yet been attained by any wide-spread class of man. Untiring industry from youth up; resolute scorn of delights where they interfere with laborious days; faithful, exact performance of every business duty, great or minute; and a sensibility of mercantile honour, which, in the beautiful words of Burke, feels a stain like a wound – all these belong to the best types of the class, especially as it exists in England.[142]

Other writers focused on the intellectual virtues promoted by commerce. Hume claimed there to be a connection between the rise of commerce and the development of intellectual labour. He thinks that repetitive work can never produce an inclination and a tendency towards it.[143] This idea was taken up by the sociologist Georg Simmel. In his *Philosophy of Money* (1900), Simmel argues that it is only through the abstract relations that the development of a monetary economy fosters that certain kinds of intellectual abilities arise.[144] Perhaps he was taking a hint from Marx and Engel's acerbic comment in *The Manifesto of the Communist Party* (1848) on the idiocy of rural life.[145] William Hutton, in his *History of Birmingham* (1781), draws these strands together, connecting commercial society with civilisation itself:

> the intercourse occasioned by traffic [commerce] gives a man a view of the world and of himself; removes the narrow limits that confine his judgement; expands the mind; opens his understanding; removes his prejudices; and polishes his manners. Civility and humanity ever the companions of trade; the man of business is the man of liberal sentiment; a barbarous and commercial people is a contradiction.[146]

It is worth noticing that while these claims for the virtues and self-reliant probity of commercial life are attractive, and attractive to Smith, they are already at some remove from the purely utilitarian considerations that are thought ultimately to legitimate the institutions of commercial society.

There are two further points to be made concerning Smith's pro-commercialism. The first is that as Smith understands the matter, it is a feature of commercial society that it does not undermine social solidarity and community as critics from Plato onwards have contended, but rather further develops, extends and deepens such bonds. This is because the very roots of community lie in the self-interest activity that finds its clearest and most pervasive expression in commercial activity:

> Society may subsist among different men, as among different merchants, from a sense of its utility, without any mutual love or affection; and though no man in it should owe any obligation, or be bound in gratitude to any other, it may still be upheld by a mercenary exchange of good offices according to an agreed valuation.[147]

And because such activity simply deepens and ramifies the bonds of interconnectedness:

> without the assistance and co-operation of many thousands, the very meanest person in a civilized country could not be provided, even according to, what we very falsely imagine, the easy and simple manner in which he is commonly accommodated.[148]

The second point is that *inequality*, which so worried earlier moralists, is no longer considered morally objectionable, but an essential part of the operations of a system in which 'a general plenty diffuses itself through all the different ranks of the society'.[149] In a passage dear to the hearts of the well-off everywhere, Smith makes the point with, for him, unusual directness:

> The rich only select from the heap what is most precious and agreeable. They consume little more than the poor, and in spite of their natural selfishness and rapacity, though they mean only their own conveniency, though the sole end which they propose from the labours of all the thousands whom they employ, be the gratification of their own vain and insatiable desires, they divide with the poor the produce of all their improvements. They are led by an invisible hand to make nearly the same distribution to the necessaries of life, which would have been made, had the earth been divided into equal portions among all its inhabitants, and thus ... advance the interest of the society, and afford means to the multiplication of the species.

When Providence divided the earth among a few lordly masters, it neither forgot nor abandoned those who seemed to have been left out of the partition. These last too enjoy their share of all that it produces.[150]

This 'green and pleasant' vision, in which all 'enjoy their share', should not be understood as resting on a notion of desert above that commercial society insists upon when it strictly correlates entitlement to available purchasing power. As Smith's contemporary, Condorcet, thinking of a dearth and famine in grains ('corn') explained, when corn merchants raise their prices under such straited circumstances, and to such a level that it 'discourages the consumption' of 'the inferior ranks of people', this should not be seen as morally pernicious or impermissible – indeed, quite the contrary; for such merchants and such prices *help to avert famine* by bringing about a 'diminution in the consumption of the poor'.[151]

There is a third significant strand of pro-commercial argument which, while it may have been suggested by Smith's approach – in particular his talk of the emergence under commercial society of a system of 'natural liberty' – derives more obviously from the thought of John Locke. On this view the justification of commercial society does not lie with its powers to increase general levels of material prosperity, nor does it lie in the way that it might generate and favour certain admirable moral or intellectual virtues; it lies rather in the fortunate (or unfortunate) fact that only commercial society accords with those fundamental human rights all people bear in virtue of their (shared) *humanity*. The implication is that *all* the casuistical moral questions that might be directed at commercial activities are to be answered by pointing to the moral legitimacy of the market *per se*.

This style of argument has found its most powerful and influential modern defence in the American philosopher Robert Nozick's single book on political theory, *Anarchy, State and Utopia*.[152] Developing his position from Lockean foundations Nozick claims that all human beings possess, in virtue of their humanity, the moral rights to life, liberty and private property. On this basis Nozick develops an 'entitlement theory of justice' which contains three elements: (i) justice in acquisition, (ii) justice in transfer and (iii) justice in rectification.[153] Justice in acquisition concerns how one might rightly come to own which was previously unowned. Justice in transfer concerns the appropriate rules for the exchange of property, while justice in rectification is concerned with the appropriate remedial actions when the requirements of just acquisition and just transfer have been violated.

Nozick's argument begins with the question of how one might justly acquire property and how, having obtained property, we may legitimately engage in trade. Life and liberty are, of course, the possessions of every person, but the right to private property does not mean that every person has a real claim on some delineated portion of the earth or its resources, or on any of its resources at all; it means only that every man has the capacity, through their labour, to acquire property to which they are then entitled. The right is not *to* property, as it is under certain socialist and egalitarian conceptions, but *to acquire* property in the appropriate way, if such (potential) property is available. This is 'justice in acquisition', and it arises whenever one mixes one's labour with a portion of the earth to which no-one else has, through their labour, a prior claim.[154]

Many issues now arise – for instance, how the labour entitlement is to be derived from the rights to life and liberty, what counts as *genuine* labour, and what to do when an acquisition is, in this sense, unjust – but these are not our concern here. Our concern is with that justice (*justice in transfer*) that emerges from the fact of legitimate ownership in acts of consensual commercial exchange.

Justice in transfer encompasses commercial exchanges that are consensual in the sense that they do not involve the violation of the rights of either of the parties concerned. They must not be tainted by any hint of force or fraud.

The theory of justice Nozick develops is, in his own words, an *unpatterned historical* theory.[155] It is *unpatterned* because unlike meritocratic theories which demand that the pattern of holdings be determined by the relative merits of citizens, or egalitarian theories which demand an equal distribution, it is not interested in any particular final pattern of holdings. It is *historical* in the sense that the history of how agents came to acquire goods matters for their entitlement. If they justly acquired them through legitimate processes – through labour and without violating anyone's rights – then they have a legitimate entitlement to them.

Nozick's categories have a taxonomical and evaluative function; they not only mark his theory out from other accounts of distributive justice but provide the basis of his criticism of those other theories.[156] Nozick argues vehemently against any patterning in the distribution of holdings.[157] Any such pattern can only be achieved and maintained by infringing on our natural liberties. Unless the state regulates every 'capitalistic act between consenting adults', then very soon the required pattern will be upset.[158] The sexual metaphor carries much of the moral weight of the argument: just as many think the state has no right to govern what people do in their bedroom, there is equally no right to interfere in the private acts of exchange in which people engage. Since patterning can only be maintained through state intervention and such intervention is morally indefensible, we must reject theories of justice that involve patterning.[159]

For Nozick, there can be no imposed 'patterning' of prices in the market, be it on the basis of need, or out of a desire to reduce inequality, or out of a suspicion of the motives of the vendor. Equally, there is nothing that – given the willingness of the exchange – cannot be appropriately exchanged in the market.

This moral defence of 'capitalist acts between consenting adults' has a number of striking consequences, not least of which is that it leaves no room for the kind of economic casuistry that wishes to draw moral distinctions within the realm of commercial activities. One might well think – as the Medievals and Socialists thought – that the moral objectionableness of force and fraud opened the door to various kinds of moralistic assessment of commercial activities, even if such activities are, in the minimal sense, consensual. After all, one may consent to something not because one takes it to be a fair or proper bargain, but because if one does not then certain adverse circumstances might foreseeably follow, such as not being able to eat. It is a truth, socialists are right to emphasise, that even choice may be a site of exploitation and power. Nozick avoids the point by insisting on a sense of coercion which is extraordinarily narrow. Thus, if one is drowning and a boat passes, there is for Nozick no question of coercion, but only of consensual choice, if one's being plucked from the water involves agreeing to provide the boatman with all the wealth one hitherto possessed.

A further consequence of his defence of consensual exchange is that there is absolutely nothing which might not be exchanged. For Nozick, one may under duress sell oneself into a slavery.[160] The person drowning in the ocean who is offered assistance on the condition that he gives up all of his material possessions is not coerced, Nozick says, for he always has the option to refuse.[161]

An even more striking consequence is that concerns about need-satisfaction and levels of inequality have no place in assessing the moral status of market exchange and outcomes. Any concern with justice-in-pricing, as with, say, anti-HIV drugs which are priced outside the reach of the majority of sufferers, is to be answered simply and conclusively by pointing to the operations of that market which delivers such prices.

Finally, let us notice something that all too often is not noticed, or if noticed, then immediately forgotten. For despite the vigour with which Nozick closes the door on moral assessments of commercial activities, that closure is itself merely conditional. For the justification of the market as a moral free-fire zone depends first on the (unargued) claim that human beings possess rights, and indeed just those rights which Nozick specifies; and second, that these rights do indeed lead to, and lead only to, commercial society of the kind Nozick envisages. In this sense the defence is not a robust one in the way implied by the Smithian claim that to truck and barter is a universal human tendency which, unleashed, will ensure the best possible material return to everyone. After all, there may be non-commercial modes of interrelationship (e.g. those of charity or of gift-exchange) which equally respect such rights; and more importantly, there may be morally defensible modes of commerce which involve their violation.[162]

But despite its conditionality, the implications of the Nozickian argument are the same as the other pro-commercial arguments: within the realm of monetarised exchange there is no room for finer moral discrimination. Indeed, desire for such discrimination is mistaken. The right to freedom of exchange over-rides whatever moral concerns one might have about various harms caused by the operations of commerce. It is a sphere beyond economic casuistry.

Concluding remarks

This brief survey of philosophers and others' reflections on the moral status of money and commercial life has led us from the anti-commercialism of the Ancients and early Church Fathers, to the initially grudging but eventually accepting attitude towards money, the merchant and trading, in the late Medievals, back to a situation in which money and commerce are to be viewed with the suspicion and hostility of a Tertullian, or to be endorsed and celebrated with the uninhibited gusto of Adam Smith and his successors. It would be pleasant to think this trajectory one of increasing insight and illumination, but insofar as the extremes stand in contradiction to each other this cannot be; and besides, the extreme positions, with their tendency to conceive of commercial life in hegemonic terms, fail to give us any account of those everyday moral and evaluative distinctions, qualms and questions, which surround us in commercial society.

Our aim is to restore a language of economic casuistry. Our approach is more akin to the Medieval stance on money and commerce, than the views of later socialists or followers of Smith; however, there is a key difference between us and the Medievals in that for us the profit-motive is not, in itself, always morally problematic in a way that means it is permissible only if it founds or subserves intrinsically valuable non-pecuniary ends. We share, however, their view that an *either/or* attitude towards money and commerce is not merely mistaken, but closes off, and prematurely, the search for self-understanding that Socrates insisted defined the philosophical enterprise.

In order to develop an economic casuistry we turn from history to philosophical analysis. For behind the sweeping condemnations and approbations of money and commerce we find a veritable tangle of argumentation. Our approach will be casuistical in the sense that it requires us to draw distinctions where others have generally preferred the broader swathes of pro- or anti-commercial rhetoric.

Our first topic will be the profit-motive. Money opens up the possibility for the pursuit of unlimited profit and, as we have seen, for many this connection provides sufficient grounds on its own for repudiating the pecuniary absolutely. Avarice, *pleonexia* and *cupiditas* were condemned in no uncertain terms. What should we make of this blanket condemnation? In the following chapter we explore the profit-motive and suggest that it is more complex than these traditional objections suggest.

3
The Profit-Motive and Morality

There are not many of us who remain sober when we have the opportunity to grow wealthy, or prefer measure to abundance. The great multitude of men are of a completely contrary temper – what they desire they desire out of all measure – when they have the option of making a reasonable one they prefer to make an exorbitant one.

Plato, *The Laws*, Bk. XI, 918d–918e

Introduction

Our attitudes towards the profit-motive are more vexed than might at first appear. On the one hand, we typically deem profit-seeking socially desirable, even necessary. We appreciate the plethora of commodities that markets, fuelled by the profit-motive, produce and, like Adam Smith, are well aware that it is not from the benevolence of the butcher or the baker that we expect to find bread or meat upon our table.

On the other hand, we often treat the *merest* hint of self-interest in another's purposes as grounds for suspicion. Those who collect for charity on the condition that they receive some percentage of the take drift into a morally dubious realm that raises suspicions, not the least of which is whether the charity will receive any of the money. To make the claim about any commercial agent that 'they are *just* doing it for profit' is typically to impugn their motives to such an extent that even merchants and financial speculators feel the need to present themselves as public benefactors. Consider the sign that appears regularly in our local butcher: *For Your Convenience We Will Be Open On Christmas Eve*. Imagine, in order to make the point more vivid, if our butcher had written instead *We Will Be Open Because We'd Rather Have Your Money Than Celebrate Christmas Eve*.

There seems to be some residual need, even in the commercial realm, to maintain the perception of unselfish public service.

Then there is the view that the profit-motive drives many to vice and not only accidentally: we are thought to be, in the words of the English poet Gerard Manley Hopkins, 'bleared and smeared by trade'. In *The Long Good-Bye*, Raymond Chandler makes a similar point, less succinctly perhaps but with more power, when he has his hard-bitten detective Bernie Ohls pronounce:

> There ain't no clean way to make a hundred million bucks. Maybe the head man thinks his hands are clean but somewhere along the line guys got pushed to the wall, nice little businesses got the ground cut from under them and had to sell out for nickels, decent people lost their jobs, stocks got rigged on the market, proxies got bought up like a pennyweight of old gold, and the five per centers and the big law firms got paid hundred grand fees for beating some law the people wanted but the rich guys didn't, on account of it cut into their profits.[1]

We all recognise that there is some truth in this hard-boiled cynicism, as did Adam Smith when he noted that it is scarce possible for three merchants to get together without perpetrating a conspiracy against the public good.[2]

We seem caught between conflicting and diametrically opposed responses to the profit-motive, between applauding its outcomes and rejecting it entirely as irredeemably tainted with vice. The first step in resolving this dilemma is to increase the resolution of our analytic microscope. Rather than speaking of '*the* profit-motive' as if it were exhaustive of our motivational resources when it comes to dealing with money, we need to consider those motivational sets or arrays within which a concern for profit may have its place.[3]

We should note that in pursuing this goal we will often leap across historical periods; the justification for doing so lies in part with our view about the continuity of those moral attitudes people have exhibited towards money.

Six objections to the profit-motive

What have been the *principal objections* to the profit-motive *per se*? We can distil six main objections, some of which are arguments from *irrationality*, *meaninglessness* and some of which are arguments from *immorality*. These objections involve (i) making an end of a means; (ii) the endless iteration of financial goals; (iii) pleonexia; (iv) sharp practice, lying and fraud; (v) the denial of amity-based relations; and (vi) exploitation.

The first objection is that the pursuit of profit is not a proper end of activity. Money and profit are simply *means*, not *ends*; yet those who pursue profit are in danger of regarding money as an end-in-itself. Aquinas, as we have seen, makes this point in the *Summa Theologiae*. It is not that pursuing profit is vicious necessarily, but that all too easily it is so.

Some writers have gone further claiming that the profit-motive is a universal substitute motive. It is not simply treated as an end but can replace all other motives as the universal goal. Keynes writes:

> Why do practical men find it more amusing to make money than to join in open conspiracy? That is why, unless they have the luck to be scientists or artists, they fall back on the grand substitute motive, the perfect *ersatz*, the anodyne for those who, in fact, want nothing at all – money.[4]

By treating money as the ultimate end, money comes to replace all other motives. One is reminded of Aristotle in the *Politics* when he suggests that some people turn every quality or art into a means of making money; this they conceive to be the end, '... as though to make money were the one aim and everything else must contribute to that aim'.[5] It has been a theme of writing on money ever since. Rousseau condemns those who only speak of money and commerce,[6] while the American economist John Kenneth Galbraith (1908–2006) points to the young financial deal-maker who 'surrenders all personal effort and conscience to pecuniary return' and measures all personal achievement by its result. Galbraith ends the passage with the comment that perhaps Aristotle should be read on Wall Street.[7]

The focus on money *as an end* is inappropriate because one's activities become mere means to the pursuit of profit and this in turn empties out the specific motivations people have for undertaking any particular task. What activities one pursues become – in terms of its content – entirely arbitrary. If one has the pursuit of profit as a goal then one might well not care what activities one undertakes in that pursuit, so long as it involves profit. In the *Republic*, Plato complains of those who 'have too many callings' [552]. The danger with the profit-motive is that it can undermine the idea of a *vocation*; any job becomes merely an opportunity for the pursuit of wealth. Money thus gives us too many callings or, perhaps, none at all.

What might be the grounds of this alleged mistake? For Aristotle it is not just an intellectual error, but also a *natural error* that derives from two sources. On the side of the agent, there is the danger of regarding money as an end-in-itself. On the side of money, it is that it stores easily and does not spoil. Both come together to make it natural to regard money as an end-in-itself.

A second objection is that the pursuit of money is a goal without a *telos*.[8] Unlike many other goals, such as the successful building of a sea-worthy boat, it has no satisfaction conditions and endlessly iterates.[9] *Genuine* activities have a realisable goal and do not endlessly iterate. A genuine human activity is one in which there is a possibility of satisfactory completion. The hoodlum, Mendez, in *The Long Good-bye* expresses this endless iteration:

> I'm a big man, Marlowe. I make lots of dough. I got to make lots of dough to juice the guys I got to juice in order to make lots of dough to juice the guys I got to juice.[10]

A similar point is made by the contemporary English philosopher David Wiggins when he discusses the Southern hog farmer who buys more land to buy more corn to feed more pigs to buy more land and so on. Wiggins is concerned with the *restlessness* of the Southern hog farmer.[11]

A bleaker variant of this objection has it that the iteration ends in *addiction*. If the pursuit of wealth is an endless activity, then one can easily become addicted to the momentary satiation which because it craves another is never satisfied. This seems to have been Plato's point in his discussions of the tyrannical man in the *Republic* and *the Gorgias*, for here we have conflict and territorial aggrandisement that result from the pursuit of unlimited wealth, and which itself stems from flouting the limits of necessity.[12]

A third objection concerns what the ancient Greeks called *pleonexia*, the Romans and Medievals, *cupiditas* or 'covetousness', and we now label 'avarice' or 'greed'. While the first two objections involve philosophical confusions about the ends of activities, here we have a concern that has long been a staple of religious and literary discussion of money. While in 1 Timothy 6:10 it is said that 'Covetousness is the root of all evils', and in Ecclesiastes 5:10 it is said that 'He who loveth silver shall not be satisfied with silver: nor he that loveth abundance with increase: this is also vanity.' Recall the quotation at the outset of this chapter from Plato's Athenian who remarks that few of us can resist the temptation to maximise.[13]

We can distinguish two forms of the 'rapacious appetite for gain'. One of these is *instrumental* in so far as it serves as a vehicle for pride and luxury, while the second is an end-in-itself. As Abraham Cowley says in his essay 'Of Avarice' (1665) that the first one is '...but of a bastard kind, and that is, the rapacious appetite of gain; not for its own sake but for the pleasure of redunding it immediately through all the channels of pride and luxury'.[14] While the second is the true kind and properly so called, 'which is a restless and unsatiable desire of riches, not for any further use, but only to hoard, and preserve, and perpetually increase them'.[15]

In the fifteenth century William of Rennes defined *cupiditas* as:

> a wanton desire for having temporal riches, not for necessary use or utility, but for curiosity, so that fancy is charmed by such, just as a magpie or a crow is enticed by coins, which they discover and hide away.[16]

For William such greed for wealth is a mortal sin. San Antonino argues that the pursuit of profit is most reprehensible because the desire for gain knows no bounds but reaches into the infinite.[17] He echoes the Stoic philosopher Epictetus who argued that once you have a passion for money, unless reason is brought to bear on this passion, it would become inflamed until it becomes a fever.[18]

In either case, the harm philosophers have discerned in *pleonexia* can be divided into the *self-regarding* and the *other-regarding*. Self-regarding harms concern the adverse impact of *pleonexia* on character and the possibilities for human flourishing, whilst other-regarding harms concern the adverse social consequences of this vice.

Self-regarding harm is captured in the King Midas myth where the all-consuming desire for wealth almost leads to Midas' demise. Here the loss of view of other things and the monomaniacal restlessness impoverishes the values that might inform one's life.[19] It is for this reason Seneca (4 BC–65 AD) says that the greedy are always in want.[20]

Pleonexia is sometimes said to give rise to a one-dimensionality that stymies human flourishing or upsets the proper balance of a well-adjusted person. For Plato the oligarchic personality was one in which the love of money, as the ruling passion, leads to a neglect of *sophrosune*, that is, of the virtue required if one's life is to be just and harmonious.

The love of money is sometimes thought to distract us from that which matters and, in particular, from religious and philosophical pursuits. St Augustine feared that trade would turn human beings from the search for God. Others, influenced by Socrates, have argued that to pursue wealth is to give up on the philosophical life.[21] Aristotle held that because the pursuit of profit is at odds with the proper intellectual orientation of a citizen, those engaged in commercial life should not be allowed to be citizens.[22]

But not all philosophical criticism focuses on one-dimensionality of profit-seeking. The German philosopher Arthur Schopenhauer (1788–1860), foreshadowing Keynes, provides a different take on the harms to the self of avarice.[23] After identifying some positive features – in particular the prudential element associated with a due concern for managing future uncertainty – he turns to its negative role as the quintessence of all vices. Since avarice survives the decay of our capacity to satisfy other vices, it thus replaces them all.

> Money, which represents the dry trunk overgrown with all the dead lusts of the flesh, which are egoism in the abstract. They come to life again in the love of Mammon. The transient pleasure of the senses has become a deliberate and calculated lust of money, which like that to which it is directed, is symbolic in its nature, and like it, indestructible.[24]

Unsurprisingly, avarice is the sin of the aged.

> This obstinate love of the pleasures of the world – a love which, as it were, outlives itself; this utterly incorrigible sin, this refined and sublimated desire of the flesh, is the abstract form in which all lusts are concentrated, and to which it stands like a general idea to individual particulars.[25]

Even when we become as angels, free from the mortal constraints of the physical, the vice of avarice may still take root in our souls.

The fourth objection is that the *other-regarding* harms of *pleonexia* involve cases where one's love of money may lead one towards exorbitant profits, exploitation, lying, sharp practice and fraud. This has been a staple of literature. The connection between moral corruption and money is a recurrent theme of those artistic works which consider the profit-motive. Consider, for instance, Frederick Duerrematt's play 'The Visit' which explores the corrosive effects of money on our morals. In the play, a rich widow, Claire Zachanassian returns to her old home town to buy justice in the form of the death of a former lover who had jilted her many years before. 'Justice cannot be bought', responds the burghermeister of the town. But as the town becomes slowly wedded to debts to Zachanassian, we discover that the townspeople can in fact be bought and chillingly, the widow buys her justice. The ex-lover is killed. Similar themes are to be found in many other playwrights; Shakespeare's *Merchant of Venice, Troillus and Cressida, Timon of Athens*, Christopher Marlowe's *The Jew of Malta*, Granville Barker's *The Voysey Inheritance* and so on.

The concern with fraud has ancient origins. Ptolemy of Lucca (d.c.1328) recalled an old saying that 'Money is from *monere* (to warn), because it warns against fraud.'[26] In the fifth century Pope Leo I (d. 461) sums things up with the phrase 'it is difficult for buyers and sellers not to fall into sin'.[27] The late Medieval philosopher and Bishop of Lisieux, Nicholas Oresme (1330–1382) distinguished three ways in which one might make money: (i) through the 'art of exchange'; (ii) through usury or interest-taking; and (iii) through the alteration of money.[28] Oresme was especially concerned with the third and wrote extensively on the dangers of the debasement of the currency, through the physical diminution of coins by the monetary authorities by shaving and other such techniques.[29] Oresme, like the philosopher and logician Jean Buridan (1295–1358), ascribed intrinsic value to the monetary metals, and so condemned as unjust the gains derived from the debasement practices of the authorities of his time.

Debasement of the coinage is but one form of sharp practice or fraud where one makes money through the production or exchange of inferior products. The profit-motive is condemned on the grounds of the seemingly irresistible temptation it provides to employ fraudulent means. Much of Plato's discussion on the perils of money in *The Laws* deals with fraud. And the Church Fathers too worried about it, as can be seen from St Ambrose's (339–397) demand that:

> In contracts it is ordered that the faults in the things which are sold be made known; and if the seller has not declared these, the contracts are held void by action for fraud, even if the property has passed into the possession of the purchaser.[30]

Peter the Chanter (d.1197) offered specific advice to priests who resided in commercial quarters and administered penance to butchers and other retailers. If a butcher deceived an unwary buyer with tainted meat, not only should he restore the price, but perform penance for homicide because he had endangered the life of his customer. Merchants who attempted to fool customers by dyeing cheap cloth to look like better material were required to return what they obtained from such practices.[31] In other places the Chanter asked to what extent the responsibility of the original seller survived subsequent re-sales of defective goods. A contemporary, Robert of Courson, proposed that prelates supervise the markets to prevent the sale of defective items such as lame horses and spoiled meat.[32]

Many critics of the profit-motive have focused on the lying that they take to be an integral part of the life of the merchant. The Biblical story of Ananias and Saphira who lied about the price of their land was one source of such criticism. In this story Ananias, with his wife Saphira, sold a piece of land and by fraud kept back part of the price of the land. The story ends tragically with both Ananias and his wife dying barely 3 hours after being chastised by the Apostle Peter.[33]

We also find this theme in classical sources. In *De Officiis*, Cicero claims that retail traders have little to gain unless they are dishonest, and San Bernardino (1380–1444) is said to have disliked the haggling of the marketplace because it was so often associated with 'lies, perjury and swearing'.[34]

The pursuit of profit may lead to forms of *insincerity*. Think of fortune hunters with their feigned love, or the used car salesmen with their insincere sales pitch who provided insincere appearances of conviviality. Marx in the 1844 Manuscripts beautifully captures this inversion of values:

> What I am and can do is not at all determined by my individuality. I am ugly, but I can buy the most beautiful women for myself. Consequently I am not ugly. . . . I am stupid, but since money is the real mind of things, how could its possessor be stupid?[35]

It is only because those whom the rich come in contact with are motivated by the love of money that such inversions of values are possible. The relations are inauthentic because they do not reflect their respective *natural* virtues and vices, but rather their relative access to money.

A fifth objection to the 'pursuit of profit' holds that profit distorts the motives of human solidarity. The idea is (roughly) that in commercial society we confront each other not as fellow beings, but as members of two nations whose interests are not merely discontinuous, but necessarily and essentially hostile.

> For where there is envy and contentiousness, there is instability and every wicked deed.
>
> (James 3:16)

The operations of the profit-motive generate social conditions in which human fellowship – human solidarity – is not merely undermined, but is fractured. Cicero (106–43 BC) says that to profit by another's loss is to strike at the 'roots of human society and fellowship'.

> For if we each of us propose to rob or injure another for our personal gain, then we are clearly going to demolish what is more emphatically nature's creation than anything else in the whole human world: namely, the link that unites every human being with every other.[36]

The British social critic and historian Thomas Carlyle (1795–1881) also rails against the destruction of fraternal bonds by commercial society. In a remarkable passage in *Past and Present*, he writes:

> We call it a Society; and go about professing openly the totalest separation, isolation. Our life is not a mutual helpfulness; but rather, cloaked under due laws-of-war, named 'fair competition' and so forth, it is a mutual hostility. We have profoundly forgotten everywhere that *Cash-payment* is not the sole relation of human beings; we think, nothing doubting, that *it* absolves and liquidates all engagements of man.[37]

The thought is that cash payment undermines the basis of shared and common values on which human moral community depends. Community disintegrates as people confront each other not as fellow beings, but as members of two separate nations, whose interests are not merely discontinuous, but necessarily and essentially hostile. In just the same way the Medieval Franciscans worried about the effect of cash payments on human relations for their vows of poverty were underpinned by the belief that money was harmful to the ideal of universal amity.[38] As Carlyle himself complained:

> Never on this earth, was the relation of man to man long carried on by Cash-payment alone. If, at any time, a philosophy of laissez-faire, Competition, and Supply-and-demand, start up as the exponent of human relations, expect that it will end soon.[39]

In this vein, R.H. Tawney remarked dryly in *Religion and the Rise of Capitalism* that affection is not very common among merchants.[40]

A sixth and final objection concerns exploitation. Many critics of the profit-motive have argued that the commercial relations it generates are necessarily exploitative, for trade is a zero-sum game. An early exponent of the view was St Jerome (347–419) who argued that if one person gains then it must be the case that the other party to the exchange loses. The idea finds its most famous and controversial expression in the writings of Marx, where the surplus value or profit of the capitalist is gained entirely at the expense of the worker.

In an associated thought, many have thought that traders do not do anything and therefore commercial relations must be exploitative. This was certainly the view of a group of seventeenth-century economic thinkers known as the 'Physiocrats'.[41] According to the Physiocrats all wealth came from the earth and from agricultural production; since trade added nothing to the value of the goods, commercial traders must of necessity be shysters and con men.

These six are the basic objections that moral philosophers have made to the profit-motive. Unlike some of our earlier writers, we do not think that the profit-motive *per se* is morally illegitimate, even when it is the final end of the action. In the rest of this chapter we develop an account of the profit-motive that allows us to draw moral distinctions between the legitimate and the illegitimate pursuit of profit.

Some cases where profit-seeking and morality seem not to collide

The objections we have discussed to the licitness of the profit-motive divide into two rough classes. One set of objections is *morally focused*: it is the immorality of exhibiting and indulging the profit-motive that attracts censure. The other set of objection is *metaphysical*: they purport to uncover something irrational, deficient, perverse or corrupt in the very logic of profit pursuit. Both kinds of objection point towards phe-nomena of which we are all too well aware, but in the end we are not inclined to think either kind of objection delivers grounds for the rejec-tion or abolition of the profit-motive. Instead, they provide grounds for a studied caution.

The first point to make is that it is not true that in commercial exchange oriented to profit the relevant motive must be characterised as *selfish*. Consider the case of a doctor who is concerned to profit from the exercise of her skills. Perhaps she is only concerned with profit in so far as it permits her some selfish pay-off (more and longer holidays, etc.), but equally perhaps she is concerned to recycle her profit into improved treatment and services, and not just so as to make more profit (and so take more and longer holidays) but to improve the health outcomes.

Consider too that the desire to profit may be essential to the effective provision of some genuinely desired good or service. Thus, if I wish, for reasons of aesthetic preference and a concern for general utility, to improve the architectural standards of my community, then the way to do this – indeed, more than likely, the only effective way of doing this – might be to establish a successful (and so remunerative) design business. Equally, if I wish for environmental reasons to reduce the need for garbage infill, then the most effective way of doing so may be to establish an efficient and competitive waste-recycling industry.

The point here is a simple one, but too often overlooked. For to pursue profit does not mean that one must see profit as an end-in-itself, just as to pursue top marks in a competitive university environment does not mean that 'coming first' is an end-in-itself. Rather the end may be excellence in a discipline, though the competitive environment, just as in the competitive market, means one cannot avoid pursuing such marks.

A different mistake is to think that if someone is pursuing a clearly self-regarding end, such pursuit is necessarily morally objectionable or, at the very least, morally questionable. That this is wrong can be seen as soon as we realise that pursuing that which one *needs* is to be engaged in self-regarding activity. After all, it can hardly be held that it is morally objectionable for a person to seek to have their needs met: and if, for any reason, it is so held, then the obvious corollary is that altruism or other-regarding actions are themselves immoral. Indeed, what is the difference between my providing for my needs and you doing so, or aiding me in doing so? If it is wrong for me to provide for myself, what is it that makes the wrongfulness of this provision turn into virtue when someone else does it? And notice that we can not say that one case is self-regarding, the other, other-regarding. For while this is true, the question is what makes the other-regardingness in this case a good thing? After all, there are other-regarding concerns (malevolence, for instance), which are clearly not morally legitimate. Thus to even distinguish between these two possible styles of other-regardingness we need to allow for some concerns of others – for instance, with the provision of what they need – a positive value.

Beneath the abolitionist approach to the pursuit of profit there is a problematic idealisation or inflation of moral standards. Of course, idealisation has deep roots in morality, and is not to be rejected out of hand.[42] For it is true, there are occasions in which idealisation plays a vital role in furthering the ends of morality. For example, the person who aspires to goodness might well find it useful to set an idealised standard of behaviour for themselves in order to encourage or facilitate their pursuit of virtue. Of course, if they idealise too much, it may be that the perceived impossibility of attaining such standards undermines their interest in heeding such standards in the first place or leads them towards hypocritical double-mindedness. Over-idealisation is a possibility and potentially a pernicious one.

Even if there is a legitimate place for appropriate idealisation in approaching one's own concern to be good or virtuous, it does not follow that it is legitimate to judge *others* against such idealised standards. It is, indeed, a staple of Christianity that such overly assertive righteousness is itself morally hazardous, and, all too often, an 'occasion for sin'.

Behind the kind of idealisation that insists that only saintliness deserves moral respect – and so that condemns all pursuit of profit – is a conception of moral purity that views any engagement with the messy world of contingency as a dirtying of our hands. The difficulty of this conception rests on a failure to appreciate that a genuine moral 'ought' implies the possibility of a genuinely empirical 'can'. And this is not an arbitrary or dispensable commitment; for without it morality and action come apart, and the idealisation of morality threatens to remove it from the world altogether. We have morality, and it has importance for us, just because we are neither all knaves nor saints, and this is just as true in the sphere of commercial life and the concern for profit as it is anywhere else.

If the aspiration for moral purity is one route to over-idealisation, another route lies with a concern at the fragility of morality. The worry is a kind of insecurity that can only be met if morality can utterly obliterate any and all self-regarding claims. But to think this is not only to encounter the problem of needs provision discussed above, but also to embrace the claim that even the *tincture* of self-concern will inevitably corrode away any genuine concern for others.

None of this is to deny that the pursuit of profit is often immoral. The earlier objections point to behaviour of which we are all too familiar. We see exploitation, fraud and avarice in our market societies every day. Our point is a *modal* one. It is not necessarily the case that profit-seeking is immoral. Indeed, there seem to be cases – think of our earlier case of the doctor – where the pursuit of profit is not merely morally neutral but in fact coincides with, and may even further, virtuous ends. What we require is an economic casuistry in which we can draw distinctions between forms of profit-seeking, between the morally permissible and the morally impermissible. To do this, we need to begin with an analysis of the relationship between self-interest and altruism.

But before doing so, we should consider the specifically *metaphysical objections* to profit-seeking. Although our concern is with money and morality, as opposed to money and the meaning of life, it is worth thinking about the charges that money's pursuit might be by its very nature meaningless and futile.

The idea is not that the pursuit of profit is a *moral* vice which reflects and encourages an indifference or competitive hostility towards others, but that it involves an agent in a pathological form of activity that damages her own flourishing or well-being. Rather than threatening vice, the profit-motive threatens to undermine, or evacuate the *meaningfulness*, by ourselves and with others, of our lives.

The linchpin of the Aristotelian argument is the idea that an action is only *well formed* to the extent that it can be *completed*. Only that which can be completed has a determinate identity; and only that which has a determinate identity can bear meaning. The pursuit of profit, however, has no natural goal or end in which it might finds completion. It *harries* agents, rather than *fulfilling* them. It is pathological in just the sense that neurotic or compulsive behaviour is pathological: indeed, in modern parlance, the Aristotelian objection is simply that the pursuit of profit is a kind of compulsive neurosis.

It is not our purpose to assess the philosophical and psychological credentials of compulsive neurosis; instead, our aim is to highlight the dubious nature of some of those ideas on which such a diagnosis of meaninglessness rests.

The first point is that even if the Aristotelian criticism of the profit-motive as pathological obtains, so that the activity in itself is 'meaningless', there are many other things one might pursue *via* that commercial activity which are meaningful. Indeed, it may well be that it is precisely because of that profit which one manages to procure in the supposedly meaningless activity that the pursuit of meaningful goals becomes possible.

The second point is that the diagnosis of meaningless rests on the idea that the *iterability* of profit-pursuing actions is somehow pathological, but clearly this cannot be a *general* truth. After all, the iterability of an action may simply reflect the fact that such actions are (say) a matter of routine necessity. Is it a matter of pathology, for instance, that we are motivated, over and over and over again, to procure food for ourselves? Or that we are motivated to go and see our football team play its next opponent?

David Wiggins – perhaps because of this lacuna in the Aristotelian argument – suggests that it is not iterability itself that generates meaninglessness, but rather the *boredom* generated by such iteration, and the *restlessness* manifest in the iterative activity itself.[43] Boredom is, however, a matter of experience, and, at least on the available evidence, it seems clear that some people do find the pursuit of profit endlessly exciting. The objection from restlessness points, presumably, to the fact that the pursuit of profit, like that of personal sustenance, is such that one cannot ever settle comfortably in the knowledge that this will not have to be done again. But, again, so what? E.M. Forster may have felt disappointed because his sexual desires did not leave him as he aged, but this surely tells us something about Forster, not the meaningfulness of sexual desire *per se*.

The Aristotelian objections rest on the view that the pursuit of profit is *necessarily* a matter of compulsive neurosis. And while it is certainly true that some people do exhibit what deserves to be called such a compulsion, it is not true that everyone who pursues profit, even in the most dedicated of fashions, is subject to such a compulsion. Just as it turned out that the moral objections to the profit-motive were best understood as indicators of morally hazardous aspects of the pursuit of profit, so too the metaphysical objections are best understood as indicating the psychologically hazardous aspects of that pursuit.

Rethinking self-interest

If the standard objections to the profit-motive are best understood as well-grounded worries about the moral hazards of dedicated profit-seeking, why it is that these objections have been thought to point to some *necessary*, and not merely *possible*, immorality? The answer lies in two common theses about the nature and moral standing of self-interest, which together feed into a problematic conception of moral virtue.

The first thesis holds that self-interest is nothing more or less than selfishness; while the second thesis, and now coming at the issue from the other side, holds that altruism cannot exist in any motivational setting in which self-interest exerts any force. In both cases the underlying conception of morality is the same: morality cannot contain, but only set itself against, self-interest. We think both theses are false and the underlying conception of morality, mistaken.

Antony Flew, in one of the very few modern philosophical discussions of the profit-motive bluffly, but never the less, effectively, dismisses the identification of self-interest and selfishness:

> This [identification] is wrong. For, although selfish actions are perhaps always interested, only some interested actions are selfish. To say that a piece of conduct was selfish is to say more than it was interested, if

it was. The point is selfishness is always and necessarily out of order. Interestedness is not, and scarcely could be.[44]

He goes on to say that when his daughters eagerly eat their dinners they are pursuing their own interests:

> But it would be monstrous to denounce them as selfish hussies, simply on that account.[45]

Flew's point is incontrovertible; and, so obviously so, that the identification of self-interest and selfishness presents a striking puzzle awaiting resolution. We offer five ways in which self-interest may find expression without lapsing into simple (and objectionable) selfishness.

In the first place, there is what deserves to be called *good* self-interest. In such cases one is certainly, in Flew's words, interested, but that interestedness is itself (and already) a moralised interest.

This, presumably, is what Kant was suggesting when he spoke of such things as 'duties towards oneself', and associated then with due *self-respect*. Kant thought we ought to be interested in the development of our capacities and potentials, rather than squander that which was given to us. Equally, there is virtue in being able to 'look after oneself', so as not to be a drag on the benevolence of others. If it is true that others should pay some attention to what one needs, it is a deeper and prior truth that, all things being equal, one ought oneself to give due attention to one's needs. Certainly, it is hard to see the gain to virtue if one sets oneself to help others at the expense of taking due care of oneself. And there is clearly something objectionable in cases in which someone simply 'lets themselves go', whether out of (mistaken) moral motives, or indolence. Reasons such as these led Bishop Joseph Butler (1692–1752) to sermonise:

> a due concern about our own interest or happiness, and a reasonable endeavour to secure and promote it. . . . is [a]virtue, and the contrary behaviour faulty and blameable; since, in the calmest way of reflection, we approve of the first and condemn the other conduct, both in ourselves and others.[46]

The idea that due self-respect underpins the virtue of prudence is predominant in the emergence of the 'protestant virtues' celebrated by John Wesley and Benjamin Franklin, and which, if Max Weber is right, played such a crucial role in the development of capitalism.[47]

Self-interest, as it emerges in a due self-respect, is neither objectionable nor selfish. Indeed, a strong case can be made that such self-interest is not merely morally permissible, even admirable, but the very foundation on which individual moral commitment emerges. After all, the person who is concerned with moral ends must found that concern on the interest they have in living as morality demands.

This rehabilitation of self-interest from selfishness is partial, for it relates only to self-regarding action, but we can just as effectively defend self-interest when it comes to other-regarding action.

It is clear that self-interested motives may run through others (in Kantian terms, motives which involve us in treating someone, and in some respects, as a *means*), without being thereby opposed or hostile towards self-interested ends. If I want to get my hair cut, then I may want to use you, as a hairdresser, as a means to a desirable outcome. In such a case my self-interested end is certainly not hostile to your ends as a hairdresser. In fact, it is more likely the case that my self-interested end furthers your self-interested ends.

In the second place, as the hairdressing example suggests, one's self-interested ends may be *compatible* with self-interest in another; either because the ends are, as in the haircutting, *complementary*, or because they simply *coincide*. For an example of the latter, take hitchhiking. When I hitchhike I have a self-interested end – my arriving at X – and what I am asking with my sign up and thumb out is for anyone else who is interested in themselves arriving at X to consider letting me along for the ride.

It is wrong to assume that self-interest means the exclusion, loss or corruption of any other motivating purpose or goal. It is true that certain motivational states may drive out all others, as when someone enters into 'blind rage', but this is not because of the motive itself so much as the emotional charge that may be associated with its expression.

Self-interest need not be, and most often is not, associated with such extreme states (we tend to speak of 'cold, calculating, self-interest'). In the normal case self-interest cohabits with other concerns. Generally, our motives are often mixed or mingled.[48] If I help you dig a ditch for your new septic tank connection, why do I do this? Well, you could do with assistance, and I would like to assist you. But I also have it in mind (or at the back of my mind) that in so doing I help ensure that you will help me when I need to do some work on my property. Besides, the job will get done quicker and easier if there are two of us, and I look forward to the pleasure I know I will take from the companionship, from the result of a job well done and from the *bonhomie* afterwards.[49]

What does the term 'mixed motives' mean in this context? Robert Nozick distinguishes between the specific or particular goal of any motive, and those values or interests or ends which might place limits on what we are prepared to do in pursuit of our primary goal.[50] Nozick calls these limiting features 'side-constraints', though they might equally be termed, as Jon Elster terms them, 'restraining principles'.[51] Whatever the favoured terminology, the point is that even where our primary goal is manifestly a matter of self-interest, that goal may well be restrained or side-constrained by certain other-regarding ends or values, just as, from the other side, a primary commitment to the well-being of another might itself be constrained by certain self-regarding ends.

The second fallacy is that altruism is only appropriately attributed to another *if, and only if,* their action or decision is untainted by self-regarding concern(s). The idea is that altruism presupposes self-abnegation is given expression in 1 *Corinthians* 10:24: 'Let no one seek his own interests, but those of his neighbour.' And in the eighteenth century Bishop Joseph Butler (1692–1752) takes it to be the standard or usual position:

> there is generally thought to be some peculiar kind of contrariety between self-love and the love of our neighbour, between the pursuit of public and of private good; insomuch that when you are recommending one of these, you are supposed to be speaking against the other.[52]

Butler acknowledges that love of oneself and love of one's neighbour are distinct *principles*, but points out that that does not make them exclusive of one another. As he says, disregard of the interests of others is no part of the *idea* of self-love, just as disregard of self-interest is no part of the *idea* of benevolence or altruism. Self-love is not exclusive of 'all regards to the good of others', and 'neither on the other hand does benevolence . . . exclude self-love'.[53] Having considered self-love and benevolence, Butler proceeds to explore the relationship between the pursuit of private interest and the pursuit of public good, arguing again that the two need not diverge. His point is not the modern claim that selfishness has good public consequences, but that self-interest, not being at odds with benevolence, means that pursuing it need not be at odds with the public interest.[54]

But that the point has been made before does not mean it is less important to make it again, since the error is so pervasive to warrant reinvoking the spirit of Bishop Butler. Like the good Bishop we suggest there is no *necessary conflict* between self-interest and public-minded benevolence, although, as a matter of fact, the two often diverge.

The divergence hides a deeper complementarity. After all, benevolence implies doing good for another, and so there must be something that one can do for another; but if we assume that all men are benevolent, and so lack any distinctive self-interested ends, then each is in the paradoxical position of wanting to help others who themselves simply want to help others. The lesson is that benevolence and altruism presuppose the legitimacy of at least some self-interested ends; for otherwise there is not the material on which these virtues work.

Profit-seeking and mixed motives

The profit-motive is a self-interested motive – one wishes profit for one-self – but, as we have established, self-interestedness does not imply selfishness. As Antony Flew writes, 'no one . . . has any business simply to assume that the desire to make a (private) profit is always and necessarily selfish and discreditable'.[55]

The second thing to note is that the pursuit of profit, and self-interestedness generally, does not rule out concern for others. One may pursue profit in order to facilitate or enable the general availability and provision of some good or service that serves or furthers the ends of others.

This possibility means repudiating the 'zero-sum' conception of commercial exchange according to which 'Whenever material gain follows exchange, for every plus there is a precisely equal minus.'[56] That one might further one's self-interested ends by furthering another's means that far from being a zero-sum game, commercial exchange may benefit both parties. As Flew colourfully puts it, 'mutually satisfactory sex is a better model [for such exchange] than poker played for money'.[57]

The pursuit of profit does not necessarily only ever involve a concern for profit. On the contrary – and as is the case with many motives – our reasons for pursuing profit are mingled or mixed. As Flew writes,

A man may invest his capital in a bassoon factory both because he wants a profitable investment; and because he wants to popularise bassoon playing; and because he wants to infuriate his unmusical aunt.[58]

This man has mixed motives. He has three reasons for investing in the bassoon industry, each or any of which may have been alone sufficient to secure his investment.

There is another sense in which motives can be mixed. Rather than there being different reasons or routes to the same action, it may be that there are one or more side-constraints on what an agent will count as the acceptable or proper pursuit of an end. Thus a man may pursue profit as his goal, but hold that there are certain things or certain routes to that goal which are forbidden, perhaps because they involve doing things to others that it would be wrong to do.

Equally, the profit-motive may itself function as a side-constraint on other ends, rather than simply as an end. Consider the dedicated musician who needs to accrue some profit from his skill so as to enable himself to dedicate himself to that skill.

The profit-motive does not imply the ubiquity of selfishness, nor that for every winner there is necessarily a loser. It is not a singular or exclusive motivating force, but typically operates as an element in a distinctively mixed motivational set. The central obstacle to a more nuanced account of the profit-motive is the tendency to treat the pursuit of profit as something monadic, for it is this that encourages that polarisation of our attitudes towards the profit-motive, according to which it must be something that is either entirely good or entirely bad. In a sense this simply repeats the standard reading of the Christian claim that one cannot serve both God and Mammon.[59]

This cannot be correct. Think of the difference between the doctor who demands upfront payment before he will treat any patient and the doctor who sends out a monthly bill. Both are animated by the pursuit of profit. Yet the fact that we can draw moral distinctions between these two acts means that there must be some descriptive difference upon which these moral differences supervene. One cannot draw moral differences between descriptively identical acts.

The profit-motive and moral hazards

The final point that we wish to make concerns what we might call *moral hazards*, an idea whose origins can be traced back to the Medieval notion of an 'occasion of sin'. The Medieval teaching suggested that while commerce was as legitimate as any other occupation, it must be carefully scrutinised and kept within bounds.[60] This was a constant in their teachings on commerce. Among the volumes which Columbus owned was a little book called *Summula Confessionis*, by the Dominican friar Antonius

Florentius, published in Venice in 1474. The *Confessionale* (as it was popularly known) was a handy pocket-sized guide to personal piety and behaviour, which went through over a 100 printed editions before 1500. The second part of this work was dedicated to methods of questioning individuals on the morality of their conduct with reference to their occupations, enabling the individual to confess his shortcomings in day-to-day affairs. Merchants and traders got a long chapter to themselves. The life of the merchant adventurer was, according to the *Confessionale*, packed with opportunities for every kind of sin.[61]

For the Medieval Schoolmen mercantile activity was an 'occasion of sin', a set of circumstances where vice is neither a necessary consequence of, nor caused by, involvement in trade. What trade provides are *opportunities* for wrongdoing. We too treat commercial activity as a moral hazard. It is not that commercial activity necessarily leads to vice, nor that it strictly causes them, rather it provides certain opportunities for vicious behaviour that, given our natures, are not easily avoided.

John Wesley on the profit-motive

While the idea that we should look at the profit-motive in terms of complex motivational sets can be found in the Medievals, there are modern precedents, of which one prominent example is John Wesley (1703–1791). In his sermon 'The Use of Money', Wesley provides an account of the different forms of the profit-motive.[62] Wesley, who was an enthusiastic advocate of commerce and the accumulation of wealth, suggests we have a *duty* to gain all we can, so that we can provide for our family and indulge charity to others. However, we should do so without 'hurting our mind any more than our body and without hurting our neighbour'.[63] He argues that the *love of money* is the root of all evil but not money itself. 'The fault does not lie in the money, but in them that use it. It may be used ill: And what may not?'[64] And so he says of commerce that, with various cautions and restrictions being observed, '... it is the bounden duty of all who engaged in worldly business to observe that first and great rule of Christian wisdom, with respect to money, "Gain all you can"'.[65] What is interesting is the thought that the ideal of gaining all you can does not mean gain *at all cost*. Money can be an end so long as 'certain cautions and restrictions' are observed.

What are these 'cautions and restrictions'? Wesley distinguishes between self-regarding and other-regarding constraints on the appropriate pursuit of profit. On the side of the former, he insists that there are two important restrictions. In the first place, 'we ought not to gain money at the expense of life, nor (which is in effect the same thing) at the expense of our health'.[66] And in the second place, we should 'preserve ... the spirit of an healthy mind', where this means 'we must not engage or continue in any sinful trade; any that is contrary to the law of God, or of our country'.[67] To pursue profit at the expense of our bodies, and at the cost of staining our conscience, is to violate the demands of a proper self-respect, and to injure by an undue concern for worldly ends, that which God has given us.

When it comes to other-regarding restriction on the pursuit of profit, Wesley says that 'if we love our neighbour as ourselves' – and we must – then there are three ways in which we might violate this absolute moral requirement. In the first place, we might, wrongly, hurt someone *'in his substance'*. By this Wesley means a person's *economic* substance, as becomes apparent when he continues:

> We cannot, consistent with brotherly love, sell our goods below the market price; we cannot study to ruin our neighbour's trade, in order to advance our own; much less can we entice away, or receive, any of his servants or workmen whom he has need of.[68]

In the second place, we may not 'gain by hurting our neighbour *in his body'*. Just as we are forbidden to harm our own bodies in the pursuit of profit, so too we are forbidden to do so at the cost of harm to others' bodies. In particular, Wesley condemns the sale of 'liquid fire, commonly called drams, or spirituous liquors', though he also has stern words for those 'Surgeons, Apothecaries, or Physicians, who play with the lives or health of men, to enlarge their own gain'.[69]

Finally, we are forbidden to pursue profits that involve 'hurting our neighbour in his soul'. We are not to engage in commercial activities which 'minister ... either directly or indirectly, to his unchastity, or intemperance'.[70]

Wesley's account of those side-constraints required is intended to show us how we might honour Jesus' injunction in Luke 16:9:

> I say unto you, Make to yourselves friends of the mammon of unrighteousness; that, when ye fail, they may receive you into everlasting habitations.

Wesley distinguishes self-regarding and other-regarding constraints, where the first reflect what he calls 'truly Christian prudence', the second the absolute moral demand that we love our neighbour as ourselves. This Christian morality gives Wesley's account a normative direction that it would be useful to eschew, and for two reasons. The first reason is that it commits us to moral values that many others, without thinking themselves as immoral or amoralists, would dispute. And the second is that Wesley's values, somewhat paradoxically, seem to involve an essential hostility to capitalism. After all, it is hard to see what kind of efficient market economy we might develop and maintain when each and every merchant or capitalist is required to respect the economic substance of his fellow merchants or capitalists, down to refusing to engage in any activity which might, at my benefit, harm the substance of my potential competitors.

Rethinking the profit-motive – or our taxonomy

With these insights in mind, let us offer a taxonomy of the profit-seeking motive.

First is what we call *Lucrepathic Action*: seeking profit is the sole or dominant consideration in an agent's all-things-considered judgements. There are no constraints upon commercial activity other than the bottom line. In lucrepathic action there is nothing that one would refrain from doing if it will increase one's profit. The whore 'Timonara' in Shakespeare's play 'Timon of Athens', who would do anything for money, provides us with an example of lucrepathic action. It involves, as the economist E.J. Mishan once said, the gross over-development of the acquisitive instinct.[71]

The second category is that of *Accumulative Action*. Now while the profit-motive is the primary aim of action, its pursuit is moderated by moral side-constraints. In this case one might refuse to trade in a certain good or service, for example pornography or nuclear bombs, since one believes that its production, provision or consumption involves significant harm to others.

The third action category we label *Stipendiary Action*. Now profit is not a goal, but functions as a side-constraint on action directed by other non-commercial goals. The aim is some non-pecuniary end, but that action is side-constrained by the necessity of profit-seeking.

Finally, there is *Lucrephobic Action*. In lucrephobic action the pursuit of profit is an evil that is to be avoided *no matter what*. In lucrephobic action profit is neither a side-constraint nor a goal. This is the kind of view we find in writers like Fourier (see Chapter 2) and in some earlier Christian writings.

While these four possibilities mark the general terrain, they do not exhaust the possibilities, nor do they delineate complete character types. We may be dedicated to one form of the profit-motive, but more often our motives will be mixed. And we can make finer distinctions. Thus lucrepathic profit-motives may be free of other-regarding side-constraints, but may or may not run entirely free of further self-regarding 'aesthetic' interests one might have in sustaining or upholding a certain valued self-conception. One can imagine a lucrepath, totally unleashed in how he pursues profit when it comes to the consequences for others, who is dedicated in pursuing that profit to maintaining a self-image as an 'aggressive venture capitalist', or 'renegade drug-dealer', which places certain self-regarding limits on his actions. There are things he will not do (*akrasia* apart) but not because he would be doing them to others.

With the *accumulative* profit-motive there is a clear distinction between those whose pursuit of profit is constrained by moral considerations that are primarily 'market-external' (in the sense that the considerations exist quite independently of the presence of market activity) and those that are refracted through a dedicated commitment to values that arise through market activity, and so are 'market-internal'. The former might refuse to trade in a certain good or service (e.g. pornography, weaponry, prostitution) because they think its production provision involves harm to others, while the latter might allow trade if it is legal and, say, it promises the highest return to shareholders.

Equally, there are two ways in which the *stipendiary* profit-motive presents itself, call the first 'romantic', the second 'realistic'. For the romantic stipendiarist profit is important only to the extent it makes available those non-market options the agent values, whereas for the realistic stipendiarist there is no commitment to resting content with acquiring the bare minimum necessary for pursuit of the relevant non-market interests. After all, a modicum of financial comfort and ease facilitate our enjoyment in pursuing these interests.

Turning to the lucrephobic motive, we may note that while it is *constitutive* of the lucrepath's motivational set that profit be the goal, it is not so constitutive of the lucrephobic motive that moral virtue be the goal. We leave it to the reader to complicate matters further.

Our claim is that the profit-motive cannot be condemned *in toto*. It is not necessarily offensively selfish, and it typically operates together with other motives. What can be condemned – and what presumably animated the hostility to the profit-motive in the first place – is the lucrepathological expression of that motive.

Moreover, in commercial society there is a strong pull towards the lucrepathological. Although, mixed motives are both possible, there is nevertheless a tendency for the commercial goals to predominate. David Hume, in an essay entitled 'Of the Dignity or Meanness of Human Nature', holds that while it is a fallacy to believe that because an act is self-interested that other espoused motives are spurious, when money and revenge are involved it is difficult to prevent them becoming the sole activating principles.[72]

Our view does not commit us to thinking that if the end of action is profit, then here we have lucrepathological action. By drawing a distinction between goals of action and side-constraints, we open up the possibility that the pursuit of profit can be morally unobjectionable if the appropriate side-constraints shape the possible routes to the desired end. This is the possibility of accumulative action and so in making room for capitalism.

It is worth contrasting our views with those of the Medievals. For writers like Aquinas the pursuit of profit is admissible only when it is a means to non-pecuniary intrinsically valuable goods. It is not permissible to pursue profit as an end-in-itself. Pure accumulative action is immoral. Similarly with Wesley, pure accumulation is not morally permissible. Wesley makes no space for activities in which profit is an end. The only legitimate ends in commerce are other-regarding; money can only be a proximate end. On our taxonomy, vice only arises with lucrepathic action. It is only unconstrained profit-seeking we should reject.

Flew's critique of economic motivationalism

The profit-motive is to be condemned when it is lucrepathological. It is not the profit-motive *per se* that should be condemned but its operation in the absence of moral constraints. It is the profit-motivational set of the lucrepath which is morally pernicious not the mere pursuit of profit. Our view might be characterised as a *motivationalist* since we judge the motives of those seeking profit.

This idea of distinguishing between different economic motives has been attacked by Antony Flew in 'The Profit Motive'. Flew argued that it was radically misguided to apply a psychology a 'categorical system originally developed in, and appropriate to economics'.[73] How ought we to respond?

Flew argues that economic motivationalism involves a *reductio ad absurdum*. He suggests that if there is a profit-motive, then there must also be a rent motive and a wages motive and so on. To illustrate the absurdity he points towards some fanciful (and facetious) remarks of

Hume which 'adorn' *A Treatise of Human Nature*. For there, in the section 'Of the Probability of Causes', Hume concludes that, upon his principles:

> a man who desires a thousand pounds, has in reality a thousand or more desires, which uniting together, seem to make only one passion; tho' the composition evidently betrays itself upon every alteration of the object, by the preference he gives to the larger number, if superior only by an unite.

Flew notes:

> Noticing the suggestive 'or more' one is tempted to go on to urge: that before decimalization, the desire for a thousand pounds was – 'in reality' – two hundred and forty thousand old penny desires; that now it has diminished to a mere hundred thousand new pence hankerings....[74]

Flew takes this to be sufficient to demonstrate the absurdity of all talks of different economic motivations.

Flew's second argument is straightforwardly utilitarian. He suggests that we should look to outcomes – presumably *social* outcomes – rather than the quality of the agent in question's motives, for he says that economic arrangements are best judged by results. We should 'concentrate on the price and quality of the product. Do not officiously probe the producer's purity of heart.'[75]

How might we defend our economic motivationalism? The first point to make is a *Lockean ad hominem*. Flew himself distinguishes between different forms of motives in the marketplace. He notes that motives are often mixed and considers the different ways in which they operate.

> For motives – if it is really motives we are considering – are notoriously apt to be mixed. Dosteoevski was not exaggerating much when he said 'No-one ever acts from a single motive.' That this is indeed one of a lady's motives by no means precludes that she has other motives also. A man may invest his capital in a bassoon factory both because he wants a profitable investment; and because he wants to popularize bassoon-playing; and because he wants to infuriate his unmusical aunt.[76]

If it were indeed impossible or wrong-headed to apply to psychology economic motives (and *vice versa*) then Flew should not be drawing these kinds of distinctions.

Second, there are reasons for thinking that his general claim about motives is mistaken, for it rests on the view that if an object (a car, for instance) can also be described in compositional terms (four wheels, a carburettor, a dipstick, an odometer, etc.), then any desire for that object must also, and at the same time, be a desire for all those objects which comprise the compositional set. This is simply to ignore the intentionality of our psychological states.

In response to Flew's comments on the necessity of focusing on consequences and not intentional states when thinking about the activities of commercial agents the first thing to say is that one can be a crude consequentialist if one wants (and especially if one wants to ignore issues of intentions and motives), but it is usually the case that such positions be defended by arguments, not merely the assertoric mood. The second thing to say is that even if one is a consequentialist, it is hard to deny that there is a non-accidental, if not always reliable or predictable, connection between kinds of outcomes and kinds of those intentional states which motivate agents' activities in the relevant arena. Indeed, even those like Mandeville (and, presumably, Flew) who focus on the socially beneficent consequences of competitive market behaviour typically do so in a way that *is* sensitive to the motivational states of market agents: they *should* vigorously pursue self-interest at the *expense* of other-regarding concerns for the well-being of others.

Concluding remarks

Sometimes when people speak derogatively of profit-seeking they label the agents in question 'mercenaries' and talk of 'mercenary motives'. But strangely enough many mercenaries, especially in the Medieval period, were saddled with various moral side-constraints. It was not true that they would do anything for money. Indeed, the English mercenary John Hawkwood had written into all of his contracts that he would not fight against his homeland. He would not do *anything* for money, but rather had various side-constraints on his commercial activities.[77] But what this tells us is that 'mercenary motives' is a place-holder for what we want to call lucrepathic motives. It is the lucrepathic motivational set that should be condemned not the profit-motive *per se*. The profit-motive itself needs to be regarded as a conglomeration of different motivational states – some of which are to be condemned, and most of which are morally neutral and some morally admirable.

4
Usury and the Ethics of Interest-Taking

Two things have to be reconciled – the one that the tooth of usury be grinded that it bite not too much; the other that there be left open a means to invite monied men to lend to the merchants for the continuing and quickening of trade.

Francis Bacon

Does it matter what we do with our money? The strange tale of Father Jeremiah O'Callaghan

In October 1819 an Irish parish priest in Ross Carberry, Cork, Father Jeremiah O'Callaghan, rediscovered the traditional Catholic hostility to interest-taking or usury.[1] That he had to rediscover it is significant in itself. It was not that the Church had officially (or even publicly) recanted its traditional hostility to usury; rather it had – as Father O'Callaghan found out to his cost – purposefully allowed the traditional position to fall from view. In effect, it was swept under the carpet. But O'Callaghan was made of sterner stuff; and, taking the doctrine seriously, he refused the Last Sacraments to a dying merchant who had:

> retailed his goods, that is, flax seed, worth not more than nine shillings, to the poor, in the Spring, for sowing, and obliged them to pay in Autumn twelve shillings and sixpence; gaining therefore three shillings and sixpence, upon every nine shillings, for six months; or more than 27% per annum. Though the seed would be certainly of less value at the time of making the payment: for it would not sell at all in the autumn.[2]

The merchant was convinced to 'remit to all his customers what he had gained or would have gained in this manner' and received absolution before he died. Father O'Callaghan, on the other hand, was suspended from his parochial duties by Bishop William Coppinger of Cloyne – his sentence read from the pulpit to his congregation – and for the next 11 years he was without a parish and spent his time trying, without noticeable success, to elicit from Rome whether he or his Bishop had the right attitude towards usurious practices. Frustrated that the Church would not back his stand, but would not deny it by declaring the taking of interest to be acceptable, the good Father departed for America, and is today celebrated by regional historians as the 'Apostle of Vermont'. He never renounced his hostility to usury.

Clearly, his Church leaders felt that objections to usury embodied in traditional Catholic doctrine were no longer important or relevant to contemporary commercial life. In taking this view they were, presumably, doing more than simply hauling up the white flag in the face of existing practice. We should attribute them a little more courage than to be involved in unwilling acquiescence to conventional practices. More likely they were subject to the emerging acceptance of usury as ethically legitimate, or if not that precisely, as an essential or necessary part of a generally desirable economic system. Capitalism encouraged economic growth, and that growth was furthered by investment loans. And then there is the point that the lender takes a risk in lending, and voluntarily gives up on certain consumption opportunities. For this, a price can rightfully be charged – and such a charge is interest on the loan. And many loans, of course, are very productive, allowing the borrower to acquire advantages he or she would otherwise have missed out on. Interest might seem a fair reward to the lender for making such opportunities available to the borrower.

But if commercial wisdom and a generalised benevolence favour such a dismissal of traditional objections to usury, this is not to say that everything is settled. For it is not true that we are unambiguously usury friendly, even if we are not as likely as Father O'Callaghan to repudiate usury *period*. We might well be put out if a friend insists on a loan with interest when we, under the duress of circumstances, ask simply for a loan. Here, at least, we might see the usurious demand as an offence against friendship and personal charity. We may be worried about 'extortionate' loans in which the creditor exploits the desperate circumstances of the debtor, either to make the loan in the first place, or to make it with extraordinary levels of interest. We are thus often concerned about the credit/debtor relationships between rich first world countries and needy third world nations. We may be worried about predatory lending and so about 'loan sharking' and such institutions as the 'pay day' loan. And finally, we are often concerned about the way that interest charges on a loan may force debtors into continuing debt-bondage, so that loan chases loan, and interest continues to accrue to the creditors.

These worries cannot be adequately dealt with by pointing to the economic necessity of usury. For there are alternative kinds of commercial contract and relationships that enable one party to access the funds of another in a mutually productive way.[3]

So while we certainly do not wish to follow Father O'Callaghan to Vermont, we do think that his respect for traditional objections to usury deserves respect. Looking at these objections provides a starting point for unifying our otherwise fragmented worries about usury and developing an account which allows us to distinguish between legitimate and illegitimate forms of interest-taking. We reserve the term 'usury' for what we take to be morally illegitimate interest.[4] The distinction between interest and usury is intended to mark the difference between predatory lending and legitimate returns.

It is important, as well, to examine the problem of usury separately from justice-in-pricing. Some writers have suggested that usury doctrine is simply just price theory applied to the sale of money. For Eric Roll, '[T]he condemnation of usury was part of the general condemnation of unjust exchange.'[5] But as the case of Father O'Callaghan reveals, this subsumption of usury doctrines into just price theory is wrong. Unlike theorists of the just price, Father O'Callaghan draws no distinction between morally licit and morally illicit forms of market activity. Father O'Callaghan repudiated all and any loans at interest. There was no moderate or just interest-taking; all interest-taking was usurious and usury was condemned, as was the usurer who endangered his immaterial soul.[6]

Leaving these historical debates to one side, there are good reasons for not subsuming ethical questions regarding the sale of money into discussion of the just price, for there are distinctive harms associated with the entrapment of interest that separate it from ordinary concerns about justice in buying and selling.

The traditional objections to usury

And since we break on the wheel, and behead highwaymen, murderers and housebreakers, how much more ought we to break on the wheel and kill ... hunt down, curse and behead all usurers.

Martin Luther [7]

Exploring the evils of usury exercised the minds of a great many Medieval philosophers, writers and artists.[8] Consider Dante's *Inferno*. As Dante descends into the depths of Hell, he discovers usurers (along with sodomites and blasphemers) in the smallest and most terrifying ring (Round 3 of Circle VII) of the Inferno.[9] Dante enquires as to the nature of the sins of the usurers and is told that their sins are classified as a kind of violence towards God because usury was an attack on the natural use for money given by God and it implied contempt for God's bounty.[10]

Dante's views are typical of the moral condemnation of his society for those who made a living out of interest.[11] These concerns have a long history. Cato (234–149 BC), for instance, reports that it was less disgraceful to have your father considered a thief than a usurer.[12] The practice of usury was not only subject to moral disapprobation; theological and legal injunctions against the practice were in force during the Medieval period over much of Europe.[13] In 1274 Gregory X, at the Council of Lyons, ordained that no community, corporation or individual should permit foreign usurers to hire houses, but that they should expel them from their territory; and the disobedient, if laymen, were to be castigated with ecclesiastical censures.[14] In 1311 the Council of Vienne, under the authority of Pope Clement, declared all secular legislation in favour of usury null and void, and branded as heresy the belief that usury was not sinful.[15] Anti-usury laws, although subjected to numerous modifications, persisted across Europe for over 500 years until the time of the Napoleonic Code. After the *Code Napoleon* had allowed the taking of interest, the Catholic Church, too, decided to abandon the old usury doctrine. It was quietly buried (although not revoked) in 1830, when the Church issued instructions to confessors not to disturb penitents who lent money at the legal rate of interest without any title other than the sanction of Civil Law.[16]

What were the grounds on which the Medieval Christian world had rejected usury? In the first place, they were Biblical; there are many passages in the Bible that clearly state that to lend to another at interest is to undermine or to deny the moral fellowship that obtains between lender and borrower. To refuse charity to one's 'brother', or to refuse to lend money to one's 'brother' without insisting that one obtain more in return, is to deny that brotherhood itself. Such a lender denies the moral obligation of compassion. If one is *not* compassionate, but is a usurer, then one is utterly condemned. So one cannot lend at interest to one's fellows. But it does not follow that one cannot lend at interest to those who are *not* one's fellows, for as it says in *Deuteronomy*, 'Thou shalt not lend to thy brother money to usury, nor corn, nor any other thing, but to the stranger' (Deut 23:19). The reason for this, presumably, is that one does not owe a duty of compassion to strangers. Such relationships are outside the morality of compassion, and so here one can certainly make a profit. Indeed, for St Ambrose, usury was not only permissible when it came to dealings with strangers, it could legitimately be used as an act of war upon one's enemies.[17]

Aside from the Biblically inspired rejection of usury as a violation of moral solidarity, there were straightforwardly philosophical objections. Many of the Medieval objections to usury had their roots in Greek philosophy, perhaps the most obvious being the 'Objection from Barrenness' famously articulated by Aristotle.[18]

Aristotle's objections to usury were based on the idea that money is sterile and hence could not naturally generate offspring, and yet usury makes the barren breed – I lend you $10, and receive in return for that amount more than $10 – and so is an 'unnatural' practice, and being 'unnatural' it is unethical. As Aristotle would have it, 'of all modes of acquisition, usury is the most unnatural'.[19]

The 'Objection from Barrenness' is expounded by Aquinas in *Summa Theologica* when he explained why '[m]oney cannot be sold for a greater sum than the amount lent, which has to be paid back'.[20] De Roover argues that it was Aquinas' discussion that placed usury at the centre of intellectual debate, and that Aquinas' account of the ills of usury exerted considerable influence over subsequent commentators.[21]

The origins of Aquinas' views lie in Aristotle's *Politics*, in what is one of the few examples of an Aristotelian joke. The Greek word *tokos* means both 'token' (in our sense of 'currency') and 'offspring'. So when Aristotle suggests that money cannot give rise to offspring and therefore is an unnatural (and immoral) activity, his argument plays upon the equivocal nature of the Greek term. But whatever its origins, the idea that money was sterile struck a chord with Medieval thinkers. We see the influence of this in Shakespeare's comment in the *Merchant of Venice* 'When did friendship make a breed of barren metal of his friend.'[22]

A second philosophical argument against usury is the *argument from consumptability*.[23] The basic idea is that one cannot separate the use of money from its consumption.[24] In the language of economics and law, money is a *fungible* good. Now the idea of fungibility is not absolutely transparent. Indeed it seems to function as a kind of catchall term for those goods that may carry one or more of the following properties.[25] In the first place, fungible goods are goods that are consumed in their use – they literally perish when used. In the second place, because they perish in use, they cannot literally be returned, but can only be returned in kind. And finally, they are goods whose value is commonly estimated by weight, number or measure. For instance, a cigarette is clearly a fungible good, and in all three senses. If I use a cigarette, it perishes, just as I might from such use, if somewhat later on. If I have 'borrowed' the cigarette from you, then whilst that cigarette has perished, I can satisfy my debt obligations by giving you another cigarette of the same kind. And, of course, cigarettes are borrowed and sold in particular numerical amounts. Contrast this cigarette with a house. A house is not a fungible good. If I use – that is, live in – a house it does not thereby perish, leaving me out in the cold. Unlike with a cigarette, where it makes no sense for me to try and sell you the use of the cigarette, but not the cigarette itself (for it is consumed in use), with a house I can sell you the use (*rent* or *lease* it to you), without having to sell the house.

We find here use of an earlier distinction in Roman Law between two kinds of loan, the *commodatum* and the *mutuum*. A *commodatum* is a loan of something not destroyed by use, like a house or a horse. A *mutuum* is the loan of something consumed in use, like a loaf of bread or a bottle of wine. The just price for a *mutuum* was thought to be the exact amount of money advanced.

According to Aquinas, money is a fungible good the *telos* or end of which is to effect exchanges.[26] Just as it would be wrong to sell a cigarette to a person, and simultaneously charge him for the use of that cigarette, equally it is inadmissible to sell money, and also to charge for its use. As with the double selling of the cigarette, this would be to double charge the buyer. The proper price of any amount of money, just as with any amount of cigarettes, is the return of that amount, no more and no less. If the seller of a fungible good charges for its use, for '[H]e selleth that thing twice, and selleth thing that nought is, for the use is full waste of a thing.'[27]

A third philosophically based objection to usury Odd Langholm calls the *argument from compulsion*. This argument directs its attention to loans made under desperate circumstances. This worry was implicit in religious concerns in which it is almost always a matter of lending or assisting the poor and needy. It was believed that the usurer took advantage of those in dire circumstances. This view was especially tempting for Ancient and Medieval authors because at the time virtually all loans were consumption loans to those suffering various kinds of distress – sickness, fire, flood, blight, pestilence and so on. To attach interest to such loans struck many as a matter of 'trafficking in the miseries of others'. It was this that helps explain the ferocity of many attacks on usury and usurers. Consider Luther:

> The heathen were able, by the light of reason, to conclude that a usurer is a double-dyed thief and murderer. We Christians, however, hold them in such honour, that we fairly worship them for the sake of their money ... Whosoever eats up, robs, and steals the nourishment of another, that man commits as great a murder (so far as in him lies) as he who starves a man or utterly undoes him. Such does a usurer, and sits the while safe on his stool, when he ought rather to be hanging on the gallows, and be eaten by as many ravens as he has stolen gilders, if only there were so much flesh on him, that so many ravens could stick their beak in and share it.[28]

One might condemn this on the Nozickian grounds that whatever we might think of the agreement between creditor and debtor, all that finally matters is that the contract be *consensual* – and certainly no one was holding a gun or sword on the other.

Well, perhaps not – but the debtor does have the gun of nature and necessity levelled at them, and the problem lies in taking advantage of this vulnerability. Thus we find Gerald Odonis (c.1290–1348) suggesting that the person who borrows from the usurer is like the person who pays ransom money not to be hanged.[29] This point was formalised by Thomas of Chobham (c.1158–1230) who used the notion of *comparative will* to counter the argument that the borrowers had freely agreed to pay the extra charge. For Chobham, it was clear that an agreement that was made only because one party was subject to some underlying necessity of a kind, in which no one should or would want to find themselves, could not truly be said to be a genuinely voluntary agreement.

Other arguments against usury included the *argument from the sale of time*, the *argument from ownership* and the *argument from unearned income*.[30] According to the former argument, the usurer sells something – time – which it is not his to sell. How does the usurer sell time? He does so by charging you the interest levied for the period of time between taking the loan and finally paying it off. Thus the loan can be seen as a matter of selling that period of time. But, of course, no person owns time. According to this line of argument, it is God's property and should be common to all.[31] John Wycliffe argued the usurer 'selles pure tyme' which is the property of God who is the 'lord of tyme'.[32]

According to the next argument, there is an essential element of fraud in demanding interest on a loan. This is because when a loan is made, ownership of money borrowed passes to the borrower and so any profit obtained with it belongs to him.[33] To demand interest then is to 'profit from what is yours, not mine'.[34] And according to the final argument to charge interest on a loan is to help oneself to unearned income. The point is that the usurer's profits are not the result of his or her 'initiative, enterprise and efficiency',[35] but of their capacity to 'tax' the initiative, enterprise and efficiency of those they lend to. It is the mark of the lenders independence from real productive activity that while the profit the borrower seeks may fluctuate, the rate of interest demanded on the loan is fixed. Thus the usurer 'earns money in his sleep'.

These arguments make no concession to interest-taking – it is always wrong, no matter what the circumstances. But while this rigorism found expression at the Councils of Lyon and Vienne, it is not true that the Church was, in practice, hostile to all interest-taking, and there were theologians (particularly among the Jesuits) who tried to find ways of softening the anti-usury stance. Father O'Callaghan, of course, had no time for such laxists.[36]

The laxists argued that there was a crucial distinction rigorist approaches ignored. For while it is certainly true that any interest charged is wrong if it arises from the lenders' desire to enrich themselves, and their exploitation of the borrowers' need for money; still there are other, external or 'extrinsic' titles which may legitimate an additional charge or cost to the borrower (the titles were said to be 'extrinsic' because they did not involve financial compensation by reason of the loan in itself, but for factors that were non-inherent in the title). One such extrinsic title was the so-called *damnum emergens* (actual damages or losses incurred by the lender by reason of having made the loan) that provided money over and above the sum of the loan for damages or losses to the creditor. Aquinas himself allowed interest for such damages.

Another exception many Medieval thinkers conceded was the *lucrum cessans* (gain forgone by the lender on an alternative investment) that we might somewhat anachronistically understand as 'opportunity cost'. To have lost the chance of gain because of lending money was another justification for taking interest.

More controversially, many Medieval theorists endorsed the *triple contract* which involved a re-description of interest as three distinct contracts between 'business partners'. The triple contract involved a complicated series of legal arrangements. First, there was an original contract of partnership. Second came the contract of insurance of the principle in which insurance was given in return for an assignment of the future possible gains from the partnership. Then a third contract was drawn by which an uncertain future gain was sold for a lesser certain gain.[37] In this way, by redefining the debtor–creditor relationship as a business partnership, the triple contract allowed almost any form of interest-taking.

Over time theologians admitted more and more exceptions to the usury doctrine. While Aquinas admitted *damnum emergens*, he refused *lucrum cessans* writing that if the latter is accepted '. . . then what remains of the usury doctrine?'[38] Grotius (1583–1645), on the other hand, writing more than 300 years after Aquinas, permitted both titles.[39] There were some deviations from this general drift towards laxism, especially amongst the sixteenth-century English opponents of usury. We find Thomas Wilson (1524–1581) in his *Discourse upon Usury* (1572) allowing none of the exceptions that were commonly conceded.[40]

Ethical concerns about interest are also to be found in the Islamic tradition of Sharia law that is regarded as providing the fundamental moral precepts in many parts of the world.

Most Western commentators focus on the category of *riba* transactions and translate this as 'usury'; however, the term is actually much broader in scope covering *gain* more generally since it means excess or addition. The word *qard* is the term used in this tradition to denote illegitimate profit from the loan of money and the moral vice of *qard* is understood in relation to the idea of *riba*. Thus it is not surprising that *riba* is often thought of as a synonym for usury.[41]

Riba is defined as an unlawful gain derived from the 'quantitative inequality of the counter-values in any transaction purporting to affect the exchange of two or more species which belong to the same genus and are governed by the same efficient cause'.[42] This requires unpacking, but the basic idea is that there should be monetary equivalence in terms of price between goods of the same class. Price is treated, in part at least, as a mechanism for aligning goods in terms of their fundamental metaphysical values. *Riba* thus describes cases where gain is obtained illicitly through trades in which goods of the same class (counter-values) bring differential prices.

This framework for distinguishing just from unjust gain applies, in the first instance, to the two precious metals (gold and silver) and four basic commodities (wheat, barley, dates and salt).[43] The analysis is then extended by analogy to a whole raft of other commodities that are adjudged to be members of the same genus or governed by the same efficient cause. Licit sale requires financial equivalence between equivalent counter-values and illicit (or *ribawi*) exchanges involve non-equivalence. Clearly, much of the work involves determining what is the relevant counter-value against which any price is to be judged.

When we turn to lending we find that loans are divided into two categories: the *ariya* which is a loan for use of non-fungible property and the *qard* which involves the loan of fungible commodities.[44] (In this, Sharia follows the Roman legal distinction already discussed between *commodatum* and *mutuum*.) While the first is viewed as a proper loan, the second is regarded as improper. Money is treated by analogy as a fungible commodity for which the borrower must restore an equal amount of the borrowed good and it must be of the same quality. To charge interest is to force the borrower to restore more than the original amount and thus is considered to be *ribawi*.

There are clearly resonances with the Western criticisms of interest-taking that hold money to be a fungible good. However, unlike the Western tradition, hostility to the taking of interest has been maintained in much Islamic social theory and there are still attempts to implement interest-free banking.[45]

Objecting to the usury doctrine

Why – eccentrics like Father Jeremiah O'Callaghan apart – did the hostility to usury largely disappear in the West?

One reason was that many were horrified at the haphazard and often hypocritical manner in which the prohibition was interpreted. Some of the Roman Catholic clergy, such as Antonio Diana (1585–1663), undermined the position through their 'laxism', particularly through the use of the triple contract.[46] Their moral laxity was regularly at the service of the powerful and at the expense of the weak. While small pawnbrokers were condemned, large bankers like the Fuggers and the Medicis were cleared of all implications of sin, despite the transparently usurious nature of their commercial practices.[47] When moral authorities spend most of their time looking for clever dodges to evade the manifest implications of their purported principles, they can hardly expect that authority to be admired or respected.

In this spirit Blaise Pascal's *Provincial Letters* contains vitriolic attacks upon the laxity of the Jesuits for permitting exceptions inconsistent with their stated principles. Pascal focused, in particular, on the notorious *Mohatra* contract, which involves a needy person purchasing some goods at a high price and on credit in order to sell them over again at the same time and to the same merchant for ready money in hand and a lower price.[48] According to Pascal's Jesuit interlocutor this is not illegal so long as in disposing of the good the lender does not exceed the highest price and in repurchasing them does not go below their lowest price. Pascal, a Jansenist and thereby an enemy of the Jesuits, caused a scandal by laying bare the reasoning of the Jesuits on this and many other issues. He did not directly criticise their reasoning but simply demonstrated through their own words that they had little real concern for morality.

But, it was more than just a concern for moral consistency that undid the usury doctrine. From the sixteenth century onwards, a number of philosophical attacks on the prohibition began to emerge, one of the most ferocious of which being that of Charles Dumoulin (1500–1566) who argued that a moderate rate of interest on loans was morally permissible. Dumoulin (who was also known by his Latinised name Molinaeus) wrote that:

> It is plain that one grants a favour of a loan from his property; the other remunerates his benefactor with part of the gain derived therefrom, without suffering any loss. Therefore the creditor lawfully receives more than his principal; and by the same reasoning, he may from the beginning covenant to this effect within legitimate limits, however, and provided that the one who covenants does not plan any fraud against his neighbour, or demand usury unfairly.[49]

From this point onwards, we find the entire usury doctrine under fire, often from opposing directions. The British utilitarian philosopher and legal reformer Jeremy Bentham (1748–1832) famously lampooned the idea in his pamphlet 'A Defence of Usury' [1787], noting facetiously in one particularly memorable passage that Aristotle:

> with all his industry, and all his penetration, notwithstanding the great number of pieces of money that had passed through his hands (more perhaps than ever passed through the hands of a philosopher before or since), and notwithstanding the uncommon pains he had bestowed on the subject of generation, had never been able to discover, in any one piece of money, any organs for generating any other such piece.[50]

Obviously, Bentham did not take the Objection from Barrenness all that seriously.

The grounds for abandoning the usury doctrine were many. First, as the passage from Bentham indicates, many opposed the thesis that money was sterile. By the eighteenth century Bentham, a child of the emerging capitalist order, is content simply to poke fun at the doctrine of the sterility of money. And if Max Weber and R.H. Tawney are right that the emergence of modern capitalism depended crucially on the legitimation of interest, then of greater significance than Bentham's frivolity is the thinking of Calvin who, in a celebrated letter written in 1545 to his friend Sachinus (and published in 1574), denied that the taking of payment was prohibited, and suggested that money would only be sterile if it were kept in a box.[51]

While Calvin rejected the Aristotelian doctrine, he nevertheless distinguished instances in which the taking of interest would become sinful, as in the case of lending at interest to needy borrowers oppressed by calamity,[52] or in demanding interest of more than 4% of the loaned amount. Many came to agree with Calvin on both the productivity of capital and the distinction he drew between legitimate interest and illegitimate interest (or usury). His work here is rightly regarded as a watershed.

It is clear that if one denies the sterility of money, then the distinction between money and other goods that are loaned or rented dissolves. If money is not sterile, then it is entirely *arbitrary* to prohibit the sale of money when other goods, such as houses, donkeys and cheese, can be sold. This 'Argument from Arbitrariness' was forcefully articulated by the pre-revolutionary French economist and Government Minister, Anne Robert Jacques Turgot (1727–1781):

> we should make no mistake about it: lending at interest is simply a kind of trading, in which the Lender is a man who sells the use of his money, and the Borrower a man who buys it.[53]

The sale of money should not be treated as any more morally troublesome than the sale of a horse or the rent of a house. We also find the idea expressed in Bentham's work when he says:

> Why a man who takes as much as he can get, be it six, or seven, or eight, or ten per cent for the use of a sum of money should be called usurer, should be loaded with an opprobrious name, any more than if he had bought an house with it, and made a proportionable profit by the house, is more than I can see.[54]

As the nineteenth-century economist Alfred Marshall argued, '. . . there is no substantial difference between the loan of the purchase price of a horse and the loan of a horse'.[55] The idea behind this would appear to be the basic principle of analogy that similar things ought to be treated similarly.[56]

Regardless, as they became aware of the productivity of investment loans, many Europeans came to regard the usury prohibition as an impediment to economic growth, and even a potential moral wrong which stood in the way of substantial improvements in the material conditions of human well-being. The counter-productive consequences of usury prohibitions became more obvious as the economies of Western Europe grew.

In considering the historical shifts in our thinking about the morality of interest-taking, it would be wrong to give the impression that all of those who opposed the traditional usury doctrine did so with the same agenda in mind. There were those, like Bentham, who rejected *any* restrictions on the practices of money-lenders *whatsoever*. His writing on this matter, inspired by a proposal to reduce the legal maximum rate from 6% to 5%, argued for the abolition of any legal maximum.

Yet there were also important historical figures, such as Francis Bacon (1561–1626) who, whilst recognising the productivity of loaned capital, nonetheless wished to retain moral side-constraints upon its conduct. These moral side-constraints were to be translated into legal sanctions on the rates of usury and the kinds of contracts that were permissible. They provide the normative basis for legislative responses to the moral hazards of usury.

The maintenance of legal constraints on interest has also been argued for on *utilitarian* grounds. Now the concern is less with questions of justice and more with the overall effectiveness of a system which has no limits on the rates or kinds of contracts into which lending parties might enter. This is where Adam Smith stands. Smith recognised, on utilitarian grounds, the necessity of interest for '[t]he lowest ordinary rate of interest must, in the same manner, be something more than sufficient to compensate the occasional losses to which lending, even with tolerable prudence, is exposed'. He suggests that if this were not the case then '. . . charity or friendship could be the only motives for lending'.[57] But he also believed that excessive interest could have counter-productive economic effects and thus defended interest-rate ceilings (which he did not believe would dampen economic activity).[58] Our concern is different from Smith's. In keeping with our economic casuistry, the focus will be with the maintenance of moral constraints on the practice of selling money.

Modern justifications of interest-taking

In the non-Islamist modern world it is difficult to find much discussion of why interest-taking might be justified, as opposed to discussions of the levels of interest attached to this or that kind of loan, at this or that time. Most economic commentators take interest for granted, though typically it is unclear whether in doing this they are assuming that such interest is morally permissible, or simply accepting that levying interest is such a central element of our economic life that we cannot sensibly imagine it away.[59] In this section we explore arguments that attempt to legitimate interest-taking as such. We are concerned with the claim that the lender can be said *truly to deserve* the interest they demand from the borrower.

If we look hard enough, we find five main modern justifications of the practice of loaning at interest that attempt to show that the lender deserves a return higher than the amount lent. These are:

  (i) Productivity theory (or fructification)
 (ii) Use theory
(iii) Abstinence theory
 (iv) *Agio* theory
  (v) Return for risk theory.

Let us consider each in its turn.[60]

The *productivity theory* holds that it is only fair that those who lend 'productive goods should receive a share of the extra wealth these goods produce'.[61] As Thomas Malthus put it, interest was 'a fair remuneration for that part of the production contributed by the capitalist'.[62] If it is said that the great majority of interest loans involve the transfer of money, the productivity theorist responds that such monies can always be transformed into producer goods and therefore should be viewed as equivalent to productive goods. The same reasoning is used to justify interest on consumer loans.

Whether or not the productivity argument holds for consumption loans, it certainly looks powerful when we are considering investment loans, but even here there is a potential circularity in the argument that might trouble us. To see this, consider the case of a person who buys outright some productive good (a tractor, for instance) and the person who must borrow to buy such a tractor. In both cases the good produced is the same – the tractor – and, assuming they are the same kind of tractor, their productivity is, all things being equal, just the same. So let us assume that both the outright purchaser and the loan-financed purchaser generate the same additional productivity. Now if it is allowed that facilitating the productive gains of another gives us some title to our share of those gains, then it seems that the person who has sold the tractor as well as the person who has supplied a loan so that the tractor may be bought deserves some of the extra benefits produced. But we do not think this with the case of outright purchase. At this point a potential circularity emerges. For if we uphold the distinction between loan-financed purchase and outright purchase, it looks as if the difference is simply that with one style of purchase interest is demanded, and in the other case it is not. But what justifies this distinction? It cannot be the additional productivity of the relevant good because that is assumed to be the same in both cases. So what is it – beyond that one is just a loan (which we simply assume legitimate), the other an outright purchase?

Well, consider the second justification is the *'use theory'* of interest. On this view, interest is the charge the lender makes for the *use* of the borrowed money (in our case, to buy a tractor). But have we really avoided circularity? After all, if I buy the tractor from you for cash, then I also have the capacity to use the tractor. Why then the difference in price between outright purchase and loan-financed purchase? Again, it can look as if we have simply assumed what the argument is intended to establish.

And so we come to the *abstinence theory*. Now the idea is not that it is the productivity or use of capital that legitimates interest-taking; it is that the provision of money for lending presupposes that the lender either has already forgone some opportunities for investment or consumption, or, by making the loan, has for the period of the loan forgone such opportunities for investment or consumption. Such abstinence – in virtue of the opportunities it opens up for the borrower – deserves its own return, the interest levied on the loan.

This idea was attacked vigorously in the nineteenth century by those on the Left, for the idea that the wealthy with excess capital somehow exhibit the virtue of abstemiousness. Marx famously parodied the notion of capitalists who are being paid for abstaining from devouring manure.[63] The point behind the satire is that while investors may forgo some immediate consumption options by lending, it is not clear in what sense it is a *sacrifice*. Given that they lend at interest – so that they shall in turn receive more money that, if they so desire, they may deploy for consumption – where exactly does the deprivation lie? It was for such reasons that Alfred Marshall preferred to speak of *waiting* rather than abstinence, though now the difficulty is to see how simply *waiting* – and for a greater amount than one has outlaid – can found the claim that one *deserves* the excess.[64] What is historically curious here is that the selling time – which in the Medieval period was seen as an objection to interest – is now viewed as a justification.[65]

But is it really true that the creditor deserves moral credit for their self-sacrificial abstinence or simply for waiting? After all, while the loan may open up opportunities for the debtor, is this because of the creditor's self-denying frugality? Surely, in most cases, those who make available monies for loan do so because – having made use of what they have to quieten the urge for consumption – they have such monies available. How is such waiting a sacrifice? Further, one might wonder why one would lend if one could get the kinds of rewards the borrower is supposed to make available by investing directly oneself. To lend in such cases would be a sacrifice, and so one might claim a deserved return in interest. But it might equally be that what we have here is no sacrifice at all, but an opportunity for the well-endowed to indulge their laziness by getting a decent return from the efforts of others.

Related to the abstinence argument is the so-called *agio* defence of interest. The idea is that we value present goods (monies, consumption, etc.) over goods that arise later. Thus when the lender gives the borrower a certain amount on the agreement that it will later be repaid, if he were to do this without adding interest returns, he would in fact (so far as his preferences go) receive back less than he had lent in the first place. The interest charge then makes up for the discounting effect involved in the 'lending now, repayment later' nexus. This is a neat argument – and it means that the lender ought to be very wary of the borrower's capacity to value present goods over later responsibilities – but the problem is the same as with the abstinence conception. For if the lender is willing to lend now, then it would seem that they do not have present alternative uses for the money that outweigh their willingness to lend. What they are after – and not as any kind of compensation for loss – is a greater amount of money at some future date.

A final argument – and as we will now appreciate, perhaps the most forceful – is the *risk defence* of interest-taking. The idea is that the creditor deserves a return in interest on the capital loaned because they are taking a risk in making the loan available in the first place. For while many loans may turn out to be productive, some will not – so there is a risk that the lender will not receive repayment even of the principal. Interest, then, can be seen as a legitimate surcharge levied on the borrower because of the risk the creditor takes in making the loan.

This is an attractive defence, but we should not overstate things and particularly not when it comes to modern lending practices. In the first place, we might doubt how many there are who will lend under hazardous conditions if they cannot afford the debtor to default or cannot afford a certain level of defaulting. If someone does lend under such hazardous circumstances, perhaps they might legitimately charge interest, though given that charitableness would already seem to be involved in assuming such a risk, interest can seem a trifle supererogatory. Typically, an individual will make a loan only if they can afford to assume the risk of default, for institutional lenders do all they can to ensure that there is no real risk attached to possible loan defaulters. They may insist that as a conditional of receiving the loan the borrower takes out loan insurance so that the creditor is repaid in full should the borrower default. They ensure that the borrower has sufficient collateral to cover the amount of the loan. They have a legal system to back up their demands for repayment. Further, they will have made intensive actuarial researches so as to reduce to the absolute minimum any risks they might face.

It may be that the desire to show that the lender *deserves* the interest levied on the loan is excessive. After all, it might be that interest-taking is permissible or even desirable, without it being true that it is deserved. There would seem to be two possibilities. First, that while the creditor does not, strictly speaking, deserve the interest charges, still they may have a proper *right* to it. And second, that while it is neither a matter of the lender deserving, or even having, a particular right to the interest levied, still there is nothing objectionable in their interest-taking in so far as the practice of loaning at interest has utilitarian benefits.

Whatever the truth of such qualifications, it is quite striking that these modern justifications of interest are not as compelling as one might have expected given the way that interest is so readily accepted today. Whether or not they adequately justify interest is an open question. That is not something that matters for our casuistic approach. Instead of focusing on desert or right we accept the usefulness of interest for the development of economies. Given various side-constraints on how interest is obtained, we accept on utilitarian grounds that there is a place for interest-taking. In general, interest is justifiable because of the social good for which it is responsible, so long as the pursuit of that social good does not involve the avoidable violation of precepts of justice. In the next section, then, we explore why we take some interest to be *usurious*.

Consumption loans and desperate exchanges: 'When Indigence bargains with Opulence'[66]

Despite the benefits that may arise from investment lending, there are good reasons for maintaining moral concerns over interest-taking. If the debtor is not a victim, driven by desperation to accept money at interest, but is – or at least aims to be – better off because of the opportunities the loan opens up for productive investment, then all other things being equal, the bargain does not seem morally troublesome. But not all borrowing is of this kind.

Recall that much of the motivation for the Medieval doctrine was a concern about those who, out of reasons of necessity, took out loans under extortionate conditions and assumed heavy, even crushing, burdens of interest repayment. It would be naïve to think that such cases are no longer pertinent.

Consider, for instance, the institution of 'Pay-Day Loans'. Such loans are widely – though not universally – available in many political jurisdictions. The idea is that when someone who with little or no resources to fall back upon, but who faces a pressing need that requires a small amount of money now if it is to be met, and who has a functioning bank account and some source of reliable income, can obtain between, for instance, $100 and $1000 immediately, if, as security on the loan, they sign a post-dated cheque to the lender for that amount plus a certain 'fee'. Typically, pay-day loans extend only to the next pay period – generally two to four weeks. At that time, either the lender cashes the cheque, or the borrower redeems the cheque for its face value with cash, or the lender simply debits the borrower's account for the agreed amount. If the borrower does not have the financial wherewithal to make the required payment, then for a substantial fee, they can roll the loan over for the next pay period. If their cheque bounces, then they assume those additional costs, face rigorously pursued legal actions on behalf of the lender, and have any future credit opportunities severely curtailed.

The annual percentage rate of such pay-day loans is generally determined by length of the repayment period. One-week loans may attract a rate of up to 911%, 2-week loans a rate of 456%, and 1-month loans a rate of 212%.[67] Given the small amounts available, and given the incredible interest rate, it is clear that such loans are typically going to reflect some necessity on the part of the borrower, and their marginal financial status. If there were any viable (non-criminal) alternative, then we would not expect anyone to agree to such a deal, short of fraud, excessive indolence or remarkable incompetence.

Many people find the institution of pay-day loans exploitative, and such lending a form of avaricious predation.[68] The pay-day lender operates in that climate of borrower compulsion Odd Langholm points to as a root of traditional hostility to usury. Pay-day loans use the vital need of the borrower to gouge extraordinary levels of interest, and in many cases they manage at the same time to perform the same successful trick of ensnarement for iterative profit. What we have is the exploitation of pressing need for monetary ends; indeed, it would seem, for largely lucrepathic ends, for there are remarkably few side-constraints such lenders accept, and they are notoriously prone to attempts at subverting or controverting those constraints that are supposed to be effective. Thus pay-day loans are typically approved in 24 hours, and on the basis of minimal financial information about the client (e.g. no formal assessment is made of their real ability to pay the loan as opposed to their nominal capacity); and pay-day lenders are prone to try and avoid common usury law limits and restrictions on small loan transactions in particular jurisdictions by such methods as affiliation with a bank chartered in a more lenient legal jurisdiction.

At this point one might be tempted, encouraged by historical events, to provide a normative evaluation of the ethics of usury based on the distinction between *consumption* and *investment*. While this was not the view of Aristotle and Aquinas who both held that all money-lending for the sake of profit to be wrong, the distinction appealed to many later writers.[69] Hilaire Belloc (1870–1953) in his essay 'On Usury' argues that consumption loans should be interest-free, but not investment or productive loans.[70] More recently, Ruston has suggested that the 'original target of the medieval usury law was the medieval equivalent of the "loan shark" [but that] the medieval theory was unsatisfactory because it could not distinguish the helpful loan from the oppressive'.[71] Consider the following passage from Aquinas' teacher, Albert the Great:

> [The borrower] accepts the loan from necessity, and in distress . . . and by hard labour has acquired something as profit on which he could live, and this the usurer, suffering no distress, spending no labour, fearing no loss of capital by misfortune, takes away, and through the distress and labour and changing luck of his neighbour collects and acquires riches for himself.[72]

Other writers make the same point about consumption loans in terms of there being two distinct circuits in which money flows, one a consumption circuit and the other a production one.[73]

The Islamic tradition makes similar distinctions. For instance, in Sir Sayyed's school *riba*, or illicit gain (typically on the sale of money), is interpreted as 'the primitive form of money lending when money was advanced for consumptional purposes'.[74] Similarly, Saleh writes:

> The Prophet here did not differentiate between situations where borrowed capitals had relieved borrower distress, or had been invested in some productive enterprise. Had God meant that differentiation, or known that it would be beneficial to mankind a relevant stipulation would not have been omitted from the Quran.[75]

But for all its neatness the distinction between the commercial and the consumption loans provides at most a first approximation of those moral concerns many have about usury. While it is doubtless true that consumption loans will tend more often to reflect the impress of material necessity rather than investment loans, this is not always the case. Just as many third world investment loans reflect a pressing desire to escape material impoverishment, so too many consumption loans are driven by the desire for luxury and status generating acquisition.

Worries about the ethics of usury cannot be adequately addressed by looking simply at what the borrower does, or intends to do, with the loan. What matters are:

 (i) the conditions under which a bargain is struck; and
(ii) the subsequent kind of relationship that is established between the lender and the borrower.

The relationship is objectionable when the lender takes advantage of the desperate circumstances of the borrower.

But this is not all there is to things 'morally speaking'. For such opportunism opens up the possibility of committing the borrower to an ongoing sequence of *debt-bondage* that may have no natural conclusion. The borrower may be caught in a 'debt-trap' from which they can never escape, but which provides an ongoing source of profit for the lender.[76]

There are other sources of debt-bondage as well as the impress of need. A borrower may be ensnared through the manipulation of our psychological propensity to 'discount the future' which often involves an optimistic over-estimation of future resources and an irrational under-estimation of future needs, thus pursuing immediate gratification in opposition to our better considered judgements.[77] Sometimes, this is compounded by the desire for the status that certain commodities are thought to confer. If our susceptibility to the immediacy of expectation and consumption can ensnare us in a debt-trap, there is a more prosaic route, through our limited cognitive capacities. We are not generally well versed at, or very comfortable with, the kinds of calculations essential to grasp properly the financial implications of a loan agreement. In particular, we are not very good at grasping the dimensions of compound interest; and while lenders might try and make everything plain to us, there remains the possibility of their not doing so; a possibility that, for obvious reasons, is not hard to exploit, and which can promise greater financial returns than pellucid honesty. Whether it be through the taking advantage of desperate circumstances, or our attitudinal and cognitive shortcoming, a cunning lender can lead us into a debt-trap from which escape is difficult.

This anxiety about *entrapment* was at the heart of Plato's condemnation of interest-taking in the *Republic*:

> these money-makers with down-bent heads, pretending not even to see them, but inserting the sting of their money into any of the remainder who do not resist, and harvesting from them in interest as it were a manifold progeny of the parent sum, foster the drone and pauper element in the state. They do indeed multiply it.[78]

A consequence of this entrapment, according to Plato, was that it set one class against another and thus was harmful to the state.[79]

Further – though neither necessary nor sufficient for wrongful lending – the kind of financial dependence that may obtain between the debt-trapped borrower and the demanding creditor can engender an obsequiousness on the part of the borrower, and an unpleasant capacity for arrogance on the part of the lender.[80]

Against this, it might be argued that debtors are prodigals and thus deserve neither sympathy nor government protection. The idea now is that debtors are feckless; so that any debt-bondage they might endure is really 'their own fault'. Bentham, for instance, argues:

> [T]hose who have resolution to sacrifice the present to future, are natural objects of envy to those who have sacrificed the future to the present. The children who have eat their cake are the natural enemies of the children who have theirs.[81]

On reflection, this is a peculiar position. It reinserts the idea of *desert* into legitimating interest, though in the opposite way than before. It seems that the debtor deserves the burden of his or her interest charges as a kind of due punishment for his/her taking a loan in the first place. The lender does not so much deserve the interest repayments, as assume the right to chastise the profligate and otherwise financially unworthy. Not only is debt-bondage not an objection to usury, the more debt-bondage there is the more the unworthy are suffering their due punishment!

What are we to say of this picture of the usurer as chastiser of the feckless? One thing, surely, is that it is untrue. Creditors typically make their lending decisions on financial grounds, not on the need to morally chastise the improvident. A more effective form of chastisement – perhaps even the final form – would be to refuse to lend anything, at any rate. And if one does lend, as a matter of deserved chastisement, what non-malicious end is served by setting in process something that might well mean that the punishment for the momentarily feckless is unending?

Justice in interest-taking: Private conscience, public policy and usury

Interest, then, is morally permissible, in so far as it gives rise to great public benefits, so long as it does not exploit the desperation of the needy or ignorant in such a way that they pay exorbitant rates of interest or find themselves caught in a net of debt-bondage. These moral concerns are of sufficient weight to warrant both the exercise of individual conscience and intervention by government in the way lending institutions function. How might we translate these into concrete moral directives and public policy?

Let us begin at the level of individual morality. What we should avoid are financial arrangements which involve exploitation of another's desperate circumstances or which trap people in debt-bondage.

In this there are similarities with a number of writers in the tradition, perhaps most notably the work of Calvin who listed seven moral constraints on the actions of those who would seek profit from money-lending, three of which are central to our discussion. First, interest must not be taken from the poor. Second, one must not be so focused on gain so as to forget one's obligations to the poor. Third, in the case of investment loans, the borrower must make equal or greater gain than the lender.[82] Significantly, Calvin did not attempt to *legislate* for these, for although excessive interest is sinful, this is a matter of individual conscience. (Indeed some commentators suggest that the result of Calvin's influence was to shift usury from being an offence for which governments were responsible to one that was simply a matter of private conscience.)[83]

Curiously, Calvin was pessimistic about the likelihood of his restraints being effective. He was well aware that his criticisms of the traditional usury doctrine would in all likelihood provide ammunition for those who would abandon any moral scrutiny on money-lending.[84] Yet he continued in the hope that 'men of good will' would see the moral hazards that lay within the walls of the money-lenders tent. But this is not how it turned out, for 'while his general approval of interest was emphasized, his reservations were ignored'.[85]

Where we differ from Calvin is in our unwillingness to rely on private conscience alone. His appeal was to the power of individual moral sentiment, but such an appeal, shorn of any regulatory embodiment, is not sufficient to prevent exploitation, for there will be those who do not heed the call of conscience. We also require a set of usury laws not merely a reliance on good citizens directed by moral exhortations.

So let us consider the general composition of such laws all of which involve intervention through either prohibition or government regulation.

Our first proposal involves the so-called *usury ceilings*, that is limits on the rates of interest that are legally permitted. Governments should legislate to prevent excessive rates of interest. What counts as 'excessive' here will depend on the current market rates for ordinary business transaction and would need to be determined in relation to those.

There is no suggestion here of a *true price* for the sale of money, as there is no natural rate of interest. There have been various projects that attempted to rely on such a rate. In Ancient Rome interest was set at 12% per annum. In the nineteenth century one writer, Mr K. Arnd, thought that the rate of interest should be at 3–4% because this was the rate at which the amount of timber in the European forests increases with their annual new growth. Marx referred to this as the 'forest primeval rate of interest'.[86]

Jeremy Bentham went further. He suggested that as there is no true rate of interest, then any *particular* rate must be arbitrary. Any rate must be simply a product of social convention, since no rate of interest can naturally be more proper than another, this being borne by the variance of interest in different places.[87] '[B]ut what basis can be more weak or unwarrantable as a ground for coercive measure, than custom resulting from free choice?'

Bentham is simply mistaken. Not only does he fail to understand the need to protect the poorer members of society from excessive interest-taking, his reasoning itself is faulty. The fact that we cannot provide an exact rate does not render whatever rate we do choose arbitrary and thereby morally indifferent.

Anti-usury laws involve interest-rate ceilings, and require that the lender properly and fully explain the implications of taking this or that loan at a certain rate of interest. It may also require the lender to ensure that the borrower is in a position to repay the loan without undue hardship, such as might lead to continuing debt-bondage.

One notorious difficulty, however, with prohibitions on desperate exchanges is that, on their own, they do not necessarily improve the situations of those who are exploited. This is what some critics refer to as the 'double bind', where simply banning a desperate exchange does nothing to improve the circumstances of the desperate.[88] By prohibiting such things as pay-day loans, we do nothing to alleviate the circumstances that make people vulnerable to extortionate loans. With the imposition of stand-alone usury limits, such people might well be deemed too high a risk to lend money to and so be without access to credit. If interest rates are kept low, then financial institutions will not necessarily extend those low rates to such high-risk borrowers. Further, usury legislation often drives such transactions underground, encouraging even more predatory and exploitative lending practices ('loan-sharking'). The lesson is that usury is an issue that must be addressed *systematically*, as part of a more general distributive policy that reduces the requirement for high-risk, high-interest, loans.[89]

This brings us to our second policy suggestion: government subsidy of high risk, low-income borrowers and government banking. This is aimed at ensuring that those who, as a consequence of our usury ceilings, would fall outside the banking system or would be vulnerable to predatory exploitation, are not excluded from access to credit nor forced into illegal sources of loans. Governments might adopt one of the two alternatives here. They might act as guarantors for low-income, high-risk borrowers. Effectively, governments would be subsidising the loans of people in such circumstances. Alternatively, they might establish central government banks that offer loans to those who fall outside the credit system. Historically, in many countries there have been central banks that have fulfilled this purpose, offering low-interest loans to those in needy circumstances. Such measures are designed to ensure that usury legislation does not harm those who are worst-off.

More recently, such strategies have been developed by the Grameen ('rural') Bank in Bangladesh; strategies for which Muhammad Yunnis recently won a Nobel Prize. The point is not that such a community lender does not charge interest on their loans – it does – but that it provides credit for those who would be denied it by ordinary banking institutions:

> Grameen Bank's objective is to bring financial services to the poor, particularly women and the poorest 3/4 to help them fight poverty, stay profitable and financially sound. It is a composite objective, coming out of social and economic visions.[90]

Thus the Grameen Bank typically charges interest (although it also has a 'Struggling (Beggar) Members Programme'), but that interest is meant (i) simply to cover business costs, and (ii) to provide some capital for non-profit-driven expansion of the desired service into new areas. A mark of this is that the Bank's interest charges are not compounded, but are simple. Further than this, the Grameen Bank does not threaten loan defaulters with enforced recouping of the loan, but allows them to reschedule their loan without cost. Of course, sometimes this will not be sufficient (though the Bank claims a 98% compliance rate), and so there is a limit to the interest that can accrue on an outstanding loan. Once the interest repayment equals the principal, no further interest is levied. The Bank treats all loans as investment loans, even when the loan is to be used for such things as, for instance, housing, sanitation, access to potable water, and coping with emergencies and disasters.[91]

Our third strategy involves a recognition that there are some needs that should not be met through lending mechanisms. Here we have in mind basic necessities such as health and education. One should not have to borrow money at interest – no matter how low the interest rate might be – in order to gain access to such things as basic health care or a decent education.[92] Such goods should instead be provided *inter alia* by the state. Of course, this does rule out additional private and commercial provision. It is simply to say that some goods are so basic to human flourishing that a level of minimal coverage is required from the state.

Freedom of contract?

It might be objected that anti-usury legislation violates freedom of contract. After all, loan agreements are not made by the creditor pointing a gun at the debtor, and saying, 'sign off or die'. Even if the pressures of need force a person into taking a loan – and perhaps taking it on rather unfavourable terms – still the loan agreement itself is consensual, even if the route to accepting the loan is one of perceived necessity. Clearly, this is a more substantial objection to our position than the former; and it meshes neatly with the claim that trying to restrain such trades will often have the perverse consequence of harming the worst-off.

What are we to say? One thing to say is that if the pressures on a debtor are such as to give them no reasonable alternative to signing onto a loan agreement they understand is generally unfavourable or harsh, then perhaps there ought to be alternatives, including the alternatives, perhaps, of simple charity or of public provision. As Bernard Williams remarked, there is often a certain bad faith in play when someone says 'there is no alternative'. He considers the case of the strong-arm standover man who says to a merchant, 'Unless you pay me this amount weekly, then you leave me no alternative but to break your legs'.[93] Of course, there is an alternative – just as charity and public provision are alternatives to desperate loans – it is just that the standover man, given his lucrepathology, has no interest at all in these alternatives. Often this seems to be just as true of those lenders who champion the legitimacy of desperate loans; there is no alternative in part because they refuse to think of any alternatives, for such alternatives may reduce their profit-taking opportunities.

The deepest worry with this contractualist position lies with the notions of coercion and consent it deploys. Can we really accept the view that circumstances might coerce us into making a contract, but that the contract (and so all it entails) is consensual in a sense that cancels out any worries about the lender 'taking advantage' of another's misery or desperation? This position has been defended by existentialists like Sartre, and has been explicitly argued by the libertarian Robert Nozick. Nozick, as the reader will recall, argues that the man who could, without significant risk to himself, rescue another who is drowning by pulling him into his boat, but insists to the drowning man that he will only do this if he agrees to transfer to the rescuer all of his wealth, is not coercing the man into an unconscionable contract. The man is free to choose – in this case to drown or not to drown and emerge much poorer – and whatever choice he makes is, given that there are alternatives in play, consensual. One immediate and natural response to this is to reject the argument out of hand. Any account of consent that licenses such cases is simply wrong, even perverse. If there can be situations in which no one would wish to find themselves, such as at risk of drowning, there are even more reasons to think no one should have to find themselves in this position with a man like Nozick making such a repugnant offer.[94]

Concluding remarks: Usury as the dog that did not bark

Usury, then, is not an antiquated normative concern, for what we do with our money when we put it out at interest is a matter of considerable moral import. Any suggestion that the Medieval writers were just mistaken in their focus on interest should be repudiated; their mistake was to ban all interest-taking. But we should still endorse their goal of protecting the vulnerable.

The great failing of Medieval doctrine was to regard all loans as desperate exchanges and not to see the potential productivity of capital. Nonetheless, their moral concern about the compulsion involved in usury contracts and the bondage that may ensure it is still a live issue today. To see this we need only consider the passion that third world debts and pay-day loans often inspire in critics of such money-lending practices.

But if exploitative lending practices are highly topical issues, this topicality is not reflected in contemporary moral theory. There is little from philosophers on the questions of what might be legitimate interest, why there might be problems with some forms of interest-taking, and how one might distinguish, if one were so inclined, between legitimate and illegitimate interest. One aim of this chapter has been to go some way towards redressing that gap in the philosophical literature.

More specifically, we make four main claims. First, we accept the general legitimacy of interest on the grounds that under non-desperate circumstances it is the product of consensual agreement and it provides great social benefits. Second, despite this, there remain genuine grounds for concern over some forms of money-lending and to these we attach the term 'usury'. Third, these concerns are of a kind with what motivated the Medieval prohibition of money-lending: predatory lending, crippling rates of interest, debt-bondage and dependency. Finally, these concerns require constraints at the level of both individual morality and public policy. It follows that the selling of money is not just like the sale of a horse or a house. *Contra* the argument from arbitrariness, loan contracts involve possibilities for bondage and exploitation that do not arise in the same way with ordinary commercial transaction. While desperate exchange is a potential feature of any commercial transaction, in the case of money-lending there are opportunities for exploitation and dependency that go way beyond those found elsewhere. Thus the idea that interest, being merely the price of money, does not warrant more concern than other forms of commerce is just wrong.

The final point is that our justification of interest-taking does not legitimate whatever amount it might be that a lender can manage to squeeze out of a debtor. Calvin's arguments were appropriated in this way, but it should be clear that ours do not absolve the money-lender of moral responsibility to avoid exploiting the desperate, nor governments of the responsibility to address such desperation. Equally, arguments about freedom of contract, harming the worst-off or debtors being prodigals or feckless, should not be thought to outweigh these concerns over exploitation and debt-bondage. We seek a point mid-way between those who would allow all loans and those who would prohibit them entirely. While this might not be an overly spectacular theoretical conclusion – and certainly not as spectacular as Father O'Callaghan's repudiation of any interest-taking, or Bentham's *laissez-faire* approach to lending – it does greater justice to our pre-theoretical intuitions, and to the political constraints that we tend actually to find embodied in various usury laws. To the extent that proper theorising in the social sciences is a matter of what John Rawls calls 'wide reflective equilibrium' – that is, it requires reflection on the relationship between our general views and our intuitions – then the loss of anything theoretically spectacular may not be a fault, but a blessing.

5
The Morality of Pricing: Just Prices and Moral Traders

Well, but what will you say to this question? (You know that there is no settled price set by God upon any Commodity that is bought or sold under the Sun; but all things that we buy and sell, do ebbe and flow, as to price, like the Tide:) How (then) shall a man of tender conscience doe, neither to wrong the seller, buyer, nor himself, in buying and selling of commodities . . . . .

John Bunyan, *The Life and Death of Mr. Badman (1680)*, 123a

Introduction: The irrationality of a just price?

A central function of money is as a unit of account and this raises moral questions; most notably, what price a good should bear. It is not a question of what things should *have* a price. That some things ought not to be priced, or that pricing them is morally hazardous, does not mean that when we come to things which can be priced, any questions morality might ask concerning that price are thereby irrelevant or mistaken.

Just this view often presents itself as economic orthodoxy or hard-headed common sense. Typical is the view of the Oxford philosopher R.G. Collingwood (1879–1943):

A just price, a just wage, a just rate of interest, is a contradiction in terms. The question what a person ought to get in return for his goods and labour is a question absolutely devoid of meaning. The only rational questions are what can he get in return for his goods or labor and whether he ought to sell them at all.[1]

In many respects, this is an extraordinary passage.[2]

What exactly is he rejecting? Well not just an idea, but also a venerable tradition. This tradition has its roots in the Ancient World but reaches its full flowering in the thought of the Medieval philosophers. The theory of the just price follows from the Medieval acceptance of the legitimacy of commerce so long as it is constrained by and furthers moral considerations. It was a natural consequence of the shift from the anti-commercialism of the early Medieval thinkers to a *moral* account of the market that accepted the necessity of trade and yet which acknowledged the moral hazards such activities involved.

As we saw in Chapter 2, for Medieval thinkers such as Aquinas, the pursuit of money was permissible so long as it was treated as a means to other morally acceptable ends, such as raising a family or for purposes of charity. Commerce is a mere means and must serve valuable non-pecuniary ends and if it is to perform its function, it must not lead to either avarice or the self-interested exploitation of the vital needs of others. The thought behind both restrictions is that human beings are readily tempted by the lures of money in such a way that there is always a danger of lucrepathology. This echoes the suggestion of Saint Augustine that we are all too prone to vice when it comes to money. In 'On the Holy Trinity', Augustine tells the story of a fairground magician who says he can tell what every person is thinking – and the answer is to buy cheap and sell dear.[3]

At the heart of the Medieval theory of the just price is the doctrine of *laesio enormis*.[4] This doctrine first appeared in the Justinian Code where it was concerned only with land sales, but the Medieval thinkers extended it to cover all sales. The doctrine of *laesio enormis* came into play when the price for a good was either double or half the standard market price. In such cases there was an obvious *prima facie* suspicion that something untoward was going on. With double the usual price the suspicion was that the vendor was somehow exploiting the prospective buyer; and with half the usual price the suspicion was either that the exploitation was running the other way, or that there was some kind of underhand collusion going on. In such cases both the buyer and the seller could call on the doctrine to legally undo or rescind the sale. Of course, exceeding the half/double criterion did not of itself – simply in virtue of the numerical ratio – condemn the relevant price as unjust or unfair. It meant that if one or other of the contracting parties felt that something was amiss with the sale price, they could call on the magistrate's authority to rescind the sale.

Perhaps the most striking thing about *laesio enormis* is the practical good sense it involves. It is an example of 'casuistical' market regulation that is neither excessively stringent nor rigid. Its whole point is to

delineate cases in which there is an obvious suspicion of something untoward going on, and, having done this, to allow the bargaining parties the
opportunity to reassess their commitment to the sale. Accordingly, no
attempt was made to ensure that every economic transaction accorded
with the just price, and so no preference for command-style economic
management is to be found.

This concern that prices not be well outside the conventional market price was one rough and ready way that the Medieval philosophers
tried to deal with the problems of price-gouging and illicit collusion in
commercial exchange. Three practices in particular attracted especial disapprobation: *forestalling, engrossing* and *regrating*. These practices were all
monopolistic in nature and inspiration. Forestalling involved the private
buying up of goods before they reached the market; engrossing meant
'cornering the market' by buying up all or most of a certain commodity;
while regrating involved the buying up of all or most of a commodity in the marketplace so as to resell that commodity in the very same
market. All of these practices were ruled illegal by Medieval commercial
law, though often enough the discovery of such practices was revealed
not by direct investigation (something that Medieval jurisdictions were
typically not well-manned to provide) but by the social consequences
such price manipulation generated.

With the advent of modern economic theory, and the work of writers such as Turgot, Smith and Condorcet, we find that the idea of
justice-in-pricing disappears. It was largely lost to 'enlightened' economic reflection. However, even if just pricing was no longer a reputable
intellectual pursuit, the *practical* manifestations of it did not vanish
entirely.

In the language of E.P. Thompson in his seminal essay on this subject,
'The Moral Economy of the English Crowd in the Eighteenth Century',[5]
while the political economists derided concerns with justice-in-pricing
as misplaced sentimentalism to be subdued if necessary by state force,
they remained an essential component of the 'moral economy of the
crowd', particularly in times of dearth. As Roger Wells, quoting Thompson, writes of the eighteenth-century crowds' conception of economic
justice:

> Much more than mere uproar, their central forms, mass imposition of
> popularly stipulated maximum subsistence prices, and enforced reser-
> vation of locally-grown foodstuffs for district, as opposed to distant
> markets, were '*legitimated by the assumption of an older moral economy
> which taught the immorality of any unfair method of forcing up the prices*

of provisions by profiteering' .... by farmers, merchants, manufacturers and retailers *'upon the necessities of the poor'.*[6]

For an example of such behaviour – demonstrating clearly that the concern is with *just pricing*, and is not a manifestation of blanket anti-commercialism, consider the following account of a local food riot taken from the *Northampton Mercury* (May 2, 1757):

> Some farmers demanded 11s. per Bushel for Wheat, and were agreeing among themselves to bring it up to 15s. and then make a stand . . . [The townsmen, however] sent their Wives in Great Numbers to Market, resolving to give no more than 6s. per Bushel, and, if they would not sell at the Price, to take it by Force; and such Wives, as did not stand by this Agreement, were to be well flogg'd by their Comrades. Having thus determined, they marched to the Corn-Market, and harangued the Farmers in such a Manner, they lowered their price to 8s. 6d. The Bakers came, and would have carried of all at that Price, but the Amazonians swore, that they would carry the first man who attempted it before the Mayor; upon which the Farmers swore they would bring no more to Market; and the sanguine Females threatened Farmers, that, if they did not, they would come and take it by Force out of their Ricks. The Farmers submitted and sold it for 6s. on which the poor Weavers and Woolcombers were content.[7]

If we are to believe George Rudé, this position – in which political economy had abandoned the idea of just pricing, but the people's 'moral economy' had not – was historically transient:

> gradually, the old protective legislation against enclosure, engrossing, and forestalling, and the export of grain, and the old laws empowering magistrates to fix prices and wages, were rescinded; and the old notions of the 'just' price and 'just' wage, imposed by authority or sanctioned by custom, gave way to the new prevailing notions of 'natural' wages and prices in a freely competitive market.[8]

But on this Rudé seems to be wrong. For we do not have to look far to find just the same concerns today with justice-in-pricing, though not always so tightly focused on the provision of foodstuffs.

For example, recent debates about the sale of HIV drugs point to the survival of a concern with the justice of pricing. In South Africa it was (successfully) argued in November 2003 that vendors of cheap locally produced replicas of HIV drugs should not be prosecuted for infringe-ment of patents since the pricing of the legally produced drugs was too high for those who have the misfortune to be both sick and poor. South Africa's Competition Commission brokered a deal with GlaxoSmithKline and Boehringer allowing HIV drug sales in all 47 sub-Saharan African states.[9]

Equally, in many political jurisdictions there are laws which limit price rises in areas that have been declared natural disaster zones. Even such things as the listing of used car prices by motoring organisations reflects a concern that buyers not be 'ripped off' or 'gouged' with unfair prices.

Nor can we argue that such views are a mark of economic primi-tives or those unacquainted, or newly acquainted, with the operations of commercial life, for even in highly commercialised and economic literate societies such as the United States and Switzerland, people still entertain and act upon what those like Collingwood say are nonsensical intuitions.

In the book *Not Just for the Money* (which we discussed briefly in the introductory chapter), the economists Bruno Frey and Werner Pom-merehne describe an experiment in which respondents were asked for their reactions to an increase in the price of a good in the face of scarcity.[10] The remarkable thing about the survey was that not less than 83% of the participants thought the hardware store owner's opportunis-tic pricing 'unfair', even if, in classes of economics, they might read, 'the question what a person ought to get in return for his goods and labor is a question absolutely devoid of meaning. The only rational questions are what can he obtain in return for his goods and whether he ought to sell them at all.'

It is central to our approach that if sophisticated members of long-established commercial societies still entertain and, as in the case of the HIV drugs and anti-price-gouging laws, act upon what those like Collingwood say are nonsensical intuitions, then there is good reason to begin by taking such concerns seriously. This is particularly so when we appreciate that the concern with just pricing is venerable, complex and continuing.

In our view its relative bad odour in many circles lies not, as Colling-wood thinks, with some essential incoherence contained in the very idea, but with the way in which that notion has been cashed out, and typi-cally by hostile critics. This hostility is not, as Collingwood suggests, a matter of pointing to a piece of blatant nonsense, but entails repudiation of both an intellectual tradition and many contemporary practices. At the very least, Collingwood owes us a powerful and persuasive account of how it is that so many, for so long, and after so much thought, can entertain what is supposedly palpable nonsense.

But if Collingwood has little to offer beyond the charge of sheer nonsense, there is a plausible historical story that can be told which allows us to see why he should think the case against the just price is obvious. Behind this story lie a series of interpretative mistakes.

Why think that justice-in-pricing is a 'contradiction in terms', absolutely devoid of meaning?

How might one cash out the claim that the just price is, as Collingwood would have it, plain irrational? Historically, there are three main sources of criticism of the just price. First, that any form of justice-in-pricing involves unwarranted normative interference in the working of the market; second, that the just price tradition reflects an attempt to maintain the social status of the aristocracy; and third, that those who defend the just price tradition are wedded to the idea of a determinate true price – a *verum pretium* – inhering in an object for sale. These criticisms are not simply intended to undermine the just price tradition, but any attempt to develop an account of justice-in-pricing.

Let us begin with the objection to normative interference in the market. There are two grounds for the view that any idea of a price beyond what one can successfully impose on a prospective buyer is mistaken, neither of which would have had any grip with Medieval thinkers.

One ground is utilitarian, and depends on the idea of the 'invisible hand' that ensures the pursuit of private ends produces public goods. This idea comes from Bernard Mandeville (1670–1733) and his *Fable of the Bees*. The point is simple: given the unmatched efficiency of the *laissez-faire* market in delivering commodities – and given that the production of such commodities generates material affluence – then any supposedly normative interference in market pricing procedures and outcomes is, in fact, morally counter-productive as it reduces utility. Such interference is morally undesirable, not the other way round. (We will explore Mandeville's ideas in great detail in Chapter 8.)

The other ground is deontological. The idea now is that normative interference in the market such as it might impact on pricing involves violating the foundational moral rights of market agents. It is not, as with the utilitarian, that consequences are what count, but that individuals' 'natural liberties' or rights are respected.

This view can be found in Adam Smith, and among its recent defenders are Robert Nozick and Milton Freidman.[11] The idea is that individual freedom is of ultimate value, and that such freedom is wrongly curtailed by any restrictions imposed on consensual exchange in the marketplace.

Both the utilitarian and deontological views rest on substantive and contentious claims. The first depends on the invisible hand thesis, the second on claims about our fundamental rights; and we take up these claims in a later chapter (Chapter 8). At this point there are two things that need to be said. The first is that despite the appeal of these two positions to many people (and although they are different, and perhaps, on occasions incompatible), it is just not true that modern economic markets are entirely free of normative restraints on pricing. The second thing to say is that we ought not immediately condemn such interference as somehow mistaken or immoral. After all, the plausibility of general moral theories such as utilitarianism or the deontology of natural liberties cannot be established independently of our everyday 'folk' moral intuitions. If our everyday intentions concerning the legitimacy of certain kinds of normative interference in the processes and practices of market pricing are firm, and if they can withstand (non-question begging) reflection, then this has implications for what more general theoretical demands we might legitimately make.

A second more historically attuned objection to the Medieval theory of just price is that it simply reflected a desire in those who proffered it to maintain *social status* in deeply hierarchical societies.[12] An object is justly priced when the price is an accurate reflection of the social standing of the agent selling it. The thought is that the structure of prices should reflect the existing pattern of income distribution within the community. The true price does not so much *inhere in the object* itself as depend upon the standing of the vending agent. Such a perception of the Medieval just price is widespread.[13] Moreover, it has been used to explain the Medieval objection to covetousness. Covetousness is said to be a sin because accumulating wealth in order to improve one's status in society was morally pernicious.[14] On this reading, Aquinas' concern with *cupidity* becomes, in the hands of writers like Barry Gordon, an objection to social stratification rather than a claim about the moral psychology of economic agents.

However, it is not at all clear that most – or even many – Medieval theorists held such a view. Aquinas, for instance, argues explicitly against it in his *Quodlibetales*.[15] Indeed, the only major Medieval figure that appears to have held this view is Henry of Langenstein (1325–1397).[16] Despite the lack of evidence, the view that the Schoolmen in general held such a position is widespread and is used as a reason for treating them in a derisory manner.[17]

Whatever the truth of these allegations regarding Medieval theory, this line of criticism has little bearing on contemporary demands for justice-in-pricing. There is no intrinsic reason to think that people who speak of justice-in-pricing are doing so because they wish to maintain a specific social hierarchy. There are two points here. The first is that it is often because they are concerned to mitigate or eliminate various inequalities that many social activists are impelled to demand constraints on the prices given by markets. The second is that a 'desire to rise' in social status through economic success is not frowned upon today as some form of 'hierarchy destroying' covetousness.

Let us turn then to what we take to be the most important route to the charge of irrationality. According to what we might call the '*Verum Pretium* Objection', the fault with the idea of the just price involves its connection to the idea of an *objective price inhering in an object*. When economic historians and philosophers discuss the idea of justice-in-pricing, they usually have in mind a theory that posits the existence of an objective or true price (the *verum pretium*) that is somehow inherent in or intrinsic to the commodity. Just price theory, on this account, is a form of *price realism*, that is the thesis that:

> For every object on the market there is a *natural price* which it bears, and which it should, in exchange, receive.

We see this view of the just price expressed in Hannah R. Sewall's *The Theory of Value Before Adam Smith* when she complains that because of the ancient Greeks' concern over right and wrong, rather than the mechanics of the economy:

> the somewhat naïve conception of value, or the worth of a thing, as a quality belonging to the thing itself, was not questioned. It was commonly held that the price ought to correspond to this quality, but that it often did not.[18]

The inherent properties that price was supposed to track were typically those properties which made the objects useful for human beings or which reflected the amount of work involved in their production.[19] It is a view that many historians of ideas have ascribed to Medieval thinkers. Yet according to contemporary economic theory, natural price is queer in the way that hobgoblins and unicorns are queer; things are worth just what they can sell for, or more precisely their marginal utility.[20] Norman S.B. Gras (1884–1956) expresses the worry in this way when he writes that:

> It was assumed that there was such a thing as an objective value, something inherent in the object rather than in the minds of the buyer and seller. We now have had enough experience and have made enough examination of the problem, of course, to know that no such value existed.[21]

Accordingly, just price theory should be repudiated on the grounds that it is committed to an account of the formation of prices that marginal utility theory has shown to be incorrect, not merely in detail, but in its very conception.

Thus, if one accepts the idea that there is a *true* or *objective* price, then one might attempt to explain the putative immorality of the actions of the shovel-vendor by pointing out that he raises the prices beyond the *verum pretium*. Such an account requires that the disgruntled consumers discern a shift from the true price the morning after the snowfall. But there is a problem here, for what they seem to have discerned is its opportunistic rise from the conventional price.

Probably, the best-known version of the *verum pretium* is the 'cost-of production' view, derived from Locke, Smith and Ricardo, and given seminal expression in Marx's labour theory of value. According to Marx, the price of an object is determined by the labour power embodied therein. Exploitation involves failing to pay workers the value of the labour embodied in the objects they produce.[22] Smith, too, believed that the natural price of a thing was set by the labour embodied in its production, but did not endorse significant or widespread interference in the workings of the market since he believed that in the long run the prices given by the market would track the natural price.

The cost-of-production account of price is often attributed to Medieval theorists such as Aquinas; indeed, it was just such a connection that led Tawney, in *Religion and the Rise of Capitalism*, to label Marx the 'last of the Schoolmen'.[23] However, the evidence with respect to Aquinas at least is equivocal; whilst in his *Commentaries on the Nicomachean Ethics of Aristotle* he endorses a cost-of-production view, in the *Summa Theologica* he views the just price as the market price.[24] One needs to look to John Duns Scotus (1266–1308) to find a Medieval truly committed to the cost-of-production view and thus to the *verum pretium*.[25]

Regardless of how one might best interpret the works of the Schoolmen, it is the cost-of-production account of *verum pretium* which contemporary economists typically discuss whenever the topic of justice-in-pricing is raised; and it is this conception of just price their criticisms address. The point is brutal: the very idea of justice-in-pricing is absurd, for the price of a commodity is set by its *marginal utility* through the mechanism of supply and demand in an adequate market. *Ex hypothesi*, the idea that the price of something is determined by some property internal to the object is nonsense and the idea that anything like a market might produce prices that capture such a property is absurd.

Whether or not the history is correct, reasons for concern with accounts of justice-in-pricing which rely on objective, inherent or natural price are readily available. Arguments about the existence of a natural price are exceedingly difficult to mount, and even harder to defend. Such properties seem to be metaphysically 'queer' in the sense that J.L. Mackie intended when he objected to the reality of moral values.[26] Regardless of whether or not one is a realist about values, in general there is certainly something queer about the idea of any good possessing intrinsically a just price.[27] Further, it is hard to understand by what epistemic means or faculty we are able to discern such objective pricing facts, and especially hard to show how such pricing 'intuitions' can distinguish themselves from the projective delusions or self-serving prejudice. The idea that there is a natural price is at odds with much of our daily experience. In general, prices appear to be determined largely by supply and demand, rather than being a function of some inherent property.

The discussion of justice-in-pricing contains, but does not resolve, an obvious tension between the *true price* and the *fair price*. One reason people find the pricing of some object unjust is not that it does not accord with what they believe the true price to be, but rather that the price makes access to the good more difficult. When consumers complain about the pricing of grain in a famine, their concern is not that the pricing does not accord with its true or natural price, but that the price charged is unfair because it makes the grain inaccessible to the poor and hungry. No reference is made to the true price, be it determined by the cost of production or some other inherent property, but to the price that is necessary if those who most need grain are to have access to it. Any understanding of justice-in-pricing based on the *verum pretium* simply fails to account for some of our most important intuitions in this area.

It is fortunate that the normative assessment of pricing does not stand or fall on the *verum pretium*. It is a mistake to think that the theory of justice-in-pricing must provide in each instance a unique magnitude. One can develop an historically adequate but metaphysically deflationary account of justice-in-pricing that is not committed to the ideas that:

(i) for every good there is a true price determined by the objective properties of the good or; (ii) the price of any good should be determined by that natural price and hence must have unique magnitude.[28] In the following section we explore three ways of doing so.

Three non-'*verum pretium*' accounts of justice-in-pricing

If the charge of irrationality rests on the *verum pretium* objection, then it is that objection we need to deflect. In this section we show that the charge of irrationality based on the *verum pretium* objection can be met since there are at least three different accounts of justice-in-pricing which do not rely on the idea of a true price, namely market conventionalism, pricing motivationalism and a needs-based account.

This section has two other functions. It is in the first instance a partial defence of the just price tradition itself, since as shall become apparent, in many cases the precedents for these non-*verum pretium* accounts of justice-in-pricing are to be found in the works of the Medievals. Second, it provides the basic material for the development of a view that makes sense of our present attitudes regarding pricing.

The first non-*verum pretium* view we consider is *market conventionalism*.[29] The thought is that justice-in-pricing is determined by previous transactions (unlike the *verum pretium* that tracks 'transaction-independent properties') and thus one appeals to the history of sales of such goods rather than anything inherent in the objects themselves. One does not focus on the spot market price, but on the conventional market price over some relevant period of time. All other things being equal, we can use the conventional price to make normative judgements about pricing. Accordingly, in such circumstances we condemn cases where it looks like the price is well outside of that typically obtained for this good. Bruno Frey's snow-shovel vendor, who increases the prices of snow-shovels when it snows, would thus be condemned either or both on the grounds that when we compare his prices with those conventionally obtained on the market, his are much higher, or they are much higher than those he charged previously. His price is unjust because it deviates significantly from the conventional market price.

It is important that this conventionalist approach not be confused with the Hobbesian 'justice-as-covenant' view. Hobbes claims in the *Leviathan* that so long as there is a 'signification of the will', then that consent is binding. Even covenants entered into by fear are 'valide'.[30] According to justice-as-covenant the just price is whatever price one can obtain through legal bargaining processes and concerns about outcomes are never worthy of consideration. This differs from forms of conventionalism in which the just price is determined by a *series* of market exchanges and wherein one can morally evaluate any particular market exchange with respect to that series.

One of the more fascinating aspects of recent debates about Medieval economics has been the shift over the past 40 years from the traditional view that justice-in-pricing for the Scholastics was determined by the *verum pretium* to the view that, except *in extremis*, it was broadly speaking the *market price*. The consensus in the literature now is that the just price was worked out, to use Aquinas' phrase, 'by common estimation', by the conventions of relevantly similar markets. It was only in extreme cases – where a price was more than double or less than half the standard market price – that norms of justice were invoked to interfere with free bargaining processes. (This is the doctrine of *laesio enormis* discussed earlier.[31]) Accordingly, no attempt was made to ensure that every economic transaction accorded with the just price, nor was there a preference for a command-style of economic management. Concerns with justice-in-pricing only became operative when a large discrepancy between a single contract and the conventional market price was discovered.

The dialectical advantages of this account of just price are obvious. First, without relying on the *verum pretium*, the conventionalist approach can make sense of the intuitions that led Frey's respondents to condemn the snow-shovel vendor. Following the conventionalist approach we can talk about the *relative* justice or injustice of transactions without committing ourselves to any idea that justice-in-pricing reflects objective properties of the good in question. Second, we are not committed to the view that there is some *unique numerical figure* that must be realised when selling any particular object or service. Justice-in-pricing will simply be a function of the average of relevant previous exchanges and will vary according to shifts in the markets. Finally, this conventionalist account of justice need not be committed to a *global normative patterning* of prices. We do not need to employ a just pricing tribunal to ensure that all prices conform to our ideal of justice. It is only when prices deviate significantly from that norm that interference might be legitimate.

A second way of avoiding a commitment to the *verum pretium* is via a pricing motivationalist approach. One interesting feature of the Medieval approach to pricing was their strong disapproval of what they viewed as the unquenchable desire for gain of those who sought money for money's sake.[32] Yet although they disapproved of such cupidity, this did not lead them to reject the pursuit of profit *per se*. In the twelfth and thirteenth centuries various Medieval thinkers, whilst condemning avaricious pursuits, allowed for the possibility of an ethically justified and moderate profit.[33] For many Medieval thinkers the morally determinate criterion of any sale was whether or not it was conducted out of the motive of *cupiditas*. While we differ from the Medievals in a great many respects – in particular the idea that the pursuit of wealth as an end-in-itself is always or inevitably sinful – nonetheless, we find the idea of examining the *motives of commercial agents* and drawing moral distinctions based in part on such an analysis suggestive.[34]

The first step in our approach, as the reader will recall from Chapter 3, is to draw a distinction between *motives* and *side-constraints*. One might pursue a certain goal with no side-constraints or, alternatively, one might pursue that goal but in so doing be constrained by various side-constraints. (Side-constraints are thus part of the motivational set.) Drawing on the discussion of the profit-motive in Chapter 3, we complicate the issue further by drawing a distinction between *pure motives* and *mixed* or *joint motives*. An action may be characterised as one motivated by a single goal or as one motivated by a number of variously related motives with one or more goals. Thus the pursuit of profit might be the sole aim of an intentional action or it might be one of a number of goals – which might be either self-regarding or other-regarding – towards which the action is oriented. For instance, a businessman who works for an environmental landscape business might hope simultaneously to make a profit and to improve the ecological standards of urban living.

With these considerations in mind, we drew a distinction, in terms of the roles the profit-motive and other-regarding moral considerations play, between a range of commercial acts. As we noted in Chapter 3, for our purposes there are three salient (and distinct) types of commercial activity, all of which involve the *profit-seeking motive*.

1. *Lucrepathic Action*: seeking profit is the sole or dominant consideration in an agent's all-things-considered judgements.
2. *Accumulative Action*: whilst the profit-motive is the primary aim of action, its pursuit is moderated by moral side-constraints.
3. *Stipendiary Action*: the profit-motive is not a goal, but rather functions as a side-constraint on action directed by other non-commercial goals.

It should be clear from this taxonomy why we believe that talk of the profit-motive *under-describes* the structure of intentional commercial acts, since in all of the cases above the pursuit of profit on the part of the agent involved is part of the action's satisfaction conditions.[35]

A third distinct approach to justice-in-pricing – though one that is often bound up in various ways with conventionalist and motivationalist accounts – is that which focuses on the connection of *pricing* and *need*. As we saw when considering E.P. Thomson's discussion, for many the problem was not, as it were, finding the precisely right or just price for a good; it was rather ensuring that pricing did not exploit 'the necessities of the poor'. When such happened, it often meant that conventional prices were abandoned for something far more remunerative to the vendor, and just as often it reflected a lucrepathic willingness to exploit the available opportunities for price-gouging; but the basic point is the same. The necessities of life ought not to be withheld from some because of the vendor's concern to make a profit.

There is a striking difference between Medieval views on pricing and need and later views that developed from the eighteenth century onwards, which reflects the increased levels of commercialisation of our lives and our general acceptance of market agency. For while earlier thinkers tended to think that in severe circumstances charity was an overriding obligation – so that in times of dearth the merchant might be required to give his stock to the needy – Thompson's crowds make a weaker demand. It is not that charity at personal loss is required – that is supererogatory – it is that the vendor must be willing to sell at no more than earlier profit levels, or, if things are really desperate, at reduced levels all the way down to just covering costs. Thus they are not required to sell at a loss.

What these three accounts demonstrate is that *there is no need for a proponent of justice-in-pricing to commit him or herself to the idea of a true price*. Further, it provides grounds for rejecting suggestions that the Medieval theory of the just price was itself committed to such an idea.

The normative foundations of justice-in-pricing: Lucrepathic motives and considerations of justice

However, we wish to go further than simply demonstrating the plausibility of an idea of justice-in-pricing or of defending the Medieval Schoolmen from criticisms of views that were not their own. Instead, we wish to explore the question of whether we are correct to be concerned with profiteering and prices that set goods outside of the reach of those who need them. Clearly, we think so. Our aim in this is to develop an account that makes sense of the intuitions that lead many of us to condemn profiteering and to condone legislation that constrains prices, particularly in times of disaster.

We begin by suggesting that all the three accounts, on their own, have problems; that is, when considered as the *sole grounds* for an account of justice-in-pricing.

Let us begin with *market conventionalism.* Conventional prices, understood as what is taken to be the customary price, may, when violated, be regarded with the suspicion of exploitation or illicit dealing as the *laesio enormis* doctrine held; but merely in itself the conventional price cannot be the standard or essence of justice-in-pricing. After all, the conventional price might well itself be the product of an extended series of exploitative acts or illicit dealings. Perhaps then, the conventional price is just if and only if it does not have such a pedigree. But that is to say that what matters for justice-in-pricing is that such prices are not exploitative or a result of illicit dealing; and that is to say that what matters are the motives which animate the deviation from the conventional price. Thus, as a matter of moral phenomenology, what matters are the motives of the price-setting agent and (rarely) of the price-taker.

So, exploitative price-setting will be, in our terms, price-setting which is lucrepathic, and which occurs in a situation in which such lucrepathic concern can find expression in a way that enables the price to significantly deviate from the customary price. And what are such circumstances? Well, typically it will be a matter of the capacity to exploit the desperate need(s) of the prospective price-taker, or their ignorance, or their simple vulnerability in the face of a monopolistic supplier. Rarely perhaps, but in a not unheard of fashion, it may also be a matter of illicit collusion between the price-setter and the taker – as, for instance, in some kind of financial or accounting trick meant to further the lucrepathic ends of both parties.

We should acknowledge, too, that the moral phenomenology of justice-in-pricing involves a continuum from cases in which while there certainly is a lucrepathic input into the price asked, we are not typically all that concerned (we may offer an expletive perhaps) to more serious cases. At the minor end of the continuum, we have no real inclination to level that kind of utter condemnation that might underpin regulatory control or legal punishment for the offending price-setter. We have already mentioned the prices typically charged at airports and sports stadia. So long as things do not get entirely out of hand, we tend to accept the higher prices in such places with a grimace, and perhaps a rueful reflection that, well, to be perfectly frank, perhaps we do not really need that beer or that hamburger. We have a monopolistic supplier, using that position to extract a premium, but so long as it is not utterly essential we purchase the relevant good, we can live with the injustice. A related case concerns the prices charged by certain corner stores. Here we might live with a touch of lucrepathology in the price-setting because, after all, we do not really need to have the relevant good here and now, so from this supplier. Perhaps we can wait until we reach the supermarket, or drive on to another store, and so forth.

Second, there is the problem of how the conventionalist deals with *need* – that is, with justice-in-pricing under conditions of sustained dearth. In famines the market price for necessary goods such as grain and meat will typically be well above a level that poorer members can afford. In such cases, the conventional market price is much higher than the price that enables the majority of the population to sustain themselves. Aquinas, in times of famine, abandons the conventional market price as the just price. Probably he is right to do so, but this is not conventionalism.

It is the last of these concerns that carries the most weight. When, for instance, Amartya Sen discusses the horror of famine, and argues that famine is rarely a natural evil, his concern is with situations of sustained shortages wherein vendors charge prices that make universal access to these necessary goods impossible.[36] The significance of cases like Sen's is that the conventionalist picture is not capable of adequately making sense of the intuitions we discussed at the outset. Thus, while the conventionalist picture is in one sense an explanatory advance upon the *verum pretium*, nonetheless it is inadequate to the task of providing a complete account of our normative intuitions regarding pricing.

Next, there is the problem of ascertaining the conventional price. Consider that in determining the conventional market price we need to decide how far back in time we must go. The conventional price of beetroot, for instance, will vary depending upon whether we consider prices over the past month, the past year, the past decade or the past century. Any choice of time-span may appear arbitrary. Yet if we do not include past market prices, and rather just simply current prices of goods, then we will have not any grounds for normative criticism. If every single one of the snow-shovel vendors in the area raises their prices simultaneously on the day of the snow-storm, then relying on *current* market prices will not provide us with any grounds for thinking the price-rise unjust.

Finally, as we have noticed, there is the strangely paradoxical consequence that a series of unjust prices can in the end sum to a just price. Imagine that one buys a house in Sydney, under extortionate circumstances, and pays something like double the going market rate. On the conventionalist model this would look like some kind of injustice-in-pricing. But imagine that whatever circumstances dictated the high price in your case are replicated all over Sydney for a period of months, so that by the end of this period the market price for a house of your type is equivalent to the price, as it happens, you paid. Given that this is the current market price, the price you paid is a just one. There is nothing particularly odd about this thus far. What is peculiar is that all of the prices that led to the change in the market price must have also been unjust, given the conventional market price at the time and yet in conjunction they give rise to a just price. How can a series of unjust pricing practices, when summed, give rise to a just price?

Price motivationalism goes deeper than mere price conventionalism when it comes to locating what it is we object to with certain price-settings, but again, it does not, by itself, capture all of what it is we might morally object to in such cases.

For instance, the motive behind certain price-settings might be equally lucrepathic, but we might still feel that there are morally important differences between certain cases. For example, it might be that certain petrol suppliers take advantage of the extra demand on public holidays and long weekends to price-gouge their customers, while certain pharmaceutical suppliers take advantage of (say) a wave of bacterial infection to price-gouge when it comes to antibiotics. All things being equal, we will tend to have a harsher reaction to the latter, and even if it is by no means a matter of life or death. Although the motives are the same, in the sense they are both equally lucrepathic, we judge the latter more harshly because the needs ignored are more pressing.

From the other side, it is equally apparent that certain kinds of undeniably vicious price-setting might not be lucrepathic at all. Consider the storekeeper who, out of racist animosity towards a certain ethnic group, insists on doubling the price of any good when a member of that ethnic group requests it. Here we may object to such prices, and on grounds of the vicious motive it expresses, but there may be no hint of lucrepathology – indeed, it may well be the case that the storekeeper's revenue is reduced because members of that ethnic community refuse to shop in his store, and he may not only be happy with this, it may have been his intention in the first place.

The point is that in order to give content to motivationalism we need to have some independent account of justice. In order to identify cases where important moral concerns are being ignored and where appropriate side-constraints on profit-seeking are missing, we need to have some sense of what those moral concerns might be.

When we turn to a *needs-based* model considered in isolation we see once again that it does not capture *all* of what is wrong with unjust pricing or which we would want to condemn on moral grounds. If we return to the case of the profiteering snow-shovel vendors, the increased prices, given sufficient levels of wealth in the community, need not prevent anyone from meeting their needs for such shovels. Considerations of need are not what are at issue. The point is that much of the moral concern we have with particular price decisions lies with the exploitation of the desperation of others – and then with the associated consequence that many who might otherwise have access to the needed good or service are now unable to purchase what they require. But in cases where that consequence is absent, moral concerns remain.

Further, considered as the sole basis for an account of justice-in-pricing, a needs-based account would seem to imply that vendors should sell at cost-price (or even a loss) when need so demands. It is no part of our morality of money – in contrast with, for instance, the Patristic Fathers – that charity trumps all, and that a vendor is required in certain circumstances to dispose of their stock at little or no profit to themselves. Such charitable intentions may well be admirable, but in the context of commercial life it is supererogatory, rather than obligatory. There is no hostility to profit-taking *per se* involved here, just a concern that such profits not be extortionate and thus excluding from the market many who would otherwise be able to purchase.

It would appear that there are weaknesses with each of the three accounts considered in isolation. Our solution is to develop a mixed account of justice-in-pricing that draws on both motivationalist and needs-based elements. We develop this by considering in turn justice-in-pricing for individuals and as a virtue of social institutions and arrangements.

Justice-in-pricing as an individual virtue

Ethical price-setting for individual commercial agents requires in the first instance that their pursuit of the profits be constrained by appropriate moral considerations. These moral side-constraints include considerations of justice, most notably those of need, though other considerations are important. If we take the case of those who charge extortionate prices for necessary medicines in developing world contexts, what is missing here is a non-exploitative concern for the needs of others. It is not that they wish to make a profit, but that their excessive desire to maximise that profit leads them to ignore morally significant human needs.

Unconstrained profit-seeking that ignores the needs of others is morally pernicious in two ways. The first is that the motive is objectionable in and of itself. We can see this is the case of Frey and Pommerhene's snow-shovel sellers. Even if the buyers can afford the extortionate prices, there is something objectionable about the motives of the sellers. The moral concern their survey uncovers is a concern with the proper structure of the price-setting agent's motivations in the marketplace. In a later work, *Economics as a Science of Human Behaviour*, Frey notes how our intuitions about justice are sensitive in just this way to profiteering. 'When a supplier raises the price for a particular commodity while keeping the prices for comparable goods constant, the price increase for this commodity is seen as proof that consumers are treated unfairly.'[37] Observing that other prices are not increased at the same time gives the impression that the seller has acted wilfully, since the price rise has not been forced by external factors such as a price rise in inputs. Raising prices in order solely to profit from an increase in demand is rightly regarded by many as illegitimate. In these cases we react to the role that the desire for profit plays in the trader's *all-things-considered* judgements.

The second pernicious element concerns the social consequences of unconstrained profit-seeking. When taking advantage of the needs of others makes the circumstances of the needy worse than they would have been, then clearly social harms have been caused.

As well as being side-constrained by concerns with needs, there are other moral considerations that should be taken into account when determining prices. For instance, one should not allow racial or religious factors to influence price. It is possible to imagine someone charging a higher price for goods to a particular religious group against whom they hold prejudicial views. Prices here would be unjust since they are formed on the basis of discriminatory attitudes. In this particular case divergence from the conventional prices provides us with an indication of injustice.

Notice three important features of our position. First, on our normative model money can be a legitimate end-in-itself of human activity. In this respect our views differ from those of the Medieval moralists for whom the appropriate pursuit of money required that it be a means to some other independently valuable end. The business person who is primarily concerned with the bottom line is not condemned so long as appropriate moral side-constraints are in place.[38] Second, the expectations on the individual to consider the needs of others have definite limits. There is no demand that commercial agents engage in charity when setting prices: doing so is supererogatory, at least *qua* commercial agents. Third, we do not attempt to provide a full account of the considerations of justice that should side-constrain the profit-motive. In this sense our account of justice-in-pricing is parasitic on a fuller account of justice.

Justice-in-pricing as a virtue of social institutions and arrangements: the role of government

Public concerns with profiteering typically bring forth more than simple exhortations for improved individual morality; often they generate demands for government action and government intervention in the operations of the market. However, the approach to justice-in-pricing must differ when we move from the private to the public realm. Governments can neither read nor regulate motives. The problem is an epistemic one. A trader might well lack any moral side-constraints on their profit-seeking and yet due to the commercial conditions price identically to someone who does possess such qualms. As far as observed behaviour goes, one cannot tell the difference between the two.

This, in no way, implies that there is no role for government; indeed to the contrary, there remains a significant role. First, in their responsibilities to the well-being and ethical lives of their citizens, governments have an obligation to lessen the *moral hazards* that commercial agents face. Economic conditions should not be such that traders have wide space for mischief. Preventing mischief will involve, amongst other things, ensuring that individuals and sets of individuals do not have undue power to determine the prices of goods and services because of monopolistic or oligopolistic conditions.

More significantly, governments have an obligation to prevent gross abuses, especially when vital need is involved. Indeed, it is when price-setting exploits vital needs – such as their requirements of basic nutrition and health – that we feel most offended, and are most prepared to take various kinds of actions against those setting prices. In particular, we may be willing to engage in government and regulatory policing and punishments of the kind that anyone who shares Collingwood's views on the sheer irrationality of concerns with justice-in-pricing will want to condemn as nonsensical and pointlessly sentimental. We, however, hold that it is an essential obligation of any government whose claim to legitimacy rests on a concern for the well-being of its citizens.

The kind of price control we have in mind here is of the minimal kind. In ordinary economic circumstances we would advocate the use of something like the Medieval doctrine of *laesio enormis*. Prices significantly above or below those standardly charged would be subject to close scrutiny on suspicion of either fraud or exploitation of another's desperate need.

Where the goods in question are the basic elements for a flourishing human life, and where we have good reason to think that pure market provision would lead to some people not having access to them, we would advocate supplemental public provision. This would not entail direct price controls on market provision, nor would it involve elimination of the market. Instead, it typically would involve additional provision of essential goods – housing, medicine and basic foodstuffs – at prices affordable to all, in order that all have access.

In cases of general extreme necessity – such as in times of famine or war – there may well be a strong case for placing limits on the maximum that can be charged for essential goods.[39] If there is a general scarcity and high prices might lead to only a few gaining these goods and public provision can only satisfy some of the demand, then governments should limit the maximum price. The force of this case is such that even Jeremy Bentham – who we have met before arguing that absolutely no limits be placed on the rate of interest – did accept a set maximum price for corn under conditions of famine and dearth in his unpublished essay, 'Defence of Maximum'.[40] In the article, which was a response to Charles Long's vigorous argument against all price controls in all circumstances, Bentham argues for 'set[ting] up a standard of right and wrong in corn-dealing which would allow a man to know whether he had charged too much for his grain or kept within the bounds of decency'.[41] But what determines the 'bounds of decency? Here Bentham – perhaps without knowing it – develops his own version of the *laesio enormis* approach to justice-in-pricing favoured by the Medievals. The maximum price for bread in a famine should be 'the exact double of the highest ordinary price at the place at which the price is highest'. This might be, perhaps, a little more permissive than Aquinas might have recommended, but still it is an example of that commonsensical approach to price determination he championed and which we suggest is a fundamental element of any sane response to these problems.

Two examples of justice-in-pricing

Our claim is that the mixed motivationalist and needs-based account we offer of justice-in-pricing goes a long way towards capturing our intuitions in the area. Reasons for holding this to be true can be found, among other familiar places, in the anti-price-gouging laws of many states of the United States, and in the story of prescription drug pricing, and in particular of the pricing of anti-HIV drug for needy recipients. In these cases the policies are aimed at lucrepathic price-setting, not at profit-taking itself, and in both cases, the concern with lucrepathic behaviour is underpinned by concerns that people's needs are met, not exploited. Consider the following two cases.

Case 1: Price-Gouging Laws in the United States

In over 20 states in the United States, price-gouging laws regulate the price level of goods and services in a jurisdiction, once it is declared a Disaster Area, or, as in the case of the state of New York, whenever there is 'an abnormal disruption of the market' such as may result from 'weather, natural disaster, energy crisis, civil disorder, national or local emergency, military action or war'.[42]

Such laws are not ancient relics, or misplaced survivors from an earlier less economically literate age, but are in the most part recent creations, as with the Florida law which was passed in 1992 after some spectacular profiteering following Hurricane Andrew, while the New York statute followed the ice storm and tornadoes that struck the state in 1998.

The laws vary in the degree of discretion they give state legal officers to determine what counts as price-gouging and what penalties it may attract. Florida laws, for example, simply forbid vendors from charging an 'unconscionable price' for their products during a declared emergency, where this is to be determined at the Attorney General's discretion, taking into account prices in the 30-day period prior to the crisis. Most other states have more stringent regimes, though the reliance on prior prices – that is to say, on market conventionalist criteria as a providing measure for lucrepathic price-setting – is common to all. For example, in Arkansas price increases are capped at 10% of the pre-emergency price as determined by averaging over the previous 30 days, while in Washington D.C. it is unlawful to increase prices in times of a declared emergency above 'more than the normal average retail price' in the jurisdiction during the '90 days prior to the emergency'.[43]

The Republican Governor Pataki of New York announced the passing of anti-price-gouging laws in his state by saying:

> Emergency situations...most often bring out the best in people. When neighbors help neighbors and friends help friends. But sometimes they also bring out the worst in some unscrupulous individuals and businesses.[44]

The worst that such situations may bring out in the unscrupulous is, of course, exploitative profit-taking. As Roy Cooper, North Carolina Attorney General, said in the aftermath of Hurricane Alex in August 2004:

> Most merchants pitch in to help their community recover following a natural disaster. However, there are some scammers who may try to take advantage of desperate times by charging outrageous prices to people when they can least afford it. That's wrong, and it's also illegal.[45]

That the laws are aimed at curbing what we label 'lucrepathic price-setting' is made even clearer when we take into account that such laws invariably allow scope for higher prices if a merchant can show that the emergency has caused their costs to rise to such a degree that the set price increase involves them selling at a loss. In such cases, as with the Arkansas laws, the seller is allowed to charge 10% above the wholesale cost plus whatever the pre-emergency mark-up was. The problem the laws address is not that of profit-taking, but is to protect consumers against those who take unfair advantage of their neighbours during natural disasters.

There are obvious possibilities for exploiting people's needs during a natural or other kind of disaster, but the concern that lucrepathic price-setting may unfairly deprive some people of what they need may find expression even outside such special circumstances. Thus, in New York, anti-gouging laws prevent supermarkets from charging any more than 200% above the price the dairy farmer received for the sale of his product.

Case 2: The Pricing of Prescription Drugs

Prescription drugs are not 'widgets'; they are not consumer goods like running shoes or vegemite. People buy them because for reasons of good or tolerable health, even for life itself. Such markets are not underpinned by a tissue of (variable) wants, but by the pressures of insistent need. Such goods, and trade in such goods, opens up the field for lucrepathic price-setting, and in a way that cannot be measured and remedied by relying on conventional price criteria.

It is hard to deny that such lucrepathic opportunities have not been taken by the manufacturers of such pharmaceuticals, and in such a way that many who need such drugs and would otherwise have the resources to access them simply cannot.

Again, let us restrict our attention to the United States. The American pharmaceutical industry has annual sales of over $200 billion. The industry ranks well above any other industry in average net returns. While the median return for other industries in the Fortune 500 is 3.3% of sales, for the pharmaceutical industry the average net return measured as a percentage of sales is 18.5%, of assets 16.3% and of shareholder equity 33.2%. These are astonishing figures, and cannot be explained away as is typically attempted by appealing to the costs of Research and Development. In fact, Research and Development consumes at most 14% of sales per annum, while 'marketing and administration' consumes 36% of sales revenues, and includes extraordinary executive salary returns. To give just one example, Charles A. Heimbold Jr., CEO of Bristol-Myers Squibb, in 2001 took home $74,890,918, not including his $76,095,611 worth of unexercised stock options![46]

For a particular instance of price-gouging in a lucrepathic market, consider the actions of Abbott Laboratories which, in 2004, announced a 400% increase in the price of Norvir, a protease inhibitor used as a booster in anti-HIV drug cocktails, and which has been available since 1996. A spokesman for Abbot defended the price hike:

> We did not make this pricing decision lightly. We carefully considered many things, and ultimately our very complex decision process allowed us to reach this difficult conclusion that this new price is necessary to be able to support our ability to continue research to bring the next generation of HIV medications to the market.[47]

Of course, if a 400% increase were suddenly necessary to realise this end, then perhaps 500% or 1000% would achieve even more.

When a producer sets prices we do not have a properly functioning market. We have, instead, an ideal environment for lucrepathic pricing. In this context it is worth noting that drug prices in the United States are substantially higher, for the same drugs made by the same manufacturers, than they are elsewhere, and not just in the developing world. It is also worth noting that both generic and brand-name manufacturers of anti-HIV drugs in Africa, Thailand and India manage to return a profit on their products while charging as low as $140 annually for an individual's drugs regime, instead of the $14,000 to $18,000 charged for the same regime in the United States.

Given a lucrepathic market, we cannot measure or remedy the problem of need exploitation by appealing to the conventional price. That is only a possibility in non-lucrepathic markets. So what can be done? Here the spokesperson for Abbott Laboratories has, if unintentionally, something to offer. Responding to charges that excessive price-setting of anti-HIV drugs means millions of people will die prematurely in the developing world, she said:

> When you're in the pharmaceutical business, you have patient assistance programs, and you ensure patients in need get the medicine when they can't afford it – that's part of what we do. But the plight of HIV in the Third World is just not the responsibility of pharmaceutical companies, it is the responsibility of this world to care for this.[48]

In many ways, this is an astounding paragraph. It asserts that the pharmaceutical industry does ensure, as 'part of what we do' – that 'patients in need get the medicine when they can't afford it', follows this with the implicit admission that this is simply not true, either in the sense of providing such drugs to the needy or of an implicit obligation to do so, then asserts that the plight of HIV suffers in the third world is 'just not' any of their responsibility, but is simply their problem and their responsibility. What the comment does imply, and surely correctly, is that attempts to measure and moderate the lucrepathic price-setting of the pharmaceutical industry will have to be imposed from outside that 'market', and that this will have to be done directly in response to matters of individual need independently of any reliance on conventional pricing as an indicator of excessive profit-taking.

Concluding remarks

We began by asking whether one could give a plausible account of the intuition that certain acts of pricing are unjust. Does talk of just and unjust prices commit one to the idea of a true price? We outlined three distinct ways whereby one might avoid any such implications. We may not have shown that there can be a just price, but we hope to have demonstrated that one can make sense of the idea of justice-in-pricing. In all the three models a commitment to justice-in-pricing neither demands a global patterning of prices, nor impugns the pursuit of wealth.

Subsequently, we developed (in outline) a mixed account of justice-in-pricing that draws on motivational and conventional elements set against an adequate background concern with adequate need provision. We argued that when setting prices for commodities, we should not act like 'lucrepaths', but instead should ensure that our pursuit of profit is side-constrained by relevant moral considerations, most notably the needs of those with whom we trade. We also argued that government policies should be devised so as to ensure that trade does not place unnecessary moral hazards in the paths of commercial agents and that the needy are not exploited. This approach to the problem of justice-in-pricing does not rely upon the existence of a *unique magnitude*. We will admit any particular price so long as the profit-motive is not overly determining in a way that is either objectionable in itself or that leads to the interests of other people being entirely overlooked.

We do not pretend that what we have provided here is a full-blown account of justice-in-pricing. However, we have laid the groundwork for such an account by repudiating the suggestion that the endeavour is irrational and by outlining what we take to be its appropriate normative elements. A full account would require a substantive theory of justice that distinguishes between essential and non-essential needs and addresses relevant distributive concerns; such a task is far beyond the scope of one chapter of a book. Justice-in-pricing is an important area for future work in the moral philosophy of money.

6
Money, Commodification and the Corrosion of Value: An Examination of the Sacred and Intrinsic Value

> *[The political economists] would dig up the charcoal foundations of the temple of Ephesus to burn as fuel for a steam-engine!*
> Samuel Taylor Coleridge, 1834[1]

Introduction

When, in the first volume of *Capital* Karl Marx thunders 'Everything becomes saleable and buyable... Not even the bones of saints, and still less are more delicate *res sacrosanctae, extra commercium hominum* are able to withstand this alchemy',[2] he is tapping into a venerable tradition that regards money as destructive or corrosive of the *sacred*. Money is the oil of the profane machinery of the reproduction of human life and ought to be kept separate from the realm of the sacred. There are some things that ought not be sold because of their sacred nature.

This concern with the sale of the sacred found a seminal expression in the writings of Martin Luther when he inveighs against the 'simoniacal' selling of spiritual grace.[3]

What is the force of this hostility towards the selling of sacred things? In tackling this question we begin by considering the battle between Church reformers and the established Catholic Church over the commodification of the sacred which reached extraordinary levels in the sixteenth century. We shall see that there are powerful moral reasons for having, or insisting on the necessity of, a non-commercial sphere of value. We shall see that the concerns that inform this demarcation of spheres of value are, in essence, concerns with the corrosive power of monetarised evaluations to eat away at other kinds of evaluation. Finally, we shall uncover an oft-overlooked temptation to defend the integrity of the sacred or intrinsically valuable as licensing – or even recommending – a complete evacuation of moral concerns from the sphere of commercial activity.

Luther, simony and the indulgences

Perhaps the most famous controversy concerning the sale of the sacred occurred with Luther's repudiation of the sale of indulgences, a repudiation which kick-started the Protestant Reformation.

According to Catholic Doctrine in every sin that is committed there is a two-fold evil. There is the personal insult or offence towards God, and there is the impersonal assault on the Divine Order of Justice. The point of this distinction is explained by the *Catholic Dictionary*.[4] Thus a child who deliberately breaks a window offends his parents and commits an injustice. His parents will forgive the child if he is sincerely penitent, but still properly demand the child make up for the (forgiven) evil by paying the cost of installing a new window. Well, the same goes for God. He may forgive the sins of the truly penitent, but still demands that the violation of the Divine Order be made good. This punishment necessitated even by forgiven sins is called *temporal punishment*, because it lasts only for a delimited period of time, and is distinguished from *eternal punishment*.

In the early Church the practice arose of commuting the purely earthly component of this temporal punishment – not the pains of purgatory – in the light of the penitent's good works or contribution to a pious cause. This possibility of remission of the temporal punishment of sin was established early in Church history (although it already contained the source of future troubles by linking the remission of Divine punishment to individuals' contributions to worthy causes (i.e. the Church)), although it was a minor element of Catholic life and excited little controversy. The changes that led to the growth of the indulgences to which Luther was opposed developed as later accretions to this original position.

One element of the change is attributable to Pope Leo IV who, in 855, attempted to counter the perceived advantage Muslim forces had in battle because of Mohammed's promise that any and all Muslims who died in battle with unbelievers would have immediate access to paradise, by promising Heaven to all Franks who themselves died in battle against the Muslims. Within 30 years Pope John VIII declared absolution of all sins and the remission of all penalties to soldiers who fought in Holy War.

These military-minded reforms of the indulgence of the early Church saw the remission extended from this worldly temporal punishments to the pains of purgatory itself; and soon saw the promise of indulgence used by the Papacy to raise money for Holy Warfare. By 1145 a penitent sinner might obtain relief from temporal punishment for sin in this world and that of purgatory by supplying sufficient money to fit out a Crusader on the same terms as if they themselves had gone.

If the age of the Crusades was over by the fourteenth century, the moneymaking aspects of the indulgence had not escaped Papal intelligence. In 1300 Boniface VIII granted a plenary indulgence to all pilgrims who made it to Rome. The rewards from the gifts supplied were such that Boniface saw fit to repeat the grant at regular intervals. All that was required was for a person to contribute to such pious causes as the Papacy saw fit to endorse. By the time of Boniface IX in 1393, papal agents were given the power to confess and absolve, and so to announce the complete remission of both guilt and penalty to the buyer.

The obvious pecuniary attractions of the practice to the Church and, in particular, the Papacy, unsurprisingly, came to be enclothed in a theory which hid any suggestion of brute avarice, but did so – and somewhat surprisingly – by even more deeply entrenching the language of money and commerce in Church Dogma. So it was that in 1343, Clement VI included in Canon Law the 'discovery' by Alexander of Hales of the Treasury of the Church, or Treasury of Merits (*thesaurus meritorum* or *thesaurus indulgentiarum*). This treasury is constituted by the merits of Christ and the saints; in modern philosophical language, it is the store of 'supererogatory virtue'.[5] It is against this stock of capital (a stock which, in the case of the saints may be of finite amount, but, with relation to Christ, of infinite amount) that the Pope, as head of the church and so chief banker, could supply as a kind of spiritual credit to whomsoever he chose; though as might be expected, such choice came increasingly to be determined by a fixed and far from insubstantial payment to the treasury from the buyer.

Despite the refinements of Church Doctrine, there lurked behind the elaborate façade a suspicion that the indulgence had become vulnerable to the charge of *simony*, a mortal sin. This is the charge that set Luther on course for his repudiation of the Catholic Church as an agency of the Papal Antichrist. But before turning to Luther, let us get clear on what it is that simony involves, and wherein lies its sinfulness.

The relevant Biblical passage (*Acts*, 8:18–24) is concerned with the actions of one Simon Magus, a magician of Samaria who had been baptised by Phillip the Deacon.

But when Simon saw that the Holy Spirit was given through the laying on of the apostles' hands, he offered them money, saying, 'Give me also this power, so that anyone on whom I lay my hands may receive the Holy Spirit.' But Peter said to him, 'Thy money go to destruction with thee, because thou hast no part or lot in this matter; for thy heart is not right before God. Repent therefore of this wickedness of thine and pray to God, that perhaps this thought of thy heart may be forgiven thee; for I see that thou art in the gall of bitterness and in the bond of iniquity.' But Simon answered, 'Do you pray for me to the Lord, that nothing of what you have said may happen to me.'

Peter's rebuke and Simon Magus' worried response make it clear that Simon wished to purchase, and so hoped Peter would sell, the gifts of the Holy Spirit. But such things, Peter insists, cannot be viewed as commodities which may change hands at an agreed upon price. Simon's sin is that of *simony of divine right*, where this is the sin of commodifying that which is *essentially* spiritual or sacred, or of commodifying those things for exchange which are *necessarily* connected to the sacred. Simony of divine right is always a mortal sin and if one dies in such a state of sin, eternal damnation awaits.

Crucially, there is a different species of simony, not always a mortal sin. *Simony of ecclesiastical law* may occur when someone sells or buys something that, while not *essentially* sacred or *necessarily* connected with the sacred, is yet imbued with such value, as with a consecrated or an indulgenced object. It occurs whenever the exchange-value of the relevant object is in some part supposedly determined by the object's sacral value. If, however, the object is exchanged at a value in accordance with its purely material or profane properties – as, say, a piece of paper or wood – there is no sin. There is no sin, because the sale operates solely on the level of profane evaluation.

Luther's assault on the simony involved in buying and selling indulgences was occasioned by the indulgence granted by Leo X to Albert of Hohenzollern in 1514. This indulgence was, in part, simply the extension to German territories of the plenary Jubilee Indulgence inaugurated by Leo's predecessor, Julius II, and intended to finance the rebuilding of the Basilica of St. Peter's in Rome. The extension was granted so that Albert – who, at 23 years of age was officially too young to assume important Church Offices – could pay for a papal dispensation enabling him to assume the Bishoprics of Magdeburg, of Halberstadt, and of Mainz. The cost to Albert of acquiring the relevant curial permissions amounted to a total of 34,000 ducats, and was paid by the German banking family, the Fuggers.[6] The deal struck with Pope Leo X was that one half of the monies collected would go to Rome for rebuilding St. Peter's, and that the other half should be retained by Albert and the Fuggers.

Driven by his extreme financial loading – and by the refusal of some German territorial princes, including Luther's Lord, Frederick the Wise of Saxony, to allow the sale in their lands – Albert sought to put as positive a spin on his holy wares as he could, even where such a spin meant sailing very close to the winds of deception. From his public advertisement for the indulgence sale, it is clear – as it was to Luther – that Albert's strategy involved what could only be intended as a purposeful effort to lead the public to think that purchase of an indulgence would provide them with an easy and guaranteed road to atonement:

> The first grace is a plenary remission of all sins, than which one might say no grace could be greater, because a sinner deprived of grace through it achieves perfect remission of sin and the grace of God anew. By which grace... the pains of purgatory are completely wiped out. The second grace for sale is a confessional letter allowing the penitent to choose his own confessor; the third is the participation in the merits of the saints. The fourth grace is for souls in purgatory, a plenary remission of all sins.... Nor is it necessary for those who contribute to the fund for this purpose to be contrite or to confess.

One of Albert's agents, Johannes Tetzel, the Prior of the Dominican monastery at Leipzig, was particularly enthusiastic, and stressed to potential buyers the ease with which, by the payment of a gulden, they could evade for themselves and their families, the torturing flames of Divine Punishment. When Tetzel preached at Juterbog and Zerbst near Wittenburg, Luther became aware of the detrimental moral effect Albert's indulgence was having on the lives of those who made the purchase. Demanding of some of his parishioners that they mend their ways, he was shocked and outraged when they responded by angrily waving Tetzel's indulgences in his face, threatening to report him to the Church authorities.[7]

Luther was not the kind of man to take well to being threatened, and his response was dramatic and seminal. On 31 October 1517, he nailed his 95 Theses to the castle church door at Wittenberg inviting learned debate on the value of indulgences. A number of the theses involved matters of theological interpretation, but the practical heart of Luther's attack is clear.

11. The erroneous opinion that canonical penance and punishment in purgatory are the same assuredly seems to be a tare sown while the bishops were asleep.

21. Therefore those preachers of indulgences err who say that a papal pardon frees a man from all penalty and assures his salvation.

22. The greater part of the people will be deceived by this undistinguishing and pretentious promise of pardon that cannot be fulfilled.

28. It is certain that avarice is fostered by money chinking in the chest, but to answer the prayers of the Church is in the power of God alone.

31. They who believe themselves made sure of salvation by papal letters will be eternally damned along with their teachers.

And in a letter to Albert, written on the same day he posted his theses, Luther is even blunter.

> Grace and mercy of God and whatever else may be and is! Forgive me, Very Reverend Father in Christ, and illustrious Lord, that I, the offscouring of men, have the temerity to think of a letter to your mightiness...

> Papal indulgences for the building of St. Peter's are hawked about under your illustrious sanction. I do not now accuse the sermons of those preachers who advertise them, for I have not seen the same, but I regret that the people have conceived about them the most erroneous ideas. Forsooth these unhappy souls believe that if they buy letters of pardon they are sure of their salvation; likewise that souls fly out of purgatory as soon as money is cast into the chest; in short, that the grace conferred is so great that there is no sin whatever which cannot be absolved thereby, even if, as they say, taking an impossible example, a man should violate the mother of God. They also believe that indulgences free them from all penalty and guilt.

Luther's assault on the commercialisation of salvation involves two interrelated themes. First, there is his stress on the dual nature of man – we are beings both sacred and profane. 'A man consists of a double nature, spiritual and corporeal; and these two are contrary, the spirit fighting the flesh, and the flesh the spirit.'[8] Second, these two natures are essentially opposed, so that the values of each sphere exclude or drive out the other. This is the lesson of Matthew 21:12–13:

And Jesus entered the temple of God, and cast out all those who were selling and buying in the temple, and he overturned the tables of the money-lenders and the seats of those who sold the doves. And he said to them, 'It is written, "My house shall be called a house of prayer"; but you have made it a den of thieves.'

It follows that as the spheres are exclusive, the proper ordering of human life involves keeping them apart. God's Justice is to be expressed and protected through the demarcation of distinct and discrete 'spheres of justice'.

For Luther the demarcation of spheres does not imply that the profane realm or, more particularly, the commercial realm is – as the early Church Fathers thought – forbidden. That 'no man can serve two masters... God and Mammon' (Matt. 6:24) does not imply that one must serve one only, that of the Sacred, unless one also imposes, as does the author of the Letter of Peter to the Gentiles, the duty for absolute and inviolable holiness:

As obedient children, do not conform to the lusts of former days when you were ignorant; but as the One who called you is holy, be you also holy in all your behaviour; for it is written, 'You shall be holy, because I am holy.'

(1 Pet. 1: 14–16)

If Luther thought that the Catholic Church's commodification of spiritual values was, on the Church's own terms, a fraudulent and sinful impossibility given that the sacred cannot be measured or captured in profane terms, his was not an unqualified call for asceticism. He thought that the profane could be employed as a means to a better appreciation of the sacred. As Preserved Smith says, Luther was 'probably appeal[ing] to her [his wife's] weaker side when he offered her a large sum to read the Bible through'.[9] Nor was the differentiation of the two spheres of value for Luther, as it was meant to be, but was not, for the Catholic Church, a 'platonic' separation of classes of people; so that the sacred was for the ascetic priesthood, and the profane for the materialistic laity. Luther generalised his attack on indulgences to an attack on the clergy itself. The claim to absolute spiritual power tended irresistibly, he thought, as an inevitable consequence of our Fallen Nature, to the corruptions of power and avarice. He looked instead, for an intra-personal division of the spheres: each person, alone and before God, had him or herself to provide what Plato had tried to achieve by a division between classes. This psychological, not sociological, attempt at demarcation was, for Luther, and later, for the Calvinists, to be achieved through the idea of a *vocation*.[10]

Traditionally, the idea had been associated with the call to the priesthood, but in Luther's nascent Protestantism the idea is extended into the profane realm. Thus when Jesus says:

> You have not chosen me, but I have chosen you, and have appointed that you should go and bear fruit.
>
> (John 15:16)

this could be, and was, taken to mean that one could have a vocation in the commercial realm, where the accumulated 'fruits' might be material and worldly, but which, as the product of God's direction, constituted also the agent's spiritual redemption.

The sacred and intrinsic value

> From Art more various are the blessing sent
> Wealth, commerce, honour, liberty content
> Yet these each other's power so strong contest
> That either seems destruction of the rest
> Where wealth and freedom reign contentment fails
> And honour sinks where commerce long prevails.[11]
>
> Oliver Goldsmith

Contemporary debates about the places where money should not go are typically undertaken under the auspices of the notion of *intrinsic value* rather than a direct appeal to the sacred. But as Ronald Dworkin, who treats the sacred and intrinsic value as synonyms, says, the hallmarks of the sacred and the intrinsically valuable are the same. Both refer to entities that are valuable merely because they exist.[12]

This is not to suggest that earlier debates on the sacred were (and are) somehow less sophisticated than contemporary debates. Both the Catholic Church and Luther's Protestantism distinguish between the sacred and the profane, as it finds expression in commercial life, but they do not simply oppose the two so that any kind of cohabitation, any mixing of commercial and sacred motives, is forbidden. The point is important, for contemporary discussions not only eschew the sacred for the intrinsically valuable, but tend to do so in a way that elides the complexities, and so the possibilities for cohabitation, found in those whose concern is unambiguous with the sacred.

As we have seen, the Catholic Church distinguishes two types of simony, that against Divine Right and that against Ecclesiastical Law. With the former any intrusion of the commercial *necessarily* destroys or irredeemably sullies the sacred value of the relevant object, while in the latter the commercial and the sacred may cohabit in the sense that, restricted to the profane properties of the relevant sacred object, there is nothing wrong with it being commercially exchanged. Equally, for Luther, while there are some things – such as personal salvation – which demand an interest that necessarily excludes any admixture of commercial interests, still there are other things, including developing a familiarity with the Word of God, which can be furthered by the judicious utilisation of commercial interests.

With this distinction made, it is clear that the sacred or intrinsically valuable might allow some room for commercial interests. It is equally clear that it is an open question whether or not there are any sacred objects or practices that necessarily involve a repudiation of any hint of the commercial. Certainly, it is tendentious to simply identify the intrinsically valuable with this, and only this, conception of the sacred.

Significant implications follow for how the intrinsically valuable is to be conceived. If, for instance, something is of the kind that any hint of the commercial necessarily occludes or sullies its value, then the only possible strategy is to radically divide off the different spheres of value, either by literally separating the two realms in the style of Aristotle who argued that, in a properly functioning polis, there must be two agoras, physically and functionally distinct from each other, so that the commercial did not taint the sacred values of proper political activity; or by instigating an internal psychological divide which ensures that here, at least, motives never mix in these troublesome ways.

If, we are dealing with the intrinsically valuable in the sense captured in the sin of simony of ecclesiastical law, there is no problem *in itself* with commercial evaluation and the evaluation of something as intrinsically valuable. What matters is ensuring that the admixture of motives does not see the exchange-values of the marketplace drive out the sense we have of the intrinsically valuable. The problem, so we argue, is one of resisting whatever *temptations* there might be for an agent to forget about, or fail to properly keep their focus on, the intrinsic value of something as they express their commercial interest in it.

We turn now to contemporary analytic discussions of the relationship between money and that which is so constituted that commodification will might violate its nature. By and large, contemporary discussions begin from the work of Immanuel Kant (1724–1804) and his characterisation of price as the certain enemy of dignity or intrinsic value and so it there we begin.

Kant on price and dignity

Born in Konigsberg to parents of Lutheran pietist stock, Kant wrote important works in cosmology and astronomy, before, in his fifties, he became acquainted with Humean scepticism, and turned his attention to matters of metaphysics and morality. The Critical Philosophy of Transcendental Metaphysics, which he developed as a response to that scepticism, is, arguably, of equal philosophical importance as Plato's transcendental realism; and today many more philosophers subscribe to Kant's views than to Plato's. For our purposes, Kant's transcendental idealism is of less importance than the distinctive moral views he develops, for it is on the basis of these views that Kant, and many later thinkers, tried to understand the nature of price and intrinsic value.[13]

In his *Groundwork*, Kant approaches the distinction between price and intrinsic value, or, as he formulates the matter, the distinction between price and *dignity*, by discussing the difference between 'things' and 'persons'. According to Kant, 'things' have only *relative* value; they are valuable in so far as someone *happens* to desire them. 'Persons', on the other hand, are *ends-in-themselves* and so possess an intrinsic worthiness or dignity.[14] For Kant, to treat a person with dignity is synonymous with treating them as an end-in-themselves. The value of a person, unlike that of a thing, is *unconditional*, in that its value is not dependent upon other ends and has priority over contingent goals; *incomparable*, in that its value is absolute and not to be compared with other beings or things; and *incalculable*, in the sense that it cannot be meaningfully assigned a determinate cardinal or ordinal value.[15] According to Kant, persons cannot have a price – that is, a value in exchange – for things with a price are *substitutable*, and such substitutability involves violating all the three requirements necessary to the attribution of dignity to persons.[16] (Note that this position is not fully anti-commercial in the way that someone like Fourier is anti-commercial. It is not opposed to all commercial activities unless one assumes that everything is intrinsically valuable.)

Kant's antagonism towards *some* market exchanges is not an idiosyncratic feature of the *Groundwork*. In the *Metaphysics of Morals*, he suggests that selling a tooth to be transplanted into another mouth or having oneself castrated in order to get an easier livelihood as a singer are ways of potentially murdering oneself.[17] He does not rule out the amputation of a dead or diseased organ when that organ endangers a person's life, nor is he concerned with cutting off parts of oneself, such as one's hair, that are not organs, although he thinks that cutting one's hair in order to sell it is 'not entirely free from blame'.[18] Kant also condemns the sale of organs (in this case, fingers and teeth) in his *Lectures on Ethics*, a discussion in which his concern lies not with murdering oneself, but with the wrongful nature of disposing of things that have a free will.

Kant is a defender of what we might call the 'Evacuation Thesis', according to which commercial concerns necessarily evacuate any intrinsic value a thing might possess. The Evacuation Thesis underpins the Catholic Church and Luther's hostility to simony of divine right, but it generalises beyond the sacred in religion. Consider the refusal of the Barcelona Football Club to allow advertising on their team's shirts, or the refusal by many to engage in cost–benefit analysis of environmental landmarks like the Great Barrier Reef.[19] It has also been a recurrent theme of much moral and political thinking about the morality of commercial exchange. Marx claimed that 'money debases all the gods of man and turns them into commodities. Money is the universal, self-constituted value of all things. It has therefore robbed the whole world, human as well as natural, of its own values.'[20] In a similar vein Hannah Arendt writes: 'The much deplored devaluation of all things, that is, the loss of all intrinsic worth, begins with their transformation into values or commodities, for from this moment on they exist only in relation to some other things which can be acquired in their stead.'[21]

Kant would take the Evacuation Thesis to rest on the requirements of unconditionality, incomparability and incalculability that he insists are a package deal. In our view this is a mistake, for the key idea is that of *unconditionality*. After all, the incomparability claim is really an injunction; it tells us we ought not to compare certain things, but it does not tell us *why* we should not do this. Further, it cannot be that we should not compare in this way because of the supposed incalculability of the relative values of the relevant items. The point is twofold. In the first place, if something has an exchange-value in the market place, then in one obvious sense its value is *not* incalculable. Its value is exactly that reflected in its relative price. Of course, this is a matter of relative or exchange-value, not intrinsic value, and it is, let us allow, quite true that the intrinsically valuable cannot be given any relative calculative equivalence value. It is presumably this point that lies behind Erasmus' ironical reflection in *Praise of Folly* on the calculations involved in the indulgence trade:

> And what am I to say about those who enjoy deluding themselves with imaginary pardons for their sins? They measure the length of their time in Purgatory as if by water-clock, counting centuries, years, months, days and hours as though there were a mathematical table to calculate them accurately.[22]

If the irony is apt, it simply reflects a prior commitment to the unconditionality of the intrinsically valuable. Properly understood, the Evacuation Thesis holds that relative evaluation involves an attitude towards something that necessarily rules out taking account of its unconditional value. And while, put this way, it may seem obviously, even definitionally, true, it is important to keep it in mind that for the Catholic Church and for Luther, this was not necessarily the case: both allowed that something might be intrinsically valued, and exchange valued, so long as certain conditions were met.

Given this we might read the Evacuation Thesis in a *causal* rather than a *logical* way. We call this formulation the 'Corrosion Thesis': the claim is that if one incorporates something with intrinsic value into the exchange relations of the marketplace, then there will be a strong *tendency* for that intrinsic value to slip from the picture. We shall say more about this thesis later, for now our interest is with the logical version of the Evacuation Thesis since this is the version Kant pursues. The claim can be usefully rewritten in conditional form as follows:

If something has a price then it is not intrinsically valued.

And contra-positively:

If something is intrinsically valued then it has no price.

Clearly then, if one finds a single case where both price and intrinsic valuation co-exist, then the Entailment Thesis is false.

Why should we think that imputing a price *must* lead to morally pernicious modes of regard? Why should the ascription of price necessarily lead to the belief that the commodified entity is substitutable for any other commodity of equivalent financial worth? Imagine that paintings by Chagall and Rembrandt bring exactly £5 million each at a London art auction. Whilst it is entirely reasonable to suppose that the two paintings are equivalent with respect to their financial value, it is not reasonable to assume that the two are thereby substitutable. Although they are substitutable *qua monetary value*, they are not substitutable in all respects. We encounter similar difficulties with the instrumentalist reading. A rational agent will certainly recognise that a thing that is bought and sold is a commodity, but will she necessarily view it *merely* as a commodity?[23]

Consider the following: Simpson owns a pony originally acquired for his children. His children are now adults and no longer live at the family home and the pony spends its days alone in the back paddock, craving the attentions of young children. Simpson advertises his pony in the local newspaper with the aim of finding a young family whose children will play with the pony and pay it the attention it so misses. In the hope of tracking down a family who will care for it he decides to charge a price for the pony. His rationale is that if the buyers pay a reasonable price for the pony, they will, at the very least, be more likely to look after it, since not to do so would be to jeopardise the well-being of their financial investment. (Although he hopes that they might well come to view the pony as more than capital.) To be sure, price cannot guarantee care, but Simpson believes that he is more likely to locate the right people by selling the pony than he is by giving it away. In this context, setting a price is his way of *expressing his own regard* for the welfare of the pony.

We should not be surprised that money can have such expressive functions. Although economists and philosophers typically treat money as being purely instrumental – and the idealised form of money exchange is purely instrumental – this is not universally true. There are many cases where money may express other values, ideals and aspirations.

We take up the expressive possibilities of pricing soon. For now the point is that Simpson's story functions as a counter-example to the claim that there is a strict entailment between the ascription of price and instrumental modes of regard. The logical version of the Evacuation Thesis cannot be true. If Simpson treated the pony *merely* as a commodity then clearly he would not be regarding it as an object worthy or respect or possessing a dignity. But that he does not regard it so is something that can be captured counter-factually. Simpson charges a price for the donkey, but he would *not* be prepared to accept a higher amount from a knacker's yard in exchange for the donkey. The *mere* ascription of price by a vendor does not license the conclusion that he believes the good to be replaceable or that the price charged expresses the value of that good.[24]

Nor need we rest the argument on the Parable of Simpson's Pony. Consider the more quotidian case discussed by Margaret Jane Radin in *Contested Commodities*. Radin directs our attention to various social attitudes towards wage labour, pointing out that not all commodified work lacks intrinsic value for those who undertake it. Although, as a matter of financial necessity, most of us must work, we do not think that other non-financial values cannot survive the commodification of work; indeed, we often find cases in which someone might, by changing their employment, obtain more money, but to not do so just because of the non-instrumental value they find in their present position. Following Hannah Arendt, Radin distinguishes between 'labour' and 'work', where 'labour' is activity which has no value for the worker other than the remuneration attached, whereas 'work' is activity in which money is not the sole motivating factor, nor does it exhaust the value of the activity.

> Work is understood not as separate from life and self, but rather as a part of the worker, and indeed constitutive of her. Nor is work understood as separate from relations with other people.[25]

Wage-labour often possesses a dignity or worth proponents of the Evacuation Thesis would have us believe impossible.

Radin's counter-example also holds against a version of the Evacuation Thesis that would restrict it to 'persons' alone. Such a respondent might argue that the Parable of Simpson's Pony does not count against the Entailment Thesis since the thesis is best understood as a claim about the evacuation of the value of *persons*, not as a general claim about the evacuation of intrinsic value *per se*; and, of course, donkeys are not persons. Such a strategy would allow us to avoid Radin's challenge too. For her argument appeals not to persons as such, but to certain of their skills, talents and labours.

With these restrictions in place the claim is that ascribing a price to a person *qua* person entails a loss of non-instrumental value. Thus, being sold as a slave *necessarily* involves an instrumental mode of regard on the part of the price-ascribing agent. Whatever the attractions of this as a defense of the Evacuation Thesis, it has its own costs. In particular, this manoeuvre would require us to repudiate the Evacuation Thesis in many circumstances where it is routinely employed, such as, for instance, in debates over the sale of bodily organs.[26] Further, even if the Evacuation Thesis is so restricted, price cannot guarantee a purely instrumental mode of regard. We can imagine a scenario in which an impoverished mother assigns a price to her newborn child for the same kinds of reasons that Simpson attaches a market price to his pony.

If the restricted reading of the Evacuation Thesis is ill-suited capturing many philosophers', including Kant's, hostility towards commodification, it is because this hostility often rests on conflation of *commodity* with *mere commodity*. When Kant asserts that everything has a price *or* a dignity, he assumes that having a price must be the same as having a *mere* price. What is perplexing is how this sits with the 'compatibilist' tradition in moral philosophy – most famously expressed by Kant himself – which allows for instrumental and non-instrumental modes of regard to co-exist. Kant's Respect for Persons formulation of the Categorical Imperative exhorts us to act in such a way as to always treat humanity 'never simply as a means but always at the same time as an end'.[27] On this formulation of the Moral Law, instrumental treatment and treating-as-an-end are not mutually exclusive, for it is permissible to treat another as a means so long as one also simultaneously treats that person as an end. Indeed, and as Kant well knew, it was essential that this compatability obtained; for if it did not, then any use of another for interested ends is impermissible. And so it is impermissible to get meat from the butcher, bread from the bakery and education from a teacher. Thus it is striking that when Kant attends to the system of commercial exchange this compatibilism is missing. Given his discussion in the *Groundwork*, one might have expected Kant to proclaim that everything has either a *mere price* or a dignity.

Equally puzzling are his comments about the pernicious role of money in the *Lectures on Ethics* when discussing the evils of prostitution:

> But to allow one's person for profit to be used by an other for the satisfaction of sexual desire, to make of oneself an Object of demand, is to dispose over oneself as over a thing and to make of oneself a thing on which another satisfies his appetite, just as he satisfies his hunger upon a steak.[28]

Why does making oneself an 'object of demand' mean that one is *only* an object of demand – a mere thing, such as a steak? Kant suggests that in commercial sex the 'inclination is directed towards one's sex and not towards one's humanity'[29] and so the compatibilist option is unavailable in the commercial realm as here to be a means is necessarily to be a *mere* means.

We draw three conclusions from this discussion of Kant on price and dignity. In the first place, ascriptions of price do not *guarantee* that the good commodified can be substituted for any other good of equivalent monetary value, nor that the price-ascribing agent believes it to be sub-stitutable in this way. Second, ascriptions of price do not *guarantee* that the price-ascribing agent is motivated solely by the desire for the accu-mulation of wealth. Third, the vice is treating an object or activity *merely* as a commodity; the mere ascription of price *per se* does not necessarily lead one to regard the commodity solely as a commodity.[30]

Where does all this leave the Evacuation Thesis? Well, perhaps we are interpreting the thesis in too literal a fashion. In the remainder of the chapter we explore alternative ways of making sense of the connection between price and non-instrumental forms of regard.

Elizabeth Anderson and expressive value

One contemporary theorist who has tried to provide a more sophisti-cated account of the modes of valuing other than the commercial is Elizabeth Anderson. In *Value in Ethics and Economics*, she endorses the Kantian idea that everything has either a price or a dignity, expanding it to include a wide array of rightful forms of regard including 'use', 'respect', 'appreciation', 'consideration' and 'love'.[31] Those goods whose proper mode of regard involves instrumental norms of use can be com-modified, whilst those with different norms might be violated in so doing. Ascertaining which goods should be commodified is a matter of determining the mode of treatment appropriate to the good in question. In contrast to neo-classical economists, Anderson argues that social pol-icy should not be oriented towards maximising outcomes but should involve analysis of the *meaning* of the goods involved; she advocates a shift from calculation to cultural interpretation.

Anderson acknowledges that markets have a vital role to play in the distribution, production and protection of many goods and services (these are the 'pure economic goods'), but there are many goods for which market norms are inappropriate. Different goods have different proper modes of treatment. To treat all goods as if they were commodities is to misunderstand the point of a number of human activities, and to diminish the quality of human relationships. Whereas 'economic' goods can be commodified, 'non-economic' goods should not be bought and sold. Economic goods are those goods whose dimensions of value are best realised within the market.[32]

In order that non-economic goods might be distinguished from the economic ones, Anderson begins by asking the following questions. First, is it the case that market norms do a better job of capturing and embodying the ways we value a particular good than norms associated with other spheres? If they do not, we should not treat them as commodities. Second, is it the case that market norms, when they control the exchange and distribution of a particular good, undermine important ideals or important interests legitimately protected by the state? If they do, then the state may act to remove that good from control by such norms.

For Anderson, it is not that there is a sphere of values as well as the sphere of money; she holds rather that the market embodies a particular conception of *freedom*, according to which it is primarily exercised in the choice and consumption of commodities. This notion of freedom is connected to the way we value commodities: the mode of valuation employed in the market is '*use*'. This can be contrasted with other modes of valuation that require constraints on use, such as '*respect*'. For Anderson, market freedom is intimately connected to the 'use' mode of valuation. Freedom in the market is freedom to use commodities *without* the kinds of constraints implied by other modes of valuing. The social relations of commercial exchange are those consistent with such impersonality.

So market relations are (i) impersonal, (ii) egoistic (in the market one is free, within the limits of the law, to pursue one's personal advantage, without concern for the interests of others), (iii) exclusive (the goods traded on the market are exclusive and hence consumption by one person diminishes the consumptive opportunities of other persons with respect to that good), (iv) want-regarding (from the standpoint of the market matters of value are entirely matters of individual taste), and (v) oriented to 'exit' rather than 'voice'.[33] These five points encapsulate Anderson's definition of an economic good or a commodity. A thing is an economic good if its production, distribution and enjoyment are governed by these five norms.[34]

To illustrate the distinction between economic and non-economic goods, Anderson contrasts the sphere of market relations with those of personal relationships and of social democracy. She holds that the ideals of these two spheres are embodied in norms of exchange that conflict with market norms and, hence, these spheres are non-economic. The goods exchanged and enjoyed in friendship are valued through modes of caring, attention and appreciation – they are 'expressions of shared understandings, affections and commitments'.[35] Given the way we value the goods proper to friendship differs from the way we value commodities, it follows that the norms which govern the exchange of these goods also differ. Personal relationships are properly governed by the spirit of *gift-exchange* and it is only when they are given as gifts that the goods of the personal sphere can be realised. For Anderson this explains why prostitution is base. The buying and selling of sexual services on the market undermines those values that should be associated with sexual relations. The good that is realised by humans in sexual relationships can only be fully brought about when sexuality is essentially reciprocal in nature. It is to be exchanged as a gift for the reason that this good is founded on the mutual recognition by the sexual partners involved that each is sexually attractive to the other. When sex becomes a market good, the kind of reciprocity required to realise human sexuality as a shared good is broken.[36] Hence it is inappropriate for market values to intrude into the realm of personal relationships; the norms of the market and those of personal relationships cannot readily intermingle because observance and pursuit of these norms secures remarkably different goods.

The justification for limiting the range of the market emerges out of her distinctive account of the social conditions of freedom and autonomy. A person is free if she has 'access to a wide range of significant options through which she can express her diverse valuations'.[37] Anderson is not speaking of *economic* freedom that consists in having a large menu of choices in the marketplace and the exclusive power to use what one buys – but rather the freedom to choose different modes of valuing.[38] By commodifying goods that have non-market modes of valuation, we limit the modes of valuing available. Accordingly, commodification of non-economic goods restricts our freedom and autonomy.

The ethical limits of the market should be determined by examining the values and meanings associated with particular goods and then ascertaining whether such meanings and values can be fully realised when treated as a commodity. Those goods whose meanings and values can be realised in the market context (economic goods) should be allowed to be bought and sold as commodities, whilst those goods whose values and meanings cannot be properly realised in such a context (non-economic goods) should not be bought and sold.

Anderson provides a language for articulating those concerns we might have about the incursions of the market into social life. For instance, she gives us a way of describing unease at the commodification of education. For Anderson, the norms of the market pose a constant threat to the autonomy of the professions and in particular the integrity of the goods internal to them.[39] Her analysis furnishes us with a language that enables us to say what might be wrong with this kind of practice.

Still, there are problems. Like Kant before her, Anderson endorses the idea that money and financial values and intrinsic value are *necessarily* at odds. The two are mutually exclusive. Thus, the objection we raised to Kant's price/dignity dictum in the form of the Parable of Simpson's Pony tells equally against her thesis. In fact, things may be even worse for Anderson than for Kant, for she explicitly licences us to view the commercial world as an arena of pure self-interest, free from the constraint of the intrinsically valuable which now exists in an hived-off sphere, just as free of the taint of the commercial as is the commercial of the moral. This may seem to save the intrinsically valued from the relatively or instrumentally valued, but it also opens up the possibility that commercial sphere may either swallow up or squeeze out such external spheres.

The Corrosion Thesis: Money as a predisposing factor?

Imagine Simpson advertises his pony with the no-frills additional offer of some free kitchen appliances (e.g. toasters and milkshake makers), to the first person that rings his toll-free number. The idea that he values the pony intrinsically is beginning to sound implausible. Indeed, the more we incorporate an activity into the profit nexus and add commercial norms (such as those associated with mass advertising), the less probable it is that intrinsic valuation will survive contact with money. By ratcheting up the degree to which commercial values are involved in the example, we can increase the likelihood that intrinsic value disappears.

An alternative response to the problem is to cast doubt upon the rationality of those for whom dignity and use are *compossible* by appealing to the judgements of ideally rational agents. The claim is that *if the agent is genuinely rational*, there will be a necessary connection between subordination to the market and a loss of dignity. Hence, it is only the irrationality of the agents that generates the apparently countervailing evidence.

On closer inspection both of these options are implausible. The first fails to capture our intuitions concerning the dangers inherent in the cash nexus when it comes to those things we value intrinsically. Such intuitions bear not only upon full-scale industrial production, but also (as we take up in the following chapter) upon the relatively uncomplicated process of ascribing a price to a thing, as public resistance to contingent valuation surveys (where we only ascribe a hypothetical or counterfactual price) testifies.[40]

The second suggestion is no more satisfactory. If work provides opportunities for the development of skills or involves goals and ideals to which the workers involved are committed, it is difficult to see that those who find meaning in such work are thereby irrational. Moreover, if 'mutual exclusivity' obtains only for ideally rational agents, and if the goods bought and sold are only to be used by less-than-fully rational agents, then anxiety about money is misplaced. So this option seems not to furnish us with the general kind of justification for worrying about the influence of money that the Evacuation Thesis is thought to provide.

We thus abandon the 'logical' construal of the Evacuation Thesis that we find in writers like Kant. What is left is a weaker version of the Evacuation Thesis according to which subordination to the market corrodes, rather than logically evacuates, the intrinsic value, which we shall call the 'Corrosion Thesis'. According to this thesis, calculating the cash value of an object *corrodes* our capacity to value goods intrinsically. The Corrosion Thesis simultaneously makes sense of our apprehension of incorporating into the commercial realm objects, activities and relationships we regard as intrinsically valuable, while accounting for the various readily available counter-examples (such as Simpson's Pony) to the claim that money or price evacuates value.

We can explicate this idea of corrosion through analogy with the medical model of diseases such as cancer, wherein alleged causal factors such as smoking are understood not as fully determining but rather as providing predisposing factors towards the disease. Likewise, money provides predisposing factors towards evacuation. As in the medical model, a *single* counter-example will not disprove the case. Thus the counter-example of a healthy octogenarian who has smoked heavily for all of his adult life does not prove that no causal relationship exists. Likewise, a single counter-example where money and intrinsic valuation co-exist will not prove the falsity of the Corrosion Thesis.[41] Rather than being a sufficient condition, money is a *predisposing factor* for the evacuation of intrinsic value.

Concluding remarks: The spheres and economic casuistry

The guiding concern of this chapter has been whether there are things whose value is such that it is corrupted or destroyed when treated as commodities? The idea that there are such things was a feature of four of the cases we used to introduce common moral concerns with money in Chapter 1. Our first case ('The Dogs of War') was concerned with what becomes of organised state violence when it becomes simply a matter of the enforcers' desire for money. Our second case ('Deciding Everything on a Dollar Basis') was concerned with whether the monetary valuation of things necessary evacuates them of their proper intrinsic value(s). Our third case ('The Bridal Register') was concerned with the effects on friendship and gift-giving of the commodification of those things given or exchanged, while our fourth case ('The Really Indecent Proposal') worried about the consequences of commodification on personal intimacy. That such worries may not merely be important, but of the greatest importance is a lesson that Luther's assault on Papal Indulgences can hardly fail to bring home to us, for his assault on the commodification of the sacred was of world historical significance.

Such worries can be explained in terms of the Corrosion Thesis. Given that money and markets tend to corrode our intrinsic evaluation of those things that we buy and sell, then we should be extremely wary of commodifying.

Does this mean we should hive off spheres of intrinsic valuation from the realm of commercial evaluation? As we saw, there may be a certain kind of unconditional value that demands so much of our attention that any intrusion of the commercial is sufficient to obliterate that value. Certainly, this was the idea behind the possibility of simony of divine right, and behind Luther's condemnation of the sale of indulgences.

There is, however, one aspect of the spheres tradition we wish to eschew: any suggestion that because we have hived off the non-commercial from the commercial realm, as a consequence, the commercial world is one in which moral evaluation is either otiose or pernicious. Such an idea is evident in the work of Walzer, whose views on the separation of spheres are notably exclusionist:

> It would be possible to give an historical account of each of the spheres along these lines...the liberation of the market from religious control (the just price, the ban on usury) and political control (mercantilism), the separation of the workplace and the household (the factory system), the walling off of church and state (religious toleration, autonomy of politics), the creation of independent schools and universities (academic freedom), the barring of kinship considerations (nepotism) from professional life and the civil service, the ban on the sale of offices and public services (simony, bribery), and so on.[42]

Like Anderson, Walzer is tempted to the view that by separating off a non-commercial realm one ends questions of the morality of commerce. This is evident in Anderson's five-point specification of the distinguishing marks of commercial exchange (impersonality, egoism, exclusivity, want-regarding, orientated to 'exit' rather than 'voice').

Such approaches may be intended to defend the intrinsically valuable, but they do so by limiting the range of issues of justice and fairness. Our approach, on the other hand, allows us to broach the kinds of questions that exercised classical and Medieval thinkers, and continue to exercise us today. By refusing the false promise of protecting the intrinsically valuable by hiving off a sphere of commercial freedom, we are able to assert the presence and dignity of values like justice and fairness within the commercial realm.

In the next chapter we shall turn our attention to *the use of money as a measuring device*, as opposed to cases where it is simply a matter of concrete buying and selling.

7
Money-Measurement as the Moral Problem

. . . . a sentimentalist is a man who sees an absurd value in everything and doesn't know the market price of any single thing.
Oscar Wilde, *Lady Windermere's Fan*[1]

Introduction: Measuring everything with money?

In 1991 an internal memo from the World Bank's Chief Economist Lawrence Summers was leaked to the world's press.[2] Uproar followed, for in the memo Summers made certain policy recommendations concerning pollution based entirely on monetary considerations. In itself this might not be thought objectionable, but Summers was talking about the morbidity and mortality associated with high levels of pollution; the third world was under polluted and so he suggested that such pollution be exported to the less developed world where human life was 'cheaper' than in more developed nations. As he pointed out, people in the less developed world did not tend to live as long or earn as much as those in the developed world. In money terms the loss, and particularly the early loss, of a productive life in the developed world far outweighed the same loss in the less developed world. True, levels of morbidity and mortality would certainly increase in less developed nations as they became the repository for the world's toxins, but such increases would hardly matter given the low monetary value of lives in these regions, and they would certainly be far outweighed by the monetary gains from healthier, longer lived people from developed nations.

This modest suggestion was not intended in the ironical spirit of Jonathan Swift, but, as the memo made clear, was an application of that cost–benefit style of analysis that generally characterises the World Bank's policy-making endeavours.

Cost–benefit analysis (CBA) is a technique for evaluating social policies in terms of their overall financial consequences, and it involves the assumption that all relevant costs and benefits can be given a monetary value.[3] In CBA the various benefits and costs of a proposed project are reduced to monetary sums and then aggregated, with total money costs subtracted from total monetary benefits. Using this approach the project is assigned a single net money amount. If the amount is positive, the project is viable; if negative, it is not.

Such analysis is a commonplace of modern governance, both in the public and the private sector, and there are those – such as the contemporary economist Gary Becker and legal theorist Richard Posner – who would countenance, even favour, extending such analysis to all areas of human life, including, for instance, the decision on whether to have children and how many.[4] Posner argues for such an expansive deployment of CBA. This criterion demands that the gains for the project could in principle compensate the losses; that is, the total gains for the project should exceed the losses.[5]

Posner has been criticised for ignoring – as does Summers – concerns with the justice of the resulting distribution of such welfare, but that criticism is really only a species of a more fundamental worry. For while there is no doubt that one of the central features of money is that it is a measure of value, indeed a measure of value that can, with the deployment of certain techniques, be extended to absolutely anything we might care about, it does not follow that such money-measurement is suited to capturing just what it is we value about such things. For example, does a CBA of the desirability of having children in any way capture what is valuable in having a family? Might such measurements in fact undermine, even destroy, what is really of value? Is CBA the decision-making technique of Oscar Wilde's cynic who knows the 'price of everything and the value of nothing'?[6]

That many people are of Wilde's persuasion on this matter is something CBA theorists know and regularly encounter when, in order to price goods or services which do not have a market-determined price, they deploy the 'contingent valuation' technique. This technique is a kind of opinion polling. It involves asking people how much they would be willing to pay for the relevant good or service. Thus: 'How much would you pay to protect the Great Barrier Reef?' The point is not that amount, whatever it is, which might emerge from such a survey; it is that many people plain refuse to answer such questions in the first place, just as one might refuse to answer the question 'Have you stopped beating your wife?'[7] The problem becomes more pointed if we ask people for a contingent valuation of what their life is worth to them. For not only do many find the question offensive, any answer is likely to be along the lines of 'An infinite amount; after all, money will mean nothing to me when I am dead!' So much for CBA.

But perhaps is this just squeamishness? Don't we in fact place a price on our life by placing a price on risks to our life? A person might take on a risky job, and do so for the 'wage premium' that attaches to such a job. That wage premium may be (say) 30 cents an hour, in which case it turns out that the value of a life is $6.3 million. And besides, CBA may be held to have significant benefits when it comes to decision-making – particularly economic and political decisions. It gives us 'more bangs for our bucks', and it promises, by reducing all value to the monetary scale, to deliver 'objectivity' and 'transparency' to decision-making.

To assess this we need to see what content can be given to those counter CBA intuitions so many people report. And, having done that, we need to think again about the 'objectivity' and 'transparency' proponents of CBA's claim their method delivers.

How might we go about explaining, if we can, the harm in measuring everything on the money scale?

The standard criticism turns on the idea of *incommensurability*. CBA assumes that money provides us with a single monistic supervalue against which all things can be judged or evaluated, but the fact is that value is *plural*, not monistic. When framed in this way the objection to CBA is best understood as an instance of the 'commodification problem' (which we discussed in the previous chapter).[8]

We take an alternative approach that takes off from Oscar Wilde's suggestive remarks about the difference between the price scale and our scale of ultimate value. It means thinking more deeply about the paradox of value. Our response involves two elements based on the following ideas : (i) the necessity of maintaining a price-independent scale of ultimate value, and (ii) that there are some things that are not substitutable.

But first, let us consider money as a tool of measurement.

That strange measuring stick called money

What exactly is it that we are measuring when we consider the relative prices of goods? One apple costs us 50 cents and another 75 cents. What does this mean? A metre ruler measures length, a rain gauge precipitation, a speedometer velocity; what is it that money measures? What does the 'price predicate' tell us about any object which is priced?

The question becomes more pressing when we consider the contemporary use of money as a *supervalue*. With money all things can be compared and goods of comparable worth can be substituted for one another. However, *in principle* we could do this with any scale. We could use weight, for instance, as a means of evaluating the relative worthiness of a public project. The heavier the goods produced the better. Gross domestic product could be measured in terms of the kilograms of goods produced each year. One might compensate a person for the loss of some item with another item of equivalent weight. This is, of course, ridiculous. But we do not think it so ridiculous when it comes to pricing, for we often compensate the loss of a good worth $1000 with the money itself. What is it that money is tracking that leads some to think it measures relevant features of sets of goods? What distinguishes it from other measuring rods? This is an important question, for if we are to use price as a tool of public policy formation – as the cost–benefit analyst would have us do – we need to know what the numbers mean.

One quite natural view is to think that the price predicate reflects or tracks some *inherent property* of the commodity in question. Consider the following scenario.

> Bridie walks into a bottle shop and buys a $30 bottle of wine. Bridie considers the $15 but then thinks, 'No, it's a special occasion – it's my mother's birthday and I want a better quality of wine', so she buys the $30 bottle. She has no information about the wines other than their respective prices.

Bridie is operating with a common folk notion of *natural value*. Relative prices are patterned in a way that reflects some inherent good making features of the wines. The pattern of ratios need not reflect a cardinal ordering. She need not expect the $30 bottle to be twice as good as the $15 one. But the expectation is that it will be better in some ordinal sense. (Perhaps Bridie does not think that she has sufficiently discriminating tastes to measure such ratios.)

The idea of natural value underpinning relative prices is usually fleshed out in terms of *utility* of the good in question. Clearly, when Bridie judges that the $30 bottle will be better, she means 'better' in terms of its capacity to give rise to pleasurable sensations.

But let us develop the story in a way that casts doubt on the idea that price tracks such inherent properties.

Bridie returns to the store later in the week and buys the $15 bottle and discovers that she finds it more pleasing to her palette. Being an empirically minded young woman she decides to buy both and test them and discovers that she consistently prefers the $15 wine.

What Bridie has stumbled on to here is the Paradox of Value that modern economists famously trace back to Adam Smith. In the *Wealth of Nations*, he discusses the odd fact that while water that is necessary for life brings nothing on the market (at least the Scottish market of his time!), a diamond, which is useless, was extremely expensive.[9] Their exchange ratios or exchange values did not reflect what Smith took to be their natural ratios in terms of utility.

Smith's Paradox of Value is a worthy utilitarian descendant of an earlier Medieval Paradox that focuses on the contrast between the intrinsic value (or the *bonitas intrinseca*) and the prices of differing goods. We find an early expression of this in St Augustine's discussion of the fact that although a horse often sold for a higher price at the market than a slave, the slave was valued more highly in the eyes of God.[10] St Thomas Aquinas commented on the fact that a pearl fetched a high price and a mouse no price at all, even though the class or genus of the mouse had been created after that of the pearl and appeared to be entitled to a higher rank in the scale of valuation.[11] Later Medieval writers discussed the contrasting prices of bags of flour and mice, in all cases the point being that the ratios of prices do not reflect the relative values of objects in terms of some absolute scale of value (in this case God's great chain of being).[12]

What the Paradox of Value illustrates, in both its guises, is that market price does not track some natural value of the goods in themselves, be it their usefulness to us or their relative worthiness in the great scheme of things. What is it then that price is measuring?

One answer that was provided by classical economists such as David Ricardo, Adam Smith and, most notoriously, Karl Marx is that price tracks the *labour* embodied in the production of the good. This is the essence of the *labour theory of value*. It states that the value of a good is determined by the amount of labour input required to produce that good.[13] To return to our *toy* example of the wine we see that on this line of thinking the difference between the prices of the bottles reflects simply a difference between the relative costs of production.

Modern economists, however, largely subscribe to the neoclassical 'marginalist' view that price simply reflects the relationship between the supply and the demand for a good.

The Marginalist Revolution in economics of the 1870s was initiated independently by William Stanley Jevons (1835–1882), Leon Walras (1834–1910) and Carl Menger (1841–1921), and it focused attention not on the inherent properties of goods but on to the relative availability and desire for them. This was re-described in terms of the marginal unit. The price we are willing to pay for a commodity – the value we place on acquiring another unit – depends not on its overall or total utility, but on its marginal utility.[14] As the contemporary economist Joseph Stiglitz says:

> Price is related to the *marginal* utility of an object; that is, the value of an additional unit of the object. Water has a low price not because the *total* value of water is low – it is obviously high, since we could not live without it – but because the marginal utility, what we would be willing to pay to be able to drink one more glass of water a year, is low.[15]

This way of viewing pricing shifts the focus from the internal good-making features of the commodity and hence away from concerns about the relationship between moral economic value.

In the 1930s marginalism became an *ordinalist* rather than a *cardinalist* doctrine, further extending the distance between value theory in economics and the concerns of moral philosophers.[16] Now the talk is of marginal rates of substitution rather than marginal utility. The concern is not with the overall usefulness of things, but our preference orderings between particular goods. Indeed, much of the history of modern economics can be understood in terms of the desire to rid the discipline of any residual connections to moral philosophy.[17]

The significance of this marginalist revolution lies in the claim that despite the pull of the intuition, the price is *not* related to the inherent properties of a good, and despite the attractiveness of the idea that it simply reflects the cost of the labour-inputs, the price does not depend on either the nature of the good or the production process itself. The price-tag does not tell us anything about the goods or the ways they are produced; it simply tells us something about how much people want it and how much of it is in supply.

The point is that price is a rather odd measuring stick. Price measures goods in the sense that it tells us how many there are and how much people want them, rather than measuring anything about the good in itself. This has a number of implications for its use in public policy formation that we explore in detail later in the chapter.

Let us return now to the topic of money-measurement as a moral problem and, in particular, CBA.

The incommensurability critique

The standard criticism of CBA, and more generally the use of money as a universal measure of value, involves a bigger story about the incommensurability of value, according to which the problem of universal money-measurement derives from the moral viciousness of universal commensuration. When we engage in CBA we commensurate, and it is this commensurating that is morally objectionable. The basic idea is that there are some values, goods or options that cannot be ranked either ordinally or cardinally.[18]

Keeping this in mind, it is possible to distinguish between 'incommensurability' and, a broader sense in which it means, 'incomparability'. Incommensurability is a matter of our inability to measure things along some cardinal scale, while incomparability refers to the inability to rank things ordinally.[19] Things are incommensurable when they cannot be measured along some cardinal scale of units of value, and incomparable when the predicates 'as good as', 'better than' and 'worse than' do not exhaust the relationships between them. For now the difference is unimportant, and in what follows we use the term 'Incommensurability Account' to cover both the ordinalist and cardinalist objections.

Advocates of the Incommensurability Account claim to derive a specifically moral charge of vice from a metaphysical claim about the (im)possibility of ordinalist and/or cardinalist rankings of that which we might value. How do they do this? Well, commensuration damages the values and ideals embodied or expressed in various goods and actions. For instance, Joseph Raz uses the term 'constitutive incommensurability' to cover cases where people feel outrage at the very idea of comparing, and where they feel that for a person to make such comparisons demonstrates a failure of understanding or character.[20] Such views involve a commitment to the plurality of value. According to the value pluralist, any attempt to reduce the range of human values to a single 'supervalue' means harming those values themselves.[21]

This has obvious implications for CBA since money-measurement involves commensuration. Money provides a common measure of value and in so doing it provides a mechanism for universal commensuration. Money provides us with precise cardinal values with which it is possible to rank goods, values or options. So money enables commensuration in cases where the values embodied are incommensurable. Given this, to suggest that money-measurement is morally neutral is absurd since often it will involve the commensuration of the incommensurable.

There are further implications, for CBA involves the assumption that all costs and benefits can be given a monetary value.[22] CBA presents the various benefits and costs of a project in monetary terms so that the money costs may be subtracted from the benefits. Whether the project is worth carrying forward or not depends on how the numbers come out. This involves the employment of a unitary method of valuation of the very kind that advocates of the Incommensurability Account repudiate. '[D]isparate spheres of society, such as the workplace, the home and the environment', writes one critic, Cass Sunstein, 'cannot be effectively valued by a single theory, such a cost–benefit analysis'.[23]

One attraction of the Incommensurability Account is that it allows us to explain what might otherwise appear puzzling, including (i) the institution of 'specific performance remedy' in law, and (ii) the widely observed resistance of many of the public to contingent valuation surveys.

Specific performance is a legal remedy that is recommended for breach of contract in cases where damages seem inadequate and where the contractor is compelled by the court to perform specifically what he has agreed to do.[24]

Suppose Mr Bond has contracted to buy a Van Gogh painting from Mr Skase, and the latter defaults on the agreement. Following a specific performance remedy the court would order Mr Skase to hand over the painting to Mr Bond, rather than pay damages. The reason is not that the damages are too low – they might be well above the market price – but rather that monetary compensation appears inadequate. Sunstein suggests that the rationale or justification for this kind of legal remedy is to be found within the Incommensurability Account.

> The specific performance remedy can be understood to stem from a resistance to commensurability. Specific performance must be awarded because the good in question is not commensurable with cash. This is not to say that it is more valuable than cash. Indeed, it is less valuable, often, than a great deal of cash.[25]

The specific performance remedy reflects the fact that the good in question is 'valued in a way that is inconsistent with cash valuation'.

Contingent valuation surveys, as we have seen, ask respondents to estimate counterfactually what they would in principle be willing to pay for various costs and benefits. However, many studies have discovered that a great many respondents refuse to engage in the requisite calculations.[26] According to the Incommensurability Account this resistance is to be explained in terms of our rejection of the idea of a single metric via which all goods and activities can be measured.

In both cases Sunstein argues that the Incommensurability Account provides the best explanation for these perplexing examples.[27] Though, as we shall see, this is not the only, or even the best, way in which one might understand these examples.

Despite the appeal of the Incommensurability Account, it is not an uncontroversial basis for developing the claim that there are some things money should not measure.[28] Some writers are sceptical about incommensurability itself, whilst other philosophers have argued that a great number of the central cases of what we ordinarily call 'incommensurability' turn out to be something entirely different.[29] Below we provide a list of cases where it would appear that it is not really incommensurability that is at issue.

First, in many cases where claims of incommensurability and incomparability are made, it does not seem to be the case that we literally cannot compare the goods in question, but rather that they are unevenly matched for the purposes of comparison. This idea is captured in the colloquial phrase 'there is no comparison'. For instance, when a wine buff asserts that there is no comparison between Grange Hermitage and other Australian wines he means that the former is unquestionably superior to the latter, not that we cannot compare them. Ruth Chang calls this *emphatic comparability*.[30]

Second, many supposed incommensurables involve *lexicographic ordering* rather than genuine incommensurability.[31] Lexicographic orderings of sets of goods, values or options arise when one set always takes precedence over another. For instance, when making choices between the interests of one's five-year-old daughter and one's pet salamander, the needs and interests of the child must be satisfied before those of the salamander.[32] It is not that they cannot be compared but rather that one of the comparators is always accorded priority. Ranking in these cases provides no evidence for incommensurable values, goods or options. Such cases provide grounds for repudiating the so-called 'axiom of continuity' rather than a universal scale of comparison. The axiom of continuity tells us that for any two bundles, where one bundle is preferred to the other, if we keep increasing the less preferred bundle then eventually we will be indifferent between the two.

Finally, there are some cases that involve *rough equality* rather than a failure of comparison. For often when we call things incomparable, the real point is that there is an element of imprecision that makes exact comparison difficult, rather than impossible. The goods in question are 'roughly equal', but the imprecision of the scale of evaluation is such that we are inclined to say they are incomparable.

Take Chang's case of a comparison in terms of creativity between Mozart and Michelangelo. Surely the comparison is impossible. But consider the comparison between Mozart and 'Talentlessi', a very bad painter. Comparing these two in terms of their respective creativity is certainly possible. But if comparison is impossible between Mozart and Michelangelo, then it should also be impossible between Mozart and Talentlessi. Since it clearly is not, we have no reason to think it impossible between Mozart and Michelangelo.[33] Chang suggests that what we really have here is 'rough equality'. And while the comparators are roughly equal, it is true that if one of the comparators increases or decreases sufficiently in skill and achievements, we can properly employ 'better than' or 'worse than' predicates.

For another example, imagine that one is forced to choose between two jobs: one that offers excellent wages and job security for what mind-numbingly boring work, and another that offers much lower pay and little security for intellectually exciting work with stimulating and friendly colleagues. We may well find ourselves unable to choose between the options, since it would require an assessment and weighting of factors that are not easily compared. However, if, in the first case, we increase the pay one hundred fold or, on the other hand, include in the second job offer an enormous amount of world travel to exotic locations, we may well have little trouble in choosing. This would seem to indicate that the dilemma reflects our inability to make comparisons in certain kinds of cases rather than the incomparable nature of the values in question.

What remains of the idea of incommensurability once such misuses are removed? Probably not a lot, although we are not denying that there may be genuine cases of incommensurability. Nonetheless, our restrictions of the field to which the term applies do diminish the appeal of the Incommensurability Account. Appreciating that many examples of 'incommensurability' reflect matters of emphatic comparability, lexicographic orderings and rough equality casts doubt on the wisdom of explicating the supposed viciousness of CBA and universal money-measurement by appealing to incommensurability.

Instead of objecting to money as a supervalue we focus on two other arguments: first, what we shall label the 'objection from substitutability'; and second, the idea that money often furnishes us the wrong scale of value.

The substitutability account

One can of beans is, in the law, *fungible* – it is replaceable with any other can of beans of the same quality. But is it true that any two goods of the same price are, because of the monetary equivalence, fungible? Can we replace any good with something of equivalent money price? This is certainly not true as far as the law goes, for there are some cases where we can only compensate by restoring the good itself. This is the very point of specific performance remedy that we discussed in the previous section.

Our first distinct concern with money-measurement is also related to replaceability or substitutability. The problem with pricing is it gives rise to *substituting modes of regard* – we can come to regard all things measured by money as replaceable by or substitutable for things of equivalent financial value.

The *Objection from Substitutability* holds that it is wrong to treat some beings, entities and activities as substitutable or fungible – the 'intrinsically valuable' – a concern that is especially relevant in the realm of human life and its relationships. The person who does not mourn the passing of his recently deceased spouse, but instead immediately begins searching for a new partner may be censured for his failure to regard his nearest and dearest as non-substitutable.

At the heart of the objection is the idea that pricing of intrinsically valuable things is morally pernicious because it insinuates attitudes of substitutability towards objects and goods where such attitudes are inappropriate. When one imputes a price to one's five-year-old daughter *in a certain sense* the child becomes substitutable *qua* commodity for either an amount of money or other bundles of goods of an equivalent monetary price. Any moral disquiet arises from the fact that she can now be viewed as replaceable.

As we see, money-measurement 'insinuates substitutability' rather than 'makes substitutable'.

Objections to substitutability have long been part of the discussion of money as a moral problem. Marx, for instance, particularly focuses on the commensurating and substituting features of money.[34] Since money serves as a 'universal measure of value', as soon as a commodity such as a table 'emerges as a commodity', it becomes comparable with all other goods.[35] Marx also holds that money makes all commodities substitutable for one another. It is the 'universal pander' for which all goods are substitutable and, conversely, which makes commodity goods substitutable for each and every other commodity.[36]

In this tradition substitutability is typically explicated in terms of the idea that money *makes things substitutable*. The mechanism for this transformation of properties is thought to be found in the equivalences that money-measurement opens up. Money-measurement not only allows us to rank objections and actions ordinally, but also enables us to posit equivalence claims between specific commodities: that is, two goods to which the same price is imputed can be said to be equivalent. As Aristotle says, money acting as a measure 'makes goods commensurate and equates them'.[37] This is the point of his discussion of the house, the bed and minae; with the advent of money we can easily calculate equivalences.[38] And it is with these equivalences that possibilities for substitutability arise and it is here that our moral objection resides.

Pricing does not change the properties of goods so that they become substitutable, but prices influence the way we regard those objects. Thus pricing encourages us to regard anything priced as ultimately substitutable. It is not any metaphysical transformation that is at issue, for it is the intentions of the trading agents that matter. Whether we trade for money alone or employ money as a medium to substitute one good for another, there is a danger we will regard the traded item as substitutable. This involves a *causal*, rather than a *necessary*, connection between money-measurement and the vice of regarding-as-substitutable. Money-measurement is psychologically corrosive rather than necessarily vicious.

Money-measurement does not necessarily lead us to regard commodities as substitutable, rather it encourages a psychologically *corrosive tendency* for us to do so. Money-measurement constitutes a 'moral hazard' or an 'occasion of sin'.[39] The moral hazard involves our attitudes. The danger is that we will use money to draw conclusions about what any good might be substituted for. So long as we accept that regarding certain goods as substitutable (in the substantive normative sense) is morally vicious, then in such cases money-measurement provides us with a moral hazard.

By way of contrast, Freud thought psychic health required that we view all the objects of one's desires as ultimately substitutable. For Freud a desire is directed towards some object or end whose attainment causes the satisfaction of the desire and the release of the energy that sustains it. However, if the object of desire cannot be attained, then the particular desire will seek release through 'substitute objects'. Now almost any object can substitute for another just as long as the person in some way associates the two.[40] For Freud we never really make contact with particular objects in a full metaphysical sense. Our view, in contrast, builds on the idea that such particularising contact with the world is of crucial – and so moral – importance to us.

Finally, we focus on the types of goods that we should not regard as substitutable rather than those that are ultimately non-substitutable. To defend the claim that pricing may encourage morally vicious attitudes we simply need to demonstrate that there are some goods that we should not regard as substitutable. We do not need to try and determine the features of an object upon which we might ground its non-substitutability.[41] Nor do we need to agree on what goods are in fact to be so regarded. All we need to demonstrate the non-neutrality of pricing is to have agreement on two matters: first, that there are at least some goods that should not be regarded as substitutable (whatever they might be); and second, that pricing is corrosive of our attitudes towards such goods.

This approach makes better sense of our intuitions that some things should not be measured by money. Consider the cases discussed earlier, beginning with the concern about contingent valuation surveys. Perhaps when we refuse to calculate how much money we would need to be paid to have the Great Barrier Reef destroyed, it is not so much that we are unwilling to accept a singular metric, as it is because of the implicit suggestion that something many of us view as irreplaceable will, given sufficient monetary recompense, be substitutable for money.

Similar points can be made if we turn to the phenomenon of specific performance remedy. If we cast our minds back to the case of the Van Gogh painting, we see that the Incommensurability explanation turned on the idea that the court gave such an order because money cannot capture the value that the person places on the painting. True, but the moral weight is carried by the fact that the Mr Bond of our story regards the good as non-substitutable, rather than because of some meta-ethical concern about commensuration and the use of a single metric. It is the painting that the plaintiff desires, not a defence of value pluralism.

Further, when we examine the writings of a number of key figures in the debate, we discover that at key points the moral weight in their accounts rests on an unacknowledged anxiety about substitutability, anxiety which does not follow directly from their value pluralism. For instance, Cass Sunstein ends his discussion of why monetary damages are sometimes inadequate and why we might prefer specific performance by saying that:

> *What the plaintiff wants, and what she is entitled to get is a good that she values in the way that she values the object for which she has contracted.* [Sunstein's emphasis] A good that she values in some sense equally – perhaps in some 'aggregate' valuation – is not a perfect substitute.[42]

In this passage it is non-substitutability that is doing the moral work rather than the idea of incommensurability.[43]

Two objections

One objection which might be raised to our account is that it violates the *axiom of continuity* which some social choice theorists have taken to be a key component of rationality. According to this axiom, given any two goods in a bundle, where one is preferred over another, it will always be possible – by increasing the quantity of the less preferred and decreasing the quantity of the more preferred – to obtain another bundle in which one is indifferent between the two. The implication is that there is no good that cannot be traded off at the margin for another. For instance, one might prefer one variety of wine to another. We might prefer Merlot to Cabernet Sauvignon. However, if we keep increasing by small degrees the price of the preferred beverage and decreasing the price of the less preferred, we will eventually reach a point where we are indifferent between the two and subsequently a point where we now prefer the Cabernet Sauvignon. According to the axiom of continuity for a person to claim that they would always prefer the Merlot, no matter what the price, is a sign of irrationality.

However, while this might be the case for bottles of wine, there are some things that we would not 'trade off at the margins', no matter what the price. These cases, which involve goods we regard as non-substitutable, provide grounds for rejecting the axiom of continuity rather than ruling out our objection from substitutability.

A second question is whether the Objection from Substitutability rules out compensation. Is the person demanding compensation guilty of a substituting mode of regard? Compensation, and particularly financial compensation, is an important social practice and although its extension to *every* area of social life might well be undesirable, it is nonetheless a necessary feature of modern society. If the substitutability account ruled out compensation then this would be an unfortunate consequence that would in all likelihood provide a *reductio ad absurdum* of our approach.

Consider the case of a woman who has lost her arm in a car accident and who subsequently applies for financial compensation. That she does so in no way implies that she regards the arm as substitutable (assuming of course that the accident was genuinely accidental). If she were given a retrospective choice, she would prefer to have the missing arm, but such a choice is not available. Since it is not, she requests a 'second best' solution which involves money. She does not in this case regard her arm as substitutable. Here we find further reason for preferring the Substitutability Account to the Incommensurability Account. The Incommensurability Account must reject all forms of compensation since such necessarily requires commensuration. For instance, if we are to compensate a citizen for the loss of an arm in an accident, we need to array the value of the missing arm along a single axis which includes *inter alia* money. Financial compensation for loss of a limb, for loss of earnings, for loss of one's home or for the loss of a family heirloom all require commensuration with monetary values. The Incommensurability Account would seem to rule this practice out. If, as we suggested earlier, financial compensation is an important social practice, then the fact that the Incommensurability Account rules it inadmissible and the Substitutability Account permits it, then this is another reason for favouring the latter.

There is also sometimes a retributive or punitive aspect to this compensation. If another person or group are causally responsible for the loss – perhaps the car company, if it was a fault in the car which caused the accident – then we may well feel that some form of punishment in the form of payment is also due. (Note that there need not be any fault for us to regard compensation to be required.) We thus compensate the person for their loss and at the same time hope to punish another for negligence, if negligence there be. This idea of fiscal punishment has a long history, with one of its most notable embodiments being the Anglo-Saxon practice of *wergild*. This was the money that had to be paid if one killed a fellow Anglo-Saxon. That the fine that would have to be paid was said to be each man, woman and child's main protection against murder in pre-Medieval society.[44] It is difficult to know how those in the time of Aelfred conceptualised this in terms of the replaceability of person, but the fact of compensation does not imply that the people involved view the object of loss as replaceable.

The wrong scale: The Paradox of Value revived

So far we have been talking about *particular* goods that should not be subject to money-measurement – but we want now to talk about cases where we might think that it is the *system* of relative ratios, *as a whole*, which is the problem.

One long-standing philosophical view about prices has it that they do not reflect an ultimate scale of value. When Jevons says –

> there is a certain sense of esteem, or desirableness, which we may have with regard to a thing apart from any distinct consciousness of the ratio in which it may exchange for other things.[45]

– he, just as surely as St Augustine and his discussion of horses and slaves, is alluding to the way that the ordering of prices does not always reflect what we might take to be the natural ordering of things.

This was the point of the Paradox of Value in all of its various guises. Adam Smith's discussion of water and diamonds focused on the curious nature of a scale of value in which water was worth nothing and diamonds a great deal. It was not that he thought this to be *causally aberrant* – as many modern economics textbooks suggest – or that it undermined his account of how prices are formed.[46] (Recall here that Smith had a labour theory of value, so when he discusses the relative prices of water and diamonds he did not do so on the grounds that prices were determined by the overall utility of the good in question.) To the contrary, he believed that it was the labour embodied that governed the price. His point is about the relationship between prices and what he took to be a fundamental scale of moral value, and it directs us towards a more general point about the relationship between prices and an ultimate scale of value. Our concern is not with the causal problem of how prices are formed – by labour, or marginal utility or total utility – but rather with the maintenance of a price-independent scale of value for assessing or evaluating the relative rankings that money ascribes to different goods.[47] Our concern is normative rather than causal.

What bearing might this have on the morality of pricing and, more specifically, the widespread use of CBA in contemporary society? We think that there are two reasons for criticism that concern money as a scale of value. In the first place the widespread usage of CBA – as well as our general immersion in a commercial culture – endangers our capacity to maintain such a distinction. In a world in which all things are open to pricing, we open the possibility that the scale of price be identified with the scale of ultimate value. By placing a price on everything (or at least a very extensive range of things), and increasing the range of social life to which monetary values are given, we risk losing our sense that there is value outside the judgements of the market. This paves the way for money to become the only goal. We see this point made forcefully by Georg Simmel in his work, *The Philosophy of Money*:

> [T]he more money becomes the sole centre of interest, the more one discovers that honour and conviction, talent and virtue, beauty and salvation of the soul, are exchanged against money and so the more a mocking and frivolous attitude will develop in relation to these higher values that are for sale for the same kind of value as groceries, and that also command a 'market price'.[48]

Simmel suggested that a blasé attitude to the world, in which our capacity for ethical and aesthetic discrimination is blunted, was most likely to be found in places with huge turnovers, such as stock exchanges, for these are the places where money is available in huge quantities and owners change readily.

Once money has become an end-in-itself, there is the danger of it becoming the only end, and of thereby evacuating any sense that price and ultimate value are distinct. To be sure, there is no necessity here, for the mere setting of prices does not automatically imply that one identifies price and ultimate value. But, as we have emphasised the con-nections need only be psychological, rather than logically necessary, in order to be morally significant. The *psychological* danger is that in a world in which everything can be given a price that we will come to regard the price as the only value to be had and in so doing impoverish our lives.

Second, beyond questions of individual moral psychology, there is the issue of how the ordinal rankings provided by money arrays goods and activities. When we use CBA the value of a good on the market is used to determine costs and benefits. But often those rankings will not capture the real values of things in terms of what we might see as an ultimate scale of value. It is possible to imagine circumstances in which saving a bottle of rare wine is more important financially than saving the life of a person in a poor region of the world. Just as it is possible, as Lawrence Summers suggests, that the marginal util-ity of pollution reduction in the first world is worth a multitude of lives (or, more accurately, deaths) in the third world. Any scale of value which would arrange the relative values of things in such a way fails to reflect the real values of those things.[49] Thus monetary considerations should not be the sole consideration taken into account when forming public policy.

Our point here is different from that of the 'incommensurabilist'. It is not that the values cannot be compared, but rather the scale of value is the wrong one. We do not deny the possibility of a single scale which ranks entities ordinally; we simply point out that money values do not reflect an ultimate scale of value and, as such, we should be wary of using them as trumps in public policy formulations. There are other non-monetary values that need to be taken into account when weighing the social benefits and costs of any project. To say this we do not need to defend the moral realist claim that there are moral values that exist independently of human valuing; although ultimately this is where our sympathies lie. All we require is an acknowledgement that, as a matter of fact, we value at least some things for more than any monetary value that might be assigned to them. Even if one holds that all values are subjective, a sensible subjectivist will recognise that people's views about the ultimate ranking of goods will often differ from their financial rankings. The point is that money provides the wrong scale for judging the ultimate worth of things, and so financial considerations should not be the sole criterion used when making public policy.

One possible response to the foregoing is that it misconstrues what is going on when we assign cash values. When we place a price on an object we are not making judgements about ultimate values; therefore we are not in this process scaling the goods in terms of their ultimate worth. Consequently, we cannot be said to be making judgements about which goods are equivalent, and thereby substitutable, since our price ranges are not judgements of ultimate worth. Accordingly, while money brings into existence a common metric and a series of equivalences, these are not to be taken as meaning anything more than what the current market will pay for these goods. In so far as we talk of equivalent worth – which many of us do – this should be read as a mere manner-of-speaking. We might sometimes talk *as if* price and ultimate value are correlated, but this is a mere figure-of-speech. Thus cash prices should not be thought of as markers of ultimate worth and to think of them as such is to misunderstand the meaning of prices.

This point is strengthened if we recall the earlier discussion of modern neo-classical price theory. Since the Marginalist Revolution of the 1870s, it has been standard for economists to argue that the price ratio simply reflects the relative relationship between supply and demand for those goods. Goods attract higher prices if they are more in demand or if they are scarcer than other goods. This, the price mechanism, should not be thought to be a marker of ultimate value; to infer that it was would be a mistake.

However, this mere figure-of-speech objection overlooks the psychological instability of 'as-if' modes of regard. There is a general point to be made here regarding the stability of as-if figures-of-speech when it comes to practical decision-making. The mere figure-of-speech objection relies heavily on people's capacity to recognise that we only ever speak 'as-if' prices were ultimate values, and that when we talk of the price value of a thing it is not an ultimate value. The economist Frank Knight once suggested that 'no-one contends that a bottle of old wine is ethically worth as much as a barrel of flour',[50] the idea being that we can maintain the distinction between ultimate value and price without any intellectual labour whatsoever. But this misrepresents what is going on in decision-making, for when we use such as-if claims as guides to action we are not treating them in a 'conditional' manner. In action such conditionals become indicatives. When Lawrence Summers made his infamous CBA-derived remarks about exporting pollution to the third world, it would have been disingenuous, at the very least, for him to suggest that he was only speaking *as-if* he was differentially valuing people.[51]

There is a second – and more significant – reason for rejecting this mere figure-of-speech approach. One of the reasons that many find CBA disconcerting is that it is employed so extensively as the basis of public decision-making. Not only is it widely used, but often it is the *only* input into decisions that have tremendous consequences for the public at large. If we use the money metric in this way, then we are implicitly saying that price captures our fundamental values, particularly if such costs and benefits are the only considerations taken into account. Indeed, if our public forms of practical reason are dominated by cash values, then it would seem that we have already lost any sense of the difference between price and ultimate value, whatever the mere figure-of-speech objection might tell us.

In many ways this simply reflects a peculiarity of the practices of modern economics where at the same time as it is asserted that prices mean nothing with respect to ultimate value, moves are made, as the foregoing illustrates, to extend the price mechanism into areas in a way which means one is effectively treating prices as ultimate values.

Another possible response to our approach travels in the opposite direction. It might be argued that money-measurement does in fact provide the correct scale of value, where value is understood in the philosopher's sense, because prices track preferences and preferences contribute what is of ultimate value. The idea is that prices reflect the relative preferences that people have for various goods, and that respecting such preferences is what matters from a moral point of view. According to this want-regarding naturalism, there is no single scale of ultimate value independent of human preferences. Whatever ranking arises in the market is a partial consequence of the relative desires that people have for various goods. Sometimes this is understood as being analogous to voting – consumers 'vote' with their dollars – and we can justify the price as a relevant scale of value in the same way that we see rankings according to numbers of votes as a relevant mechanism for electing politicians.

There are several problems with this approach, the first of which is distributive. In the market some consumers have greater voting power and so prices will reflect the preferences of the wealthy to a greater extent than it does the preferences of the poor. The preferences of different individuals are thus not given equal weighting; it is not a matter of 'one person, one first preference'. In so far as prices are a reflection of human preferences, they lean heavily in favour of the preferences of the wealthy. Moreover, those without any financial resources at all cannot buy and hence not 'vote'. So their preferences are not being tracked at all.

Then there is the problem of 'externalities'. An externality is a cost or benefit arising from a commercial transaction that is borne or enjoyed by people not directly involved in the transaction. As the preceding definition implies, there are both positive and negative externalities: the former concerns cases where a benefit is enjoyed and the latter where some burden or cost is imposed on the non-transacting party.[52] The existence of externalities means that the moral consequences of a commercial activity is not always reflected in the pricing system and, accordingly, prices fail to reflect the relative moral value of different goods and activities. The scale of relative values produced by prices then will often not reflect what we take to be the ultimate value of things.

In summary, CBA should not be taken to be the sole determinant of public policy since the scale of relative values achieved through money-measurement does not always reflect what we take to be the scale of ultimate values.

Concluding remarks

At the outset of this chapter we asked about the proper limits of money-measurement and whether it might at least sometimes be wrong to assign monetary values to some goods and activities. Our discussion does not rule out its use, but it does provide grounds for caution.

At the level of private morality, we should be wary that we do not allow the use of money to lead us either to regard it as a scale of ultimate value or to regard all goods as substitutable. It is important to maintain the distinction between ultimate value and price, just as it is important that we not regard all things as replaceable for others.

At the level of public morality money should not be used as an unproblematic device for practical reasoning. We do not rule out the use of CBA – indeed, we think it is a useful tool – but the point is that at a level of public policy formation it should not be the sole consideration.

8
The Charge of 'Economic Moralism': Might the Invisible Hand Eliminate the Need for a Morality of Money?

> Then leave Complaints: Fools only Strive
> To make a Great and Honest Hive.
> T' enjoy the World's Conveniences,
> Be fam'd in War, yet live in Ease,
> Without great Vices, is a vain
> UTOPIA seated in the Brain.
> Fraud, Luxury and Pride must live,
> While we the Benefits receive.
>
> Bernard Mandeville,
> *The Fable of the Bees*

Is this all just unnecessary moralism?

Our central claim has been that our commercial dealings should be subject to moral scrutiny. In our use of money there should be a strong moral component, for commerce is not a morality free zone. In this we differ from outright critics, such as Fourier, for whom money and the market are irremediably corrupt and we differ from those unabashed advocates of commercial life for whom money generates no moral concerns whatsoever. Our line is that while commerce is morally permissible it needs to be morally constrained.

But perhaps all of this talk of morality is redundant or even worse counter-productive. Might we not be accused of *economic moralism*?

Moralism, in its pejorative sense, involves an undue concern for morality. It covers cases where the exploration of the moral status of actions – and in particular the actions of others – seems unnecessary. As Robert Fullinwider says, the moralist indiscriminately places 'every grain of dust' under the moral magnifying glass, no matter how inconsequential or trivial.[1] It involves an excessive examination of the ethical standing of human action. As well as over-analysis, moralism typically involves self-appointment, unwarranted meddling in others' affairs and a sanctimonious tone. Our interest is in what we call *economic moralism* which we confine to the idea of a moral analysis of commercial affairs that is either pointless or counter-productive.

This charge of economic moralism might be levelled at our approach from one of two, distinctly opposed, directions: one from the traditional Left and one from the traditional Right. The first is from the Left and, in particular, the Marxist Left. Think here of Bertolt Brecht's poem 'What Keeps Mankind Alive'.

> You gentlemen who think they have a mission
> To purge us of the seven deadly sins
> Must first work out the basic food position
> That is where it all begins.[2]

All that matters is managing to live – all else is frippery. Morally speaking, then, absolutely anything is permissible if it is what is needed to 'work out the basic food position'. To hold otherwise is moralism, pure and simple.

This view is doubtless a pressing one when it is literally a matter of surviving or starving, but thankfully this is not the case for many of us. Our problems are not from whence the next mouthful comes, but are questions about the pursuit and disposal of money, or questions about whether or not something has, or should have, a price, or has the right price and so on.

Brecht's cynicism is not that different from that of Marx. Marx too – at least on the basis of his official metaphysics of historical materialism – decries economic moralism as pointless at best, and dangerously ideological at worst. Given that the all of human history (or, as Marx would have it 'pre-history') is the product of modes and relations of production, it follows that morality is itself such a derivative 'superstructural' phenomenon. What we should do – if, indeed, we should do anything – is to see through such illusions and look straight at the real economic forces in operation.

We have already made it clear (in Chapter 2) that we see little to recommend this extreme reductivism, but in fact Marx's ultimate attitudes towards economic moralism are more complex and conflicted than his official theory would allow.

In the first place, Marx is often inclined to evaluate positively the impact of monetarisation and markets. His economic determinism is eschatological. It is only through the complete development of capitalism that genuine human flourishing is made possible. Thus Marx's view turns out to share a variant of the invisible hand account of the market according to which the good consequences of the system answer all and any legitimate moral questions that might be directed at the economic sphere. The central difference between his position and that of a Friedman or Hayek is that they take the relevant consequences to be available now, while Marx locates them someway ahead in the future.

And in the second place, Marx is himself prone to make just those kinds of moral assessments of money and commerce that we think perfectly legitimate, but that the eschatological economic determinism on which he insists is illegitimate. *Capital* is full of such cases. Consider, for instance, his scathing condemnation of the wage-labour nexus as exploitative, or of child labour, or of the corrosive effects of commodification on religion, sexuality, the family and so forth.

If there is any lesson to be learnt in all these, it is surely not that when morality turns to money it lapses into sheer moralism; rather the lesson is that the very idea that it does lapse into moralism is itself deeply flawed. We can morally assess the economic realm and the cases and relationships it instantiates, just as Marx found himself doing on so many occasions. Morality looks inescapable here.

But perhaps our views on the necessity of morality in commerce are mistaken from another direction. Imagine an evil demon who changes our world in such a way that the overall material wealth of society increases whenever we act badly towards one another. It is not virtue that is rewarded but rather vice. Mineral resources, food stocks and technological products all increase whenever we lie, cheat, defraud and defame one another. Conversely, when we act well these resources all diminish significantly. In such circumstances, moral exhortation to the citizenry to act virtuously towards one another would not only be counter-productive but harmful to the overall welfare of society. Moral sermons about the need for good behaviour would be regarded both as unnecessary and ultimately self-defeating.

While this is in one sense a rather bizarre scenario, it is analogous in relevant ways to the Right Wing charge of economic moralism that is sometimes laid at the feet of those who would adopt an approach like ours. The Right's characterisation of economic casuistry as a form of unhelpful moralism is more plausible than that supplied by the Left since it does not rest on anything eschatological, but rather on the view that the consequences of economic self-interest are such that they morally legitimate self-interested and even vicious commercial behaviour. This tradition concentrates on the idea of the Invisible Hand according to which a morality of money is unnecessary because of the benefits of individuals pursuing their own self-interest in the marketplace. This point is given robust expression by Samuel J. Tilden at a testimonial dinner for John Pierpont Morgan's father, Junius Morgan:

> You are, doubtless in some degree, clinging to the illusion that you are working for yourselves, but it is my pleasure to claim you are working for the public. [Applause]. While you are scheming for your own selfish ends, there is an overruling and wise Providence directing that the most of all you do should inure to the benefit of the people. Men of colossal fortunes are in effect, if not in fact, trustees for the public.[3]

In this chapter we explore attempts from Bernard de Mandeville and Adam Smith onwards to give philosophical sense to the kinds of ideas that Tilden expresses. We begin with an analysis of the invisible hand.

Invisible hand explanations and the profit-motive

'Invisible Hand' explanations, says Robert Nozick, are explanations of institutional, or systemic, or collective outcomes, which 'explain what looks to be the product of someone's intentional design as not being brought about by anyone's intentions'.[4] The specification is neat, but potentially misleading, for as Adam Smith says, 'in the great chessboard of human society, every single piece has a principle of motion of its own'.[5]

An institutional outcome that 'looks to be the product of intentional design' is certainly a product of intentional agency, it is just that the agents involved do not aim at that outcome. Invisible Hand arguments deal in unintended consequences, but these consequences are those of agents as they act together, and so one of the interesting things about such explanations concerns the character of that intentional agency as it must be to generate those consequences.

Our concern is about the intentional agency invoked in Invisible Hand accounts of the collective outcomes generated by economic activity in the competitive market; that is to say, with *the profit-motive*. We begin by looking at how that motive is specified in the exemplary Invisible Hand accounts offered by Bernard Mandeville and Adam Smith. Both may be read, and within neo-classical circles typically are read, as offering accounts of the profit-motive that purge it of other-regarding elements.[6] The Invisible Hand produces the desired collective outcomes only if those who operate the institution pursue their 'advantages', and with a knowing determination beyond the call of a virtue attentive to the 'necessities' of others.

The Invisible Hand explanation is typically understood to have two connected implications for morality as it confronts economic agents and the economic system. We shall refer to this typical understanding as the *Mandevillean Conceit*. The first implication is obvious: explanations of agents' economic actions, as they inform the operations of the Invisible Hand mechanism, eschew all constitutive appeals to moral considerations. At the very least morality is, on this level, simply redundant. The second implication takes us further, for now such moralism is not simply irrelevant, but, from a more adequate view, morally self-defeating, even pernicious, in so far as the mechanism it undermines produces outcomes which are collectively desirable, and so, from a perspective that takes other-regarding concerns with due seriousness, morally desirable.[7] Moral judgement directed at individual motivations as they fuel the Invisible Hand's production of collective benefits is at best redundant, and at worst a destructive and self-defeating attack on a morally valuable social process.[8]

We reject the Mandevillean Conceit, and we do so because we reject the understanding of the profit-motive on which it arises. It is simply untrue that the profit-motive operates independently of other-regarding concerns, nor does it follow as a 'matter of logic' from the beneficent operations of the Invisible Hand mechanism that it must be so independent.[9] We provide a template for the various ways in which other-regarding considerations may, and do, inform and constrain the pursuit of profit. This template has two functions. In part, it constitutes our evidence that the profit-motive is not always, even usually, a manifestation of avarice alone. It does this by specifying a variety of ways the concern for profit may manifest itself in an agent's deliberations outside the *merely* avaricious. And it constitutes a contribution to the philosophy of action as it bears on economic activity in the market. It is intended to rectify the striking fact that the sophisticated analyses we find in the philosophy of action, generally, are missing when it comes to thinking about money.[10]

Having rejected the *avarice-only* reading of the profit-motive, we reject also the implications for morality supposedly contained in the Mandevillean Conceit. We suggest that the avarice-only profit-motive may not fuel, but may in fact threaten, the production of those 'unintended consequences' the Invisible Hand argument celebrates, for it may undermine those mutual expectations on which depend the possibility of rational agents engaging in consensual capitalist acts.[11] Far from moral judgement directed at agents as they operate in the market constituting either a moralistic irrelevancy or an assault on a morally desirable collective process, such judgement might itself have a crucial part to play in informing and sustaining the process. Indeed, if the morally positive evaluation of the Invisible Hand mechanism is to go through, it *must* be the case that we are concerned with more than self-regarding avarice, for otherwise we lack the required resources on which such an evaluation draws. (And notice that it does not matter the *kind* of positive evaluation on offer, so long as the evaluation targets economic agents understood as the avarice-only reading has it, it cannot succeed.)

Bernard Mandeville and the moral status of the profit-motive

The pro-commercial argument with which we are concerned is often said to derive from Bernard Mandeville's *Fable of the Bees*,[12] though the attribution is dubious. As Goldsmith points out, Mandeville was only marginally an economic theorist: 'he wrote no discourse on trade or credit or the balance of payments',[13] but concerned himself more broadly with the emergence of organised society from the state of nature. And what little he did have to say on specifically economic matters would appear, as Cook argues, to fall pretty squarely into the 'mercantilist school of economic philosophers'.[14]

As a mercantilist, Mandeville was no friend of the competitive market. He was not at all adverse to monopoly, and his concern for the economic good of the state saw him committed to economic policies that aimed at ensuring that the nation sold more than it bought. In part so that it could accumulate bullion at home, but more importantly (and here differing from most of his fellow mercantilists) so that there would be an adequate money supply for a full employment economy powered by the luxurious consumption of the few.

The emphasis on full employment should not fool us into thinking Mandeville was overly concerned with the well-being of the majority, let alone with that of each and every individual. The national wealth, he insists, 'consists not in money but in "a Multitude of Laborious Poor"',[15] for only such a multitude ensures that the demand for imported goods does not become excessive in relation to export income, would maximise that income by keeping the costs of domestic production as low as possible, and, through the incentive for effort poverty provides, would maximise productive efficiency.

It is in all likelihood wrong-headed to read Mandeville's Invisible Hand argument in the light of a concern for the efficient operations and collective benefits of a modern capitalist market economy. After all, he is not in favour of such an economy, and the collective benefits of the economic system he defends manifest no general benevolence of the kind theorists since Smith have drawn upon. But what should not be, often is. For Roger Scruton in his *Dictionary of Political Thought*, Adam Smith's later formulation of the argument in *Wealth of Nations* is simply 'a more optimistic formulation of the slogan "private vices, public benefits", given prominence by Mandeville'.[16] While for Nathan Rosenberg in *The New Palgrave*:

> there is [in Mandeville] the clear assertion that the unregulated market provides a system of signals and inducements such that that interactions of purely egoistic motives will somehow produce results that will advance the public good.[17]

Read in an unashamedly anachronistic fashion, the essentials of the Mandevillean conception of the profit-motive, as it frees itself from the call of virtue and pays homage to vice, is captured in the following couplet from *The Fable of the Bees*:

Fraud, Luxury and Pride must live/While we the Benefits receive.[18]

The beneficent Invisible Hand does not only *exclude* the vices of fraud, luxury and pride as these fuel the avaricious pursuit of wealth, but would appear to be an essential concomitant. To have 'Knaves turn'd Honest', Mandeville says, may provide a momentary self-indulgent glow of virtue to the foolish, but it means disaster to the 'Hive'. The profit-motive is, and should be, a self-interest that is not merely indifferent to vice but does not hesitate even before fraud. We might call this the *infernal* or *villainous* conception of the profit-motive, and while Mandeville did not consistently hold to it, on occasion he seems to embrace such a view.

> I flatter myself to have demonstrated that, neither the Friendly Qualities and kind Affections that are natural to man, nor the real Virtues he is capable of acquiring by Reason and Self-denial, are the Foundation of Society; but that what we call Evil in this World,

Moral as well as Natural, is the great Principle that makes us sociable Creatures, the solid Basis, the Life and Support of all Trades and Manufactures without Exception.[19]

Perhaps this goes too far. After all, one can defend the socially productive role of self-interested economic agents without likewise defending market criminality.

The concept of vice in play is ambiguous between the merely self-interested and the positively vicious, and this is quite correct. But the challenge for Mandeville is how to acquire the resources necessary for disambiguating the merely self-interested and the plainly vicious when it comes to activities in the marketplace. Such a distinction would seem to imply the effective operations of constraining (legal and moral) values. But now the crux of the problem: where, on the account offered, do these values come from and how do they obtain force for the kinds of beings presumed necessary for the beneficent operations of the Invisible Hand?

Adam Smith and the profit-motive

Turning to Adam Smith (whose views we considered in some detail in Chapter 2), we find a thinker who certainly is committed to the operations of a competitive commercial system. We can see his formulation of the profit-motive as it fuels the Invisible Hand for collectively desirable outcomes as 'more optimistic' in Scruton's sense only in so far as the avarice it celebrates is less obviously connected with *overt* vice. Smith, indeed, was familiar with, and well disposed towards, Mandeville's ideas. While he was occasionally critical of Mandeville's thought, in general he restricted his criticism to the temper of Mandeville's remarks, rather than their content, condemning them not as mistaken or misguided, but as 'splenetic', that is to say, ill-humoured, testy and irascible.[20]

The key passages in Smith's account are to be found in *Wealth of Nations* and *Theory of the Moral Sentiments*. Taken together, the lessons they offer contain his analysis of the Invisible Hand mechanism, and his justification of that mechanism.

The natural effort of every individual to better his own condition . . . is so powerful a principle, that it is alone, and without any assistance, not only capable of carrying on the society to wealth and prosperity, but of surmounting a hundred impertinent obstructions with which the folly of human laws too often incumbers its operations . . . [21]

From this passage we can draw the first lesson: Everyone's deepest desire is to 'better their position', and this desire has the capacity, against formidable political and legal obstacles, to carry society to 'wealth and prosperity'.

> It is not from the benevolence of the butcher, the brewer, or the baker, that we expect our dinner, but from their regard to their own interest. We address ourselves, not to their humanity but their self-love, and never talk to them of our necessities but of their advantages.[22]

The second lesson is that the desire to 'better oneself' as it manifests itself in the economic sphere is simply a matter of 'self-love', not other-regarding moral concern:

> every individual necessarily labours to render the annual revenue of the society as great as he can. He generally, indeed, neither intends to promote the publick interest, nor knows how much he is promoting it . . . he intends only his own gain, and he is in this, as in many other cases, led by an invisible hand to promote an end which was no part of his intention.[23]

Now the first element of the Mandevillean Conceit is in place: by eschewing moral concern and pursuing personal gain, agents produce collective gain. This is the Invisible Hand in operation.

> They [the rich] are led by an invisible hand to make nearly the same distribution to the necessaries of life, which would have been made, had the earth been divided into equal portions among all its inhabitants, and thus without intending it, without knowing it, advance the interest of the society, and afford means to the multiplication of the species. When Providence divided the earth among a few lordly masters, it neither forgot nor abandoned those who seemed to have been left out of the partition.[24]

The second element of the Mandevillean Conceit is now in place.[25] For while the Invisible Hand is fuelled by individual acts of 'self-love', the system it embodies is morally legitimated to the extent that the worst-off are materially better off than they would be under alternative economic arrangements.

Smith's view of the profit-motive as it fuels the operations of the Invisible Hand is clear. It arises from, and is exhausted by, every agent's desire to 'better his condition', where this is a matter, and generally known to be a matter, of a 'natural selfishness and rapacity' which sees each agent determined entirely on his 'own gain'. Other-regarding concerns for the 'necessities' or needs of others do not, in this realm of life, constrain our activities, and rightly so; for the profit-motive 'is so powerful, that it is alone, and without any assistance' *is* 'capable of carrying on the society to wealth and prosperity' (first element of the Mandevillean Conceit). It does so in crucial degree through the 'vain and insatiable desires' of the rich, for those desires see the useful and remunerative employment of the less well-off, thereby making the latter better off than they would be otherwise.[26] It is this that provides the Invisible Hand with its moral justification (second element of the Mandevillean Conceit). For who, except the vice-ridden, could object to a system of economic arrangements that, as Samuel Johnson said, makes it true that:

> though the perseverance and address of the Indian excite our admiration, they nevertheless cannot procure him the conveniences which are enjoyed by the vagrant beggar of a civilised country?[27]

As Mandeville's celebration of vice insinuates, but now in a more appealing form, at least as regards its consequences if not its inherent nature, *greed is good*.[28]

Self interest, selfishness and the open question argument

This conclusion concerning the goodness of greed is shaped by a fundamental and exclusive dichotomy between morality and private advantage, or benevolence and self-interest. Mandeville and Smith's contemporary, Francis Hutcheson, makes the point in a particularly blunt fashion.

> As to the love of benevolence, the very name excludes self-interest. We never call that man benevolent who is in fact useful to others, but at the same time intends his own interest, without any ultimate desire for the good of others. If there be any benevolence at all, it must be disinterested; for the most useful action imaginable loses all appearance of benevolence, as soon as we discern it flowed only from self-love or interest.[29]

We are not concerned here with the reasons for this radical opposition between economic interest and moral value. It is enough that it is there, and shapes Mandeville and Smith's account of the profit-motive. What is perhaps most puzzling is that even philosophers who are not, in general, subject to such a radical opposition often succumb when they come to consider economic activities. As we saw earlier, Kant, whose third formulation of the Categorical Imperative, 'Act always so as to treat others as ends-in-themselves, *never merely* as means', shows him to be in general a *compatibilist* between the claims of interest and moral respect, is not a compatibilist when price comes into play. Price, he insists, is positively inimical to dignity, and there is the end of it.[30]

We suspect this anti-commercial bias owes more to the *history* of philosophy – to its aristocratic bias among the Ancients, and its ascetic bias under Christianity – than to anything more substantial, but it is enough that the opposition forces on us an either/or choice, so that one is either, to coin our own terms, an unrestricted profit-seeker or an agent for whom any concern with profit is anathema. For the latter, to pursue profit would necessarily evacuate virtue.

Recall that earlier in Chapter 3 we complicated the traditional account of the profit-motive by taking from the philosophy of action the language of *goals* and *side-constraints*, and distinguishing four kinds of profit-motive: the lucrepathic, the accumulative, the stipendiary and the lucrephobic. Our suggestion at this point is that the mere possibility of there being accumulators and stipendiarists means the Mandevillean Conceit's appeal to what we might call the *avarice-only* specification of the profit-motive is, as it stands, unwarranted. The radical divide it presupposes between a concern for profit and that for virtue is simply mistaken. A concern for profit may be subject to moral side-constraints, or such a concern may itself constitute a side-constraint in the pursuit of non-commercial ends. We have no reason to prefer the Invisible Hand that relies on the activities of lucrepaths to that of its more restrained cousins, since all involve the profit-motive.

Of course, this is not to say that the Invisible Hand can operate effectively on the basis of accumulative or stipendiary motives alone. Certainly, there are reasons for thinking that weak variant of profit-seeking will not do the job if only because the role profit plays in such agents' motivational economy is not primary, merely facilitatory. In such cases we may doubt that the 'natural effort of every individual to better his condition... is so powerful, that it is alone, and without any assistance... capable of carrying on the society to wealth and prosperity'. However, there seems little reason to think accumulator will not do the job given that the concern for profit is primary, if constrained. Let us call this the Open Question Argument for it remains an open empirical question as to what kind of profit-motive best fosters social benefits.

Ad hoc defences of the commercial realm

There is no doubt that Mandeville and Smith engage in *ad hoc* forms of defence of their positions whenever the brutal consequences of uncon-strained self-interest become too apparent. Worried at the potentially market-devastating consequences of the predatory behaviour it might seem to licence – force and fraud, monopolistic and oligopolistic strate-gies, and so on – they aim to domesticate the market through externally imposed legal regulation. This manoeuvre raises two problems. The first is that we would appear to have abandoned an Invisible Hand explana-tion, or at least severely circumscribed its explanatory range, for such legal regulation would seem to involve the *intentional* provision of the valued public benefits. Rather than 'explaining what looks to be the product of someone's intentional design as not being brought about by anyone's intentions', the explanation of market outcomes now crucially appeals to the product of someone's intentions and does so by setting the profit-motive and in a broader and more adequate perspective. The sec-ond problem concerns the sources of commitment to such a regulatory regime given the assumption of lucrepathology.

Take the first question: for all of Mandeville's celebration of 'private vice', he insists that it is the role of government to further the mer-cantilist interest by instigating and defending commercial monopolies and, by force if necessary, to ensure the harsh conditions and docility of the poor.

> Private Vices by the dexterous Management of a skillful Politician may be turn'd into Public Benefits.[31]

And so too Smith, as he waxes eloquent on the necessity to an effective and efficient market economy of the Sovereign Power as guarantor of the Rule of Law. The duty of the Sovereign is to protect 'every member of the society from the injustice and oppression of every other member of it' through the 'exact administration of justice'.[32] As for why there is this need, Smith could not be clearer. The successful market competitor, and just because of his success:

> is at all times surrounded by unknown enemies, whom, though he never provoked, he can never appease, and from whose injustice he can be protected only by the powerful arm of the civil magistrate continually held up to chastise it.[33]

At this point we have left behind the Invisible Hand for an argument very much in the traditional Platonic mode of wise and benevolent rulers who have the good of the political community in mind. Good intentions become necessary for the realisation of the good society. We now have the wise rulers, just like Plato's Guardians in the *Republic*, legislating for the public good – granting monopolies and ensuring the poverty of the masses for Mandeville, generating laws against monopoly, force and fraud, for Smith – and the Auxiliary Magistrates dedicated to applying and defending those constraints on economic agents as they participate in market exchange.

Not only does this involve abandoning the Invisible Hand explanation, resting as it does on the Guardians' and Auxilleries' personal virtue and dedicated commitment to the production of collective ends, it is anyway a failure. For while Plato might have been able to divide his society into three distinct classes, with reflection on the public good monopolised by one class, another defending and implementing the results of such reflection, and the economic motives such reflection licenses unleashed only by another, subservient class, today we all of us are reflective economic agents deeply implicated in the logic and activities of the marketplace. If we are to be constrained, it cannot be by external command and coercion alone, but must be to a significant degree a matter of *inner commitment*, and certainly this is how Smith speaks of our commitment to the Rule of Law.[34]

The availability problem

But now we confront the second problem with idea that the realisation of the benefits of the market requires our economic actors to be entirely devoid of concern for their fellow beings. Let us call this second concern for the 'lucrepathological' interpretation of economic agency the 'Availability Problem'. The problem is to see how we can invoke the claims of Justice and the Rule of Law to provide effective constraints on the pursuit of self-interest when those it is to constrain are thought, as with Mandeville, to be villainously avaricious, or, with Smith, as acting wholly for personal advantage, and so without regard for the public good. On what might the required commitment to justice and law arise? It is not enough that given our lucrepathology such a commitment might be necessary if the Invisible Hand is to deliver the collective goods, for *ex hypothesi* we are not, in the market, motivated by such other-regarding concerns. If the Invisible Hand of lucrepathology strikes us as a surprising paradox, it is surely more paradoxical to expect a commitment to justice and the rule of law from 'Knaves', or from butchers, bakers and brewers who think only in terms of personal advantage. How is a commitment to public good or justice available to an agent who 'neither intends to promote the public interest nor knows how much he promoting it'? Some things, we might think, are simply too mysterious.[35]

The mystery is not removed by the one argument that can be extracted from Smith that might be thought aimed at this very question. Thus the contemporary theorist Christopher Berry – while admitting that the argument is 'implicit, not explicit'[36] – suggests that Smith felt that his Invisible Hand was practically 'robust' because he thought that the required commitment to justice and its rules would arise in 'commercial society' because economic interactions there are largely those between *strangers*, and 'it is the stranger rather than the friend who is more like the impartial spectator'[37] whose perspective constitutes the moral point of view.

We do not at all reject – if this really is his line of approach – Smith's appeal to the moral point of view to explain the required commitment to justice. But we do reject the argument offered, and for a rather obvious reason. After all, the strangers Smith is talking of are not impartial spectators concerned, as Hume put it, to view matters from a 'steady and general' point of view, but self-interested economic agents, just as we are. And our relations are not those of morally concerned beings, of bearers of a common 'humanity' but, as we all know, of self-loving advantage seekers. We might at this point reconstruct what Smith did say, or should have said, in terms of the demand for public respect. But this would confuse a desire for celebrity with a concern for morality. Certainly, the desire for celebrity is a desire to impress strangers, rather than acquaintances, and such a desire would seem, on contemporary evidence, to underpin a robust system of fame, but such a desire can be served just as well by a reputation for notoriety as for virtue.

Would a society of lucrepaths generate the good society?

Rather than attempt to save the lucrepathic reading of the profit-motive by *ad hocery*, we would be better advised to rethink our understanding of that motive. Far from there being, as the Mandevillean Conceit requires, but does not provide, an independent argument against those manifestations of the profit-motive that involve a moral component, there seem to be very good reasons, of the kind Mandeville and Smith implicitly allow, for thinking lucrepathology inimical to the proper operations of that mechanism, and so for thinking that accumulative action and not lucrepathology oils the wheels. Recall Adam Smith's words:

> It is not from the benevolence of the butcher, the brewer, or the baker, that we expect our dinner, but from their regard to their own interest. We address ourselves not to their humanity but their self-love, and never talk to them of our necessities but of their advantages.[38]

It is true that it is pointless to appeal to the benevolence of the butcher, brewer or baker, for our dinner, if that is to be provided through the market. The benevolent agent, as Hutchinson describes them, is a self-abnegating super-altruist who refuses to serve their own interests when others' interests are in play. He or she is forbidden consenting capitalist acts, for even if these *are* consensual, they are so because each party thinks he or she is obtaining some benefit for themselves, and this is what the lucrephobe refuses to do.

What might we expect if our potential provider is a lucrepath? Well – and assuming that price-gouging has not put such a purchase beyond our limited reach – we might get our dinner; but we might not get the dinner we wanted or expected. It may be that there is more profit to be made by selling us adulterated or substandard, or otherwise dangerous goods, than those of a decent quality.

This is no idle possibility, and it was one that, unsurprisingly, strongly engaged Marx's acerbic attention in one of his glorious outbursts in *Capital*, Volume 1:

> The incredible adulteration of bread, especially in London, was first revealed by the House of Commons Committee 'on the adulteration of articles of food' (1855–56) and Dr. Hassall's work, 'Adulteration detected'. The consequence of these revelations was the Act of August 6th, 1860, 'for preventing the adulteration of articles of food and drink,' an inoperative law, as it naturally shows the tenderest consideration for every Free-trader who determines by the buying or selling of adulterated commodities 'to turn an honest penny.'

He continues:

> The Committee itself formulated more or less naively its conviction that Free trade meant essentially trade with adulterated, or as the English ingeniously put it, 'sophisticated' goods. In fact this kind of

sophistry knows better than Protagoras how to make white black, and black white, and even better than the Eleatics how to determine *ad oculos* that everything is only appearance.[39]

A Mandevillean merchant would not hesitate to perpetrate a fraud if the returns promise to be right, and there is no reason to expect more from Smith's vendors. As he says – and doubtless as Marx knew he said, and was giving an oblique comment – merchants and artificers act 'merely from a view to their own interest and in the pursuit of their own pedlar principle of turning a penny whenever a penny was to be got'.[40]

Perhaps we might expect more because Smith's sellers pursue profit in the light of their *enlightened* self-interest, and this tells them that doing us down now may well harm their long-term interests in profit-maximisation. Smith would seem to be making this kind of point when he suggests that society can 'subsist among different men, as among different merchants, *from a sense of its utility*, without any mutual love or affection'. Even though no person in that society feels any sense of obligation, it may still be maintained 'by a mercenary exchange of good offices according to an agreed valuation'.[41] There is something to this, clearly, but we must be careful. If by 'sense of utility' Smith means to invoke economic agents' concern for *general utility*, then the claim is vulnerable to the objections raised earlier against *ad hoc* responses; that is, it is no longer the Invisible Hand being theorised, and the move from a concern for personal to general utility is a *non sequitur*. Any plausible reading must therefore draw everything required out of agents' concern for their utility.

Think again of our baker. How am I to decide, in the shop, my stomach rumbling, the kids screaming, whether or not in this case, here and now, the seller's enlightened self-interest will do the job I hope, even that he has any long-term interests of the relevant kind? Perhaps he has been diagnosed with a soon to be fatal disorder, or he is to retire from business the next day, or perhaps he thinks I will not notice the substitution, particularly given the kids, or perhaps he takes me to be a passing traveller and makes the opportunistic decision, and so on. The point is not that I must think we are likely to be poisoned, but that it is a possibility that cannot be discounted. And given that it cannot be discounted, it cannot be ignored.

If one is, and knows oneself to be, dealing with lucrepaths, the transaction costs of buying (and selling) will be reliably higher than they would be otherwise. And they may be so high as to threaten to stultify market exchange *period*. For if everyone is out to maximise personal returns, and is willing to do so at any cost to those others he deals with, then we have not merely a *low trust*, but a *no trust* environment. And in no trust interactions, as game theory tells us, 'defection' is all too likely to be the dominant strategy, in which case we do not have the beneficent Invisible Hand in operation, but a vicious deformation, which is characterised by its *counterfinality*, where this marks the tendency of an act or policy to thwart its own (if, in the particular case, unintended) aim.[42]

Certainly, it means that the traditional Rawlsian-style justification of the Invisible Hand, as it concerns itself with making the worst-off better off than they would be under alternate arrangements, does not go through. If Johnson thought Smith had legitimated the operations of the competitive market economy on the grounds that the 'perseverance and address of the Indian excite our admiration' and that they cannot obtain for him the 'conveniences which are enjoyed by the vagrant beggar of a civilised country', then he had not thought about our lucrepathic baker. For it would be a hard saying indeed to hold that it is better to be dead on poisoned bread than a Johnsonian 'indian', however, enmeshed in the so-called 'barbarism'.

We do not want to get too sentimental. After all, we might prefer our baker to be an accumulator, rather than a stipendiarist. For the accumulator can be expected to be committed, and committed out of his now side-constrained self-interest, to producing and providing me with the cheapest and best quality goods the market will bear. That way he may hope to maximise his returns, whereas as a stipendiarist might well be less concerned with these matters, so long as he earns enough to continue pursuing his non-profit-centred interests.

Recall too the problem of legal coercion as a solution to the problems of lucrepathology. In a society of lucrepaths such a solution is unavailable. A society of accumulators and stipendiarists has a place for such coercion, and a place not subject to the Platonic demand for distinct functional classes. For the accumulator possesses the necessary other-regarding concerns, be they market-external or market-internal, on which such a solution might build the necessary commitment. Our 'Availability Problem' does not arise. Still they will tend to favour such a solution, for while they are, in the right circumstances, susceptible to lucrepathic temptation, it is just this temptation they are motivated to avoid succumbing to. Here is the place, and possibility, for legal regulation and coercion,[43] and it may well be a further place in which the accumulator/stipendiarist distinction is important. It may be that the regulatory environment in which accumulators flourish, so unleashing the Invisible Hand as it delivers its collective benefits, is better and more effectively manned by stipendiarist rather than their more temptation-ridden strong cousins. And notice that only under the economy of either the accumulator or the stipendiarist is there the possibility for a justification of the market economy of the kind Smith celebrates. The collective benefits the Invisible Hand delivers serve to legitimate the operations of the system to accumulators and stipendiarists, for only they, unlike the lucrepath or the lucrephobe, bear the necessary moral concerns on which such legitimation draws.

Concluding remarks

We have argued that while the Invisible Hand analysis of competitive markets is often, in the form of the Mandevillean Conceit, employed to justify the evacuation of moral concerns from the commercial realm, both on grounds of their irrelevancy and their capacity to endanger the collective payoffs otherwise morally valued, this evacuation is mistaken and inconsistent. It is mistaken because the avarice-only reading of the profit-motive is not the only way of characterising that motive, and without further investigation there is no reason to believe that morally constrained versions of the profit-motive may not be responsible for whatever benefits the Invisible Hand provides. Even more worryingly for those enamoured of the Mandevillean Conceit, there are some positive reasons to think the benefits the pursuit of profit produces are better attributed to the accumulator than to his vicious cousin, the 'filthy lucrepath', and the accumulator just *is* subject to, and so (sometimes) motivated by, other-regarding concerns.

Complicating the traditional lucrepathic conception of the profit-motive does not merely place the Mandevillean Conceit under great pressure, just as importantly it opens up a whole new terrain for moral and economic exploration, for by legitimating a moralising focus on economic agents' motivations it enables us to address those questions of justice in economic life, in pricing and profit-taking and so forth, which exercise us in everyday life, and which constitute the interface between morality, politics and economics; and to do so without the imputation of a bad conscience, as if such reflections itself undermined what might be valued in economic life.

Epilogue

What is so uncertain as something that rolls away? It is appropriate that money is round, because it never stays in one place.
Saint Augustine, *Enarratio in Psalmos*, 83, 3.

We began this book with a series of cases in which we might be – and many of us undoubtedly are – concerned about the role that money played therein. We raised questions about the appropriateness of such practices as bridal registers, cost–benefit analysis and the payment of honoraria; we asked whether there might be instances where the prices charged for goods and for money itself should be subject to moral constraint. Our puzzle was whether such concerns and worries had anything substantial to them, or if they were simply irrational or misguided sentimentalism. After all, charges of sentimentalism and the like are the kinds of reactions we are likely to find from those schooled in much modern economic orthodoxy.

We discovered two things about these 'toy' cases. In the first place, we discovered that the particular concerns to which our examples drew attention were not themselves isolated concerns. Instead, we saw that such concerns have been a staple of human life and reflection about money since its very emergence, and that these worries are underpinned by deeply felt moral concerns about pricing, lending, commercial exchange and commodification. Philosophers, playwrights, poets, film-makers, novelists and religious thinkers have all explored issues concerning the morality of money. We find the concerns explored in the works of Aristotle and Aquinas just as we find them in the plays of Shakespeare and the writings of John Wesley.

In the second place, we discovered that while concerns with the morality of money had such venerable roots, the intellectual background against which they emerge and made sense had been occluded by certain historically specific views about the nature of money, markets and economic life. Since Adam Smith, this tradition virtually disappeared from intellectual view – though as our examples indicated, they had not fallen into practical desuetude; they are still part of our everyday folk morality.

It turned out that far from moral concerns about money being merely sentimental or irrational, the very fact that they might appear so is an artefact of a dislocation between the intellectual frameworks we employ to explain and interpret the world and our everyday folk moral intuitions, based as they are on our practices in the world of money.

The consequences of these discoveries are welcome indeed. Not only we have overcome an unnecessary and obfuscating divide between our theory and everyday social practice – and in so doing been able to understand better what it is we are doing or reacting to when money comes into the picture – we have been able to recover a whole intellectual tradition whose riches and insights have been so negligently ignored by modern social theorists.

The recovery of this tradition means recovering a moral psychology of money, albeit in a different form from that of earlier philosophers, for the Ancients and Medievals spoke of vices such as greed, avarice and cupidity, while we have preferred to explore the structure of the motives which animate those pursuing profit. This is not because we rescind from the moralism of their analyses, but because we have needed to introduce more fine-grained distinctions between the legitimate and the illegitimate ways of pursuing profit. Further, unlike some of these earlier approaches, our moralism is not set against the pursuit of profit for its own sake. We have no bones to pick with such pursuit so long as it is side-constrained by certain substantive moral values, in particular by a sensitivity to the necessities and vulnerabilities of need provision.

The moral psychology of money we developed involves a sensitivity to the way money concerns can *corrode* other kinds of evaluations; it is the natural capacity of money, because of its ability to commensurate and deliver a potentially endless array of commodities, to drive other modes of evaluation from the Temple of Value, and to do so in a way that fails even to register what it is that has been lost. Our Corrosion Thesis captures just this very idea. This moral psychology is practically oriented, for we suggest that if we can manage to develop an account of the morality of money that makes sense of the evaluative pangs we may feel as it spreads itself through and across our lives, then we will be far better placed not merely for self-understanding, but for reflecting sensitively and intelligently on how we might, and might not, want money to operate in our lives.

With this moral psychology in place, and allied with standard accounts of the role of need in determinations of justice, we have explored a number of practical issues of great social import, most notably the proper range of cost–benefit analysis, the just price and constraints on money lending. We have cautioned that our use of cost–benefit analysis should not in any way lead us to regard those things we regard as sacred or intrinsically valuable as mere instrumental substitutes, nor should it lead us to the view that monetary evaluations are some kind of stand-in for an ultimate scale of value. Equally, we have argued that when setting prices either for commodities or for money itself, we should not act as would the 'lucrepath', but instead ensure that our pursuit of profit is side-constrained by relevant moral considerations, most notably the needs of those with whom we trade. Equally, our government policies should be formulated so as to ensure that trade does not place unnecessary moral hazards in the paths of mercantile agents and that the needy and indigent are not exploited.

In many ways this book is only a launching pad – a prolegomenon if you like – for more substantive work in the moral philosophy of money. Each of the practical issues we have considered, the just price, the ethics of interest-taking and the relationship between money and the sacred, is worthy of more detailed examinations in their own right. Equally, new issues will arise to which we have not attended, for although money is no longer simply the round object it was in Augustine's day, nonetheless he is still correct that it does not remain long in one place. There is a restlessness about money that mirrors the restlessness of the wanton commercial agent. A challenge for future work on the moral philosophy of money will be to capture in greater detail the role that money plays in transforming our self-understanding and the moral worlds we inhabit.

Notes

1 Introduction

1. From Raymond Postgate (ed.), *The Conversations of Dr. Johnson* (New York: Taplinger Publishing Company, 1970), p. 136.
2. G. Simmel, *The Philosophy of Money*, 2nd enlarged edition, D. Frisby (ed.) (London: Routledge, 1990), p. 286.
3. Simmel writes of the now free peasant: 'He would thereby gain freedom from something, not freedom to something. We understand our own times better if we realise that the possession of money confers purely negative freedom with respect to everyone else, while making us depend on the condition that we hold it and use it...there is less and less place for that intimate connection, fusion, commitment which assign constraining boundaries to the personality, yet at the same time give it substance and sense.' Ibid., pp. 67–68.
4. B. Frey, *Not Just For the Money* (Brookfield, Vt.: Edward Elgar, 1997); and Richard Thaler, *The Winner's Curse: Paradoxes and Anomalies of Economic Life* (Princeton, N.J.: Princeton University Press, 1994).
5. Frey, *Not Just For the Money*, pp. 1–2.
6. Later, in Chapter 5, we discuss just this very case.
7. Plato, 'The Sophist' in *The Dialogues of Plato*, trans. B. Jowett, 4th edition (Oxford: Clarendon Press, 1953), [233], p. 382.
8. D. Hume, *Enquiries Concerning the Human Understanding and Concerning the Principles of Morals*, L.A. Selby-Begged (ed.), 2nd edition (Oxford: Clarendon Press, 1902), Section 1, 5, p. 11.
9. K. Marx, *Capital*, Vol. 1 (Moscow: Progress Publishers, 1954), p. 145.
10. R. Seaford, *Money and the Early Greek Mind: Homer, Philosophy and Tragedy* (Cambridge: Cambridge University Press, 2004).
11. K. Marx and F. Engels, *Manifesto of the Communist Party* (Peking: Foreign Languages Press, 1970), p. 55.
12. Some might argue that the 'moralization of the market' is not a new phenomenon at all. Those historically minded sceptics might draw our attention to the moral 'embeddedness' of Ancient or Medieval markets – or, in fact, of all markets – and toe the importance of ethical considerations in the various economic theories. (Cf. Adrian Walsh, 'The Morality of the Market and the Medieval Schoolmen', *Politics, Philosophy and Economics*, 3, no. 2 (2004), pp. 241–259). But the histories of the Ancient and Medieval markets seem to be of little help when we try to understand the contemporary phenomenon of the 'moralization of the markets'. *The Moralization of the Markets*, ed. Nico Stehr, Christopher Henning and Bernd Weiler (New Brunswick, N.J.: Transaction Publishers, 2006).
13. Cf. J.M. Keynes, *A Treatise on Money*, Vol. 1 (London: Macmillan, 1930), pp. 3–5.
14. L. Robbins, *An Essay on the Nature and Significance of Economic Science* (London: Macmillan, 1935), p. 31.

15. D. Hume, 'Of Money', in E. Rotwein (ed.), *David Hume: Writings on Economics* (Edinburgh: Nelson, 1955), p. 33.
16. T. Veblen, 'The Limitations of Marginal Utility Theory', in D.M. Hausman (ed.), *The Philosophy of Economics* (Cambridge: Cambridge University Press, 1984), p. 154. Keynes discusses all the four roles and insists that money of account is the most fundamental.
17. K. Marx, 'On the Jewish Question', in R. Tucker (ed.), *The Marx–Engels Reader*, 2nd edition (New York: W.W. Norton and Co, 1972), p. 50. Cf. Timothy 6.10.
18. H.J. Paton, *The Moral Law or Kant's Groundwork of the Metaphysics of Morals* (London: Hutchinson, 1946), p. 102.
19. Aristotle, *Nicomachean Ethics* (Cambridge: Cambridge University Press, 2000), trans. R. Crisp, [1133b], p. 91.
20. Cited in J. Kaye, *Economy and Nature in the Fourteenth Century: Money, Market Exchange, and the Emergence of Scientific Thought* (Cambridge: Cambridge University Press, 1998), p. 97.
21. Aristotle, *Nicomachean Ethics* (Cambridge: Cambridge University Press, 2000), trans. Roger Crisp, [1133b], p. 91.
22. K. Marx, *Capital*, Vol. 1 (Moscow: Progress Publishers, 1954), p. 97.
23. Marx, ibid., pp. 163–164.
24. See E. Anderson, *Value in Ethics and Economics* (Cambridge, Mass.: Harvard University Press, 1993); and C.R. Sunstein, 'Incommensurability and valuation in law', *Michigan Law Review*, February, 1994, 92, no. 4, pp. 779–861.
25. Plato, *The Laws*, translated with an introduction by T.J. Saunders (Harmondsworth, Middlesex: Penguin, 1970), [918–919].
26. J. Locke, *Two Treatises of Civil Government* (London: J.M. Dent, 1924), p. 139.
27. Locke, ibid., p. 139. Cf. Matthew 6:19–20.
28. Locke, ibid., p. 139.
29. Curiously, John Stuart Mill claims that money does not in fact have these powers, suggesting to the contrary that it is labour which allows us to maintain value. Mill argues that the money measure of value gives a false idea of its permanency. He writes, 'The greater part in value of the wealth now existing in England has been produced by human hands within the last 12 months. A very small proportion indeed of that large aggregate was in existence ten years ago; of the present productive capital of the country scarcely any part, except farm houses and manufactories, and a few ships and machines, and even those would not in most cases have survived so long if fresh labour had not been employed within that period in putting them into repair... capital is kept in existence from age to age, not by preservation but by perpetual reproduction.' J.S. Mill, *Principles of Political Economy* (London: Green, Reader and Dyer, 1878), p. 46.
30. Aristotle, *The Politics of Aristotle*, trans. Ernest Barker (Oxford: Clarendon Press, 1946), Bk.1, [1257a–1258a], pp. 25–26.
31. In the same spirit Tawney notes that engraved over the entrance to the Antwerp Market is the motto *ad usum mercatrorum cuiusque gentis ac linguae*, indicating that the market was open to all. See R.H. Tawney, *Religion and the Rise of Capitalism* (London: John Murray, 1926), p. 75.
32. D. Defoe, *Moll Flanders* (London: J.M. Dent and Sons, 1930), p. 153.
33. T. Parks, *Medici Money: Banking, Metaphysics and Art in Fifteenth-Century Florence* (London: Profile Books Ltd, 2006), p. 35.

34. In *The Wealth of Nations*, Adam Smith has presented a quite detailed discussion of the economic effects of sumptuary laws. See A. Smith, *An Inquiry into the Nature and Causes of the Wealth of Nations*, Vol. 1, R.H. Campbell and A.S. Skinner (General Editors), A. Todd (Textual Editor) (Oxford: Clarendon Press, 1976), pp. 260–264.

35. Cf. E. Anderson, 'The Ethical Limitations of the Market', *Economics and Philosophy*, 6 (1990), p. 182.

36. See M. Schofield, 'Aristotle on the imagination', in J. Barnes, M. Schofield and R. Sorabji (eds), *Articles on Aristotle. 4: Psychology and Aesthetics* (London: 1979), p. 123. Schofield focuses on Aristotle's enthusiasm for philosophising on the basis of *endoxa*. Terrence Irwin discusses the dialectical nature of Aristotle's method of first philosophy, which being from common beliefs, and cross-examines them. See Terrence Irwin, *Aristotle's First Principles* (Oxford: Clarendon, 1980), p. 19. However, there is some scholarly debate on how much of a role Aristotle wanted to accord to our common beliefs. For a dissenting view, see Stephen Everson, *Aristotle on Perception* (Oxford: Clarendon Press, 1997), pp. 171–172.

37. Cited in T. Irwin, *Aristotle's First Principles* (*Top*. 110a: 18–21), p. 36.

38. Aristotle, *The Politics of Aristotle*, trans. Ernest Barker (Oxford: Clarendon Press, 1946), Bk.1, [1257a–1258b], pp. 23–27.

39. We should not think that moral claims require entailments in order to be of philosophical interest or morally significant.

40. See T.S. Dorsch (ed.), *Classical Literary Criticism*; Aristotle, *On the Art of Poetry*; Horace, *On the Art of Poetry* (Harmondsworth: Penguin Books, 1965), p. 157.

2   Money, commerce and moral theory

1. J.W. Baldwin, *Masters, Princes and Merchants: The Social Views of Peter the Chanter and His Circle* (Princeton: Princeton University Press, 1970), pp. 262–263. See also M.M. Austin and P. Vidal-Naquet, *Economic and Social History of Ancient Greece; An Introduction* (London: B.T. Batsford, 1977), pp. 44, 73.

2. Judas, unlike King Midas, did not manage to survive his avarice – and the manner of his death makes it clear that his initial weakness was that, and not a settled disposition. He tried to return to 30 pieces of silver to the High Priests who refused to accept it.

3. The legend has it that from that day he detested gold and riches and spent his life in a simple way, wandering around the country and enjoying his freedom.

4. For a very different account of the Ancients' attitude towards commerce, see S.M. Laurence (ed.), *Economic Thought in Spain: Selected Essays of Marjorie Grice-Hutchison* (Brookfield, Vermont.: Edward Elgar, 1993), pp. 126–142.

5. D. Laertius, *The Lives and Opinions of Eminent Philosophers*, trans. C.D. Yonge (London: Henry G. Bone, 1853), p. 15. See also Aristotle, *The Politics of Aristotle*, trans. E. Barker (Oxford: Clarendon Press, 1946), [1259a].

6. Plato, *The Laws*, translated with an introduction by T.J. Saunders (Harmondsworth, Middl.: Penguin, 1970), [705], p. 159.

7. Plato, 'The Republic', in *The Dialogues of Plato*, Vol. II, trans. B. Jowett, 4th edition (Oxford: Clarendon Press, 1953), [554b], p. 421.
8. Ibid., [554c], p. 421.
9. Ibid., [554d], p. 421.
10. Ibid., [553d], p. 420.
11. Ibid., [591d–591e], pp. 466–467.
12. Ibid., [445], pp. 299–300.
13. In *The Laws*, Plato discusses *inter alia* commercial law (Book 11), and rules for the possession of money (Book 5) as well as outlining laws for the regulations of markets (Book 8).
14. Plato, *The Laws*, [919d].
15. Coleridge suggests that Lycurgus was anti-commercial, whereas Solon was simply uncommercial. See S.T. Coleridge, in R.J. White (ed.), *Collected Works*, Vol. 6 (London: Routledge and Kegan Paul, 1972), p. 223.
16. Plato, *The Laws*, [919], p. 458.
17. Ibid., [919], p. 459.
18. Ibid., [919], p. 459.
19. Ibid., [742], p. 210.
20. Ibid., [918], p. 457.
21. Ibid., [918–919], pp. 457–458.
22. Ibid., [745], p. 215.
23. Plato, *The Republic*, [550c], p. 416.
24. Ibid., [551d], pp. 417–418.
25. C.J. Berry, *The Idea of Luxury: A Conceptual and Historical Investigation* (Cambridge: Cambridge University Press, 1994), p. 49.
26. Aristotle, *Nicomachean Ethics*, trans. R. Crisp (Cambridge: Cambridge University Press, 2000), [1133b], p. 91.
27. Or a world in which there are relatively few beds and many houses.
28. J. Kaye, *Economy and Nature in the Fourteenth Century: Money, Market Exchange, and the Emergence of Scientific Thought* (Cambridge: Cambridge University Press, 1998).
29. This opposition to the spendthrift and the miser can be found in many later writers, including Smith, Johnson and Keynes.
30. Aristotle, *Nicomachean Ethics*, trans. Sir D. Ross (London: Oxford University Press, 1969), Bk. I, 5, [1096], p. 7.
31. The only moral issues with barter would have to be something related to religious views, such as divine providentialism.
32. Aristotle, *The Politics of Aristotle*, Bk. I, [1257b], pp. 25–26.
33. Somewhat anachronistically, we might describe this in Marxian terms as a defence of C-M-C (Commodity-Money-Commodity) and a repudiation of M-C-M (Money-Commodity-Money).
34. Scott Meikle notes that Aristotle's point is that 'whether they are greedy or not, this is an activity, whose *end* is without a limit', p. 158. S. Meikle, 'Aristotle on Money', in J. Smithin (ed.), *What is Money?* (London: Routledge, 2000), pp. 157–173.
35. Cicero, *Cicero on Moral Obligation: A New Translation of Cicero's 'De Officiis'*, trans. J. Higgenbottham (Berkeley: University of California Press, 1967), p. 92.
36. Ibid. If Marcus Terentius Varro (116–127 BC) is to be trusted on etymological matters, the 'very word for money (*pecunia*) comes from *pecus*, cattle, which

is the foundation of all wealth'. M.T. Varro, *Roman Farm Management: the Treatises of Cato and Varro* (Mila, U.S.A.: Kessinger Publishing, 2004), p. 83.

37. Suetonius, *The Lives of the Twelve Caesars, Caius Caesar Caligula* (Harvard: Loeb Classical Library, 1913), p. 471.
38. Cited in N. Rudd, 'Introduction', *Horace: Satires and Epistles. Persius: Satires* (Harmondsworth: Penguin, 1997), p. 13.
39. Ibid., p. 116.
40. Ibid., p. 130.
41. Ibid., p. 134.
42. Ibid., p. 154
43. Juvenal's views were outlined in this form by Samuel Johnson in his 1749 translation *cum* adaptation, *The Vanity of Human Wishes*. S. Johnson, *Poetry and Prose*, in M. Wilson (ed.) (London: Rupert Hart-Davis, 1969), p. 161.
44. See K. Pribram, *A History of Economic Reasoning* (Baltimore: The Johns Hopkins University Press, 1983), p. 634.
45. The roots of such antagonism to trade are not wholly Christian. Cicero, for instance, condemns usury and various forms of merchant activity, although admittedly not with the same venom as our Patristic Fathers. See Cicero, *Cicero on Moral Obligation*, p. 92.
46. Baldwin notes that, in the broadest sense, *turpe lucrum* included all forms of greediness, and was almost synonymous with avarice. In a narrower sense, it was often connected with such crimes as simony, usury and price profiteering. On some occasions it was distinguished from usury and referred to immoral gains generally from exorbitant prices. See J. Baldwin, 'The Medieval Theories of Just Price: Romanists, Canonists, and Theologians in the Twelfth and Thirteenth Centuries', *Transactions of the American Philosophical Society*, 49, part 4, 1959, pp. 32–33.
47. Ibid., p. 39.
48. Ibid., p. 14.
49. Ibid., p. 38.
50. Ibid., p. 14.
51. Ibid.
52. Ibid., p. 37.
53. Ibid., p. 14.
54. G. O'Brien, *An Essay on Medieval Economic Teachings* (London: A.M. Kelley, 1920), p. 45.
55. Cf. B. Gordon, *Economic Analysis Before Adam Smith* (London: Macmillan, 1975), pp. 91–96.
56. O'Brien, *An Essay on Medieval Economic Teachings*, p. 44.
57. Ibid., p. 59.
58. Ibid., p. 61. Pelagius also courted controversy with his denial of the transmission of original sin and thus his claim that baptism is not necessary for freedom from original sin. Pelagius' views here were one of Augustine's principal targets and he had Pelagius' doctrine declared heretical in 416.
59. O'Brien, *An Essay on Medieval Economic Teachings*, p. 60.
60. Ibid., p. 60.
61. Ibid., p. 52.
62. R. De Roover, *San Bernardino of Siena and Sant'anonino of Florence: The Two Great Economic Thinkers of the Middle Ages* (Boston: Baker Library, 1967), p. 9.
63. J. Locke, *Two Treatises of Civil Government* (London: J.M. Dent, 1924), p. 129.

64. Locke's argument may have performed a service in the end of counter-
    ing the anti-commercialism of his religious predecessors, but it was, in the
    end, rather a poor argument. For it rested on the mistaken belief that the
    accumulation of money was, although crucially different with regards
    the perishability of what is stored, just the same kind of activity as the
    accumulation of apples. Ibid., p. 139.
65. R.C. Solomon, 'Business Ethics', in P. Singer (ed.), *A Companion to Ethics*
    (Cambridge: Blackwell, 1991), p. 355.
66. E. Roll, *A History of Economic Thought* (London: Faber and Faber, 1938), pp.
    47–48.
67. Baldwin, *The Medieval Theories of Just Price*, p. 15.
68. Ibid., pp. 262–266.
69. Rufinas realised that a closer analysis of economic processes of buying and
    selling was necessary in order to apply a more intelligent moral evaluation
    of these functions. Ibid., p. 39.
70. Ibid., p. 39.
71. Ibid., p. 63.
72. John Baldwin notes the tendency of economic historians to paint the eco-
    nomic life of the Middle Ages as a pre-capitalist age. See Baldwin, *The Medieval
    Theories of the Just Price*, p. 6.
73. William Addis, for instance, writes, 'Scholastic philosophy . . . was the philos-
    ophy of Aristotle interpreted, developed and reconciled with the Christian
    faith.' W. Addis, *A Catholic Dictionary Containing Some Account of the Doc-
    trine, Discipline, Rites, Ceremonies, Councils and Religious Orders of the Catholic
    Church* (London: Virtue, 1916), p. 732.
74. Aristotle, *The Politics* (1946). Bk. 1 Ch. ix, [1257b], p. 25.
75. Though it should also be noted that Aquinas suggests in *De Regime Primcipum*
    that increase in affluence through fertility rather than commerce was more
    admirable. See O'Brien, *An Essay on Medieval Economic Teachings*, p. 147.
76. T. Aquinas, *Summa Theologica*, 2a 2ae, 77, art. 4 (London: Blackfriars, 1963).
    See page 15 of Pribram, *A History of Economic Reasoning*, for a brief discussion
    of the Medieval condemnation of the pursuit of gain for its own sake.
77. Ibid., 2a 2ae, 77.
78. Baldwin, *The Medieval Theory of the Just Price*, p. 58.
79. Ibid., p. 65.
80. R.H. Tawney, *Religion and the Rise of Capitalism* (London: John Murray, 1926),
    p. 34.
81. Baldwin, *The Medieval Theory of the Just Price*, p. 48.
82. Ibid., p. 67.
83. Cited in B.W. Dempsey, 'Just Price in a Functional Economy', *American
    Economic Review*, 1935, 25, p. 483.
84. O'Brien, *An Essay on Medieval Economic Teachings*, p. 154.
85. Leo XIII, *Rerum Novarum*, 'On the Conditions of the Working Classes'
    (Sydney: Pauline Books, 2000 [1891]), para. 20.
86. See C.L. Degler, *Out of Our Past* (New York: Harper Colophon, 1984), p. 8.
87. B. Franklin, *The Means and Manner of Obtaining Virtue* (Harmondsworth:
    Penguin, 1986), pp. 28–29.
88. Quoted in A.R. Humphreys, *The Augustan World: Society, Thought, and Letters
    in Eighteenth Century England* (New York: Harper & Row, 1963), p. 88.

89. Jean Jacques Rousseau, *The Social Contract and Other Later Political Writings*, ed. and trans. V. Gourevitch (Cambridge: Cambridge University Press, 1997), pp. 261–262.

90. Cited in F.E. Manuel, *Prophets of Paris* (New York: Harper & Row, 1965), p. 200.

91. C. Fourier, *Harmonian Man: Selected Writings of Charles Fourier*, Edited with an Introduction by M. Poster (New York: Anchor Books, 1971), p. 150.

92. Ibid., p. 160.

93. O. Wilde, 'The Soul of Man Under Socialism', *De Profundis: and Other Writings* (Harmondsworth: Penguin, 1986), p. 25.

94. Fourier, *Harmonian Man*, p. 257.

95. Ibid., pp. 257–258.

96. Ibid., p. 237.

97. See R.D. Laing and A. Esterton, *Sanity, Madness and the Family* (London: Penguin, 1964); and D. Cooper, *The Death of the Family* (London: Allen Lane, 1971).

98. Fourier, *Harmonian Man*, p. 17.

99. Ibid., p. 203.

100. Ibid., p. 153.

101. Ibid., p. 155.

102. If it is hard to tell just how much Marx's views on capitalism and its over-coming in communism rest on his philosophy of history, or how much the latter arises as a justifying rationalisation for views which emerge from Marx's horror at the operations of contemporary society, it is easier to see Fourier's philosophy of history as a kind of ornament to views which, as he said, emerge from his vow against commerce. Certainly, his views are weird enough: not only is the universe biological, but the planets engage in constant sexual intercourse. Further, history has a cycle of 80 000 years, the first 40 000 of which is a period of 'ascending vibrations', the latter of 'descending vibrations'. Capitalism emerges at the end of the cycle of ascending vibrations, and its demise inaugurates the period of descending vibrations in which the 'passionate intensity' of the earth will increase, and to such a degree that sea water will become a delicious lemonade flavour, and all human pests be transmogrified into their opposite, so that anti-fleas replace fleas, anti-lions, lions, and so forth.

103. Fourier, *Harmonian Man*, p. 181.

104. K. Marx, *Capital*, Vol. 1 (Moscow: Progress Publishers, 1954), p. 44.

105. Ibid., p. 151.

106. Ibid., p. 150.

107. K. Marx, *Manifesto of the Communist Party* (Peking: Foreign Languages Press, 1970), p. 31.

108. Ibid., p. 40.

109. P. Larkin, 'Toads', in *The Less Deceived* (Hessle, Yorkshire: The Marvell Press, 1955), pp. 32–33.

110. K. Marx, 'The German Ideology', in R.C. Tucker (ed.), *The Marx-Engels Reader*, 2nd edition (New York: W.W. Norton and Co, 1972), p. 160.

111. Marx, *Capital*, Vol. 1, pp. 711–712.

112. Ibid., p. 714.

113. Ibid., p. 604.

114. K. Marx and F. Engels, *Manifesto of the Communist Party* (Peking: Foreign Languages Press, 1970), pp. 33–34.
115. Marx, *Capital*, Vol. 1, p. 238.
116. Ibid., p. 557.
117. K. Marx, *Capital*, Vol. 3 (Moscow: Progress Publishers, 1959), p. 827.
118. Cited in I. Meszaros, 'Conceptual Structure of Marx's Theory of Alienation', in E.K. Hunt and J.G. Schwartz (eds) *A Critique of Economic Theory* (Harmondsworth, Middl.: Penguin, 1971), p. 169.
119. Meszaros, ibid., p. 320.
120. K. Marx, *Grundrisse: Foundations of the Critique of Political Economy*, trans. M. Nicolaus (Harmondsworth, Middl.: Penguin, 1973), p. 488.
121. Marx, *Capital*, Vol. 1, p. 555.
122. Rather like Bishop Usher (1581–1656) who calculated the exact date when the world was created, using evidence from the Bible. See Bishop J. Usher, *The Annals of the World* (Green Forest A.R.: Master Books, 2003).
123. Curiously after his visit in 1920 Bertrand Russell thought Lenin's state rather more like Plato's *Republic*. See B. Russell, 'Impressions of Bolshevik Russia', *Collected Papers of Bertrand Russell*, Vol. 15 (London: Routledge, 2000), p. 180.
124. Marx, *Capital*, Vol. 1, p. 88.
125. K. Marx, *Critique of the Gotha Programme* (Peking: Foreign Languages Press, 1976), pp. 17–18.
126. S. Lukes, *Marxism and Morality* (Oxford: Clarendon Press, 1985), p. 141.
127. Ellen Meiksins Wood too argues vigorously that capitalism involves a transition to a new and entirely *sui generis* form of society. She rejects the idea that capitalism evolves out of pre-existing social and psychological propensities. See E.M. Wood, *Democracy against Capitalism* (Cambridge: Cambridge University Press, 1995), pp. 114–115.
128. A.N. Whitehead, *Process and Reality* (New York: Free Press, 1979), p. 39.
129. Quoted by D. Winch, 'Adam Smith: Scottish Moral Philosopher as Political Economist', in H. Mizuta and C. Sugiyama (eds), *Adam Smith: International Perspectives* (New York: St. Martin's Press, 1993), p. 85.
130. A. Smith, *An Inquiry into the Nature and Causes of the Wealth of Nations*, Vol. 1, R.H. Campbell and A.S. Skinner (General Editors), Textual Editor, A. Todd (Textual Editors) (Oxford: Clarendon Press, 1976), II.iii.31, p. 343.
131. Ibid., p. 25.
132. Ibid., pp. 26–27.
133. A. Smith, *The Theory of Moral Sentiments*, in D.D. Raphael and A.L. Macfie (eds) (Oxford: Clarendon Press, 1976), p. 215.
134. T. Reid, *Essays on the Active Powers of Man* (New York and London: Garland Press, 1977 [1788]), p. 223.
135. T. Hobbes, *Leviathan* (Harmondsworth, Middl.: Penguin, 1968 [1651]), p. 300.
136. Smith, *An Inquiry into the Nature and Causes of the Wealth of Nations*, p. 456.
137. S. Johnson, *The Adventurer*, no. 67, quoted in D. Winch, *Riches and Poverty: An Intellectual History of Political Economy in Britain, 1750–1834* (Cambridge: Cambridge University Press, 1996), p. 57.
138. G.B. Hill (ed.), *Boswell's Life of Johnson*, Vol. III (Oxford: Clarendon Press, 1934), p. 56.
139. Adam Smith is dismissive of the moral economy of the general populace. He writes: 'The popular fear of engrossing and forestalling may be compared

to the popular terrors and suspicions of witchcraft.' Smith, *The Wealth of Nations*, p. 534.

140. Smith, *Wealth of Nations*, Vol. 2, Bk. ix, Ch. IV, p. 687.
141. His aim appears to be the distinction between commerce and gambling.
142. J. Lalor, *Money and Morals: A Book for Our Times* (London: John Chapman, 1852), p. 80.
143. From D. Hume, *David Hume: Writings on Economics*, edited and introduced by E. Rotwein (London: Nelson, 1955), pp. xxx–xxxi.
144. 'The growth of intellectual abilities and of abstract thought characterizes the age in which money becomes more and more a mere symbol, neutral as regards its intrinsic value.' G. Simmel, *The Philosophy of Money*, 2nd enlarged edition, D. Frisby (ed.) (London: Routledge, 1990), p. 152.
145. Marx and Engels, *The Manifesto of the Communist Party*, p. 36. See also Karl Marx, 'The Eighteenth Brumaire of Louis Bonaparte', in R.C. Tucker (ed.), *The Marx-Engels Reader*, 2nd edition (New York: W.W. Norton and Co., 1978), pp. 594–617.
146. Humphreys, *The Augustan World: Society, Thought, and Letters in Eighteenth Century England*, p. 87.
147. Smith, *The Theory of Moral Sentiments*, p. 86.
148. Smith, *Wealth of Nations*, I.i, p. 23.
149. Ibid., p. 22.
150. Smith, *The Theory of Moral Sentiments*, pp. 184–185.
151. E. Rothschild, *Economic Sentiments: Adam Smith, Condorcet, and the Enlightenment* (Cambridge, Mass.: Harvard University Press, 2001), p. 75.
152. R. Nozick, *Anarchy, State and Utopia* (New York: Basic Books, 1975).
153. Ibid., pp. 150–153.
154. Ibid., p. 160.
155. Ibid., pp. 155–164. For a useful discussion, see J. Wolff, *Robert Nozick: Property, Justice and the Minimal State* (Cambridge: Polity, 1991).
156. Nozick, *Anarchy, State and Utopia*, pp. 164–231. In these sections he attacks both Rawls' theory of justice and Amartya Sen's normative work.
157. Ibid., pp. 16–64.
158. Ibid., p. 163.
159. Cf. Wolff, *Robert Nozick*, pp. 79–83.
160. Nozick, *Anarchy, State and Utopia*, p. 331.
161. R. Nozick, 'Coercion', in S. Morgenbesser, P. Suppes and M. White (eds), *Philosophy, Science and Method: Essays in Honor of Ernest Nagel* (New York: St. Martin's Press, 1969), pp. 440–472.
162. Indeed, such systems might be more desirable on utilitarian grounds.

3 The profit-motive and morality

1. R. Chandler, 'The Long Good-bye', in *The Chandler Collection*, Vol. 2 (London: Picador, 1983), p. 403.
2. A. Smith, *An Inquiry into the Nature and Causes of the Wealth of Nations*, Vol. 1, R.H. Campbell and A.S. Skinner (General Editors), A. Todd (Textual Editor) (Oxford: Clarendon Press, 1976), p. 145.

3. As H. Grotius wrote in *The Law of War and Peace* (New York: Bobbs-Merrill, 1962), 'Acts are of a mixed character, either in their essential elements or through the association of another act. Thus [for instance] if I knowingly buy a thing at a price higher than it is worth, and give the excess in price to the seller, the act will be partly gift, partly purchase' (p. 346). It requires drawing distinctions within the marketplace to generate *varieties* of profit-motives.

4. Cited in G. Dostaler and B. Maris, 'Dr. Freud and Mr. Keynes on Money and Capitalism', in J. Smithin (ed.), *What is Money?* (London: Routledge, 2000), p. 249.

5. Aristotle, *The Politics of Aristotle*, trans. E. Barker (Oxford: Clarendon Press, 1946), Bk. I, Ch. IX, [1257b28], p. 27.

6. Cited in E. Rothschild, *Economic Sentiments: Adam Smith, Condorcet and the Enlightenment* (Cambridge, Mass.: Harvard University Press, 2001), p. 21.

7. J.K. Galbraith, *Economics in Perspective: A Critical History* (Boston: Houghton Miflin Company, 1987), p. 15.

8. Interestingly in the *Gorgias* [494–495], Callicles has a conception of pleasure in which endlessness is a constitutive feature. Callicles suggests that the pleasure of living depends on maintaining the largest possible influx. See Plato, *The Collected Dialogues*, in E. Hamilton and H. Cairns (eds) (Princeton: Princeton University Press, 1961).

9. The Medieval thinkers later suggested that action undertaken for the sake of wealth has no limits. See J. Baldwin, 'The Medieval Theories of Just Price: Romanists, Canonists, and Theologians in the Twelfth and Thirteenth Centuries', *Transactions of the American Philosophical Society*, 49, part 4, 1959, p. 13.

10. Chandler, *The Chandler Collection*, p. 253.

11. Interestingly Keynes used a similar argument, but in his case it involved banana-farmers. See J.M. Keynes, *A Treatise on Money*, Vol. 1 (London: Macmillan, 1930), p. 176.

12. Plato, 'The Republic', in *The Dialogues of Plato*, Vol. II, trans. B. Jowett, 4th edition (Oxford: Clarendon Press, 1953), [373e].

13. Plato, *The Laws*, translated with an introduction by T.J. Saunders (Harmondsworth, Middl.: Penguin, 1970), Bk. X, [918d–918e].

14. A. Cowley, 'Of Avarice' [1665], in J. Gross (ed.), *The Oxford Book of Essays* (Oxford: Oxford University Press, 1991), pp. 27–28.

15. Ibid., p. 27.

16. Baldwin, *Transactions of the American Philosophical Society*, p. 48.

17. R. De Roover, *San Bernadino of Sienna and Sant'antonino of Florence: The Two Great Economic Thinkers of the Middle Ages* (Boston: Baker Library, 1967), p. 14.

18. From A.A. Long, *Epictetus: A Stoic and Socratic Guide to Life* (Oxford: Oxford University Press, 2002), p. 115.

19. As might be expected, in the Medieval context one often finds economics discussed in connection with avarice. Medieval moralists, not to speak of saints like Sant'antonino (Saint Anthony), tended to frown upon acquisitiveness because they felt it lead to sin and perdition. See De Roover, *San Bernardino of Siena and Sant'anonino of Florence*, p. 2.

20. See C.J. Berry, *The Idea of Luxury: A Conceptual and Historical Investigation* (Cambridge: Cambridge University Press, 1994), p. 67.

21. See E. Roll, *A History of Economic Thought* (London: Faber and Faber, 1938).

22. Berry, *The Idea of Luxury*, p. 45.

23. A. Schopenhauer, 'Human Nature', in *The Essays of Arthur Schopenhauer*, trans. T.B. Saunders (Mila, U.S.A.: Kessing Press, 2004), p. 8.

24. Ibid.

25. Ibid.

26. D. Wood, *Medieval Economic Thought* (Cambridge: Cambridge University Press, 2002), p. 102.

27. Baldwin, *Transactions of the American Philosophical Society*, p. 14.

28. R. Leachman, *A History of Economic Ideas* (New York: Harper & Row, 1959).

29. Pribram suggests that Oresme was the first theologian to deal in a separate treatise with a specific economic problem, the original nature of economies and their debasement. See K. Pribram, *A History of Economic Reasoning* (Baltimore: The Johns Hopkins University Press, 1983), p. 24.

30. Cited in Grotius, *The Law of War and Peace*, p. 347.

31. Ibid., Bk. II, Ch. XII, 'On Contracts'.

32. J.W. Baldwin, *Masters, Princes and Merchants: The Social Views of Peter the Chanter and His Circle* (Princeton, N.J.: Princeton University Press, 1970), p. 265.

33. *Acts* (5: 1–11).

34. De Roover, *San Bernadino of Sienna and Sant'antonino of Florence*, p. 14.

35. K. Marx, *Early Writings [1], Economic and Philosophical Manuscripts*, trans. T.B. Bottomore (London: Watts, 1963), p. 191.

36. Cicero, 'On Duties' III, *Cicero, Selected Works* (Harmondsworth, Middl.: Penguin, 1974), pp. 166–167.

37. T. Carlyle, 'The Gospel of Mammonism', in *Past and Present* (London: Champan and Hall, 1843), p. 126.

38. Janet Coleman, 'Property and Poverty', in J.H. Burns (ed.), *The Cambridge History of Medieval Political Thought* (Cambridge: Cambridge University Press, 1988), p. 631.

39. Carlyle, *Past and Present*, p. 235.

40. R.H. Tawney, *Religion and the Rise of Capitalism* (London: John Murray, 1926), p. 35.

41. See Pribram, *A History of Economic Reasoning*, pp. 103–114.

42. See T. Lynch, 'Temperance, Temptation and Silence', *Philosophy*, April 2001, 76, no. 296, pp. 251–269.

43. D. Wiggins, 'Truth Invention and the Meaning of Life', in *Needs, Values, Truth: Essays in the Philosophy of Value*, 3rd edition (Oxford: Clarendon Press, 1998), p. 100.

44. A. Flew, 'The Profit Motive', *Ethics*, 1976, 86, p. 314.

45. Ibid.

46. Bishop Butler, *Fifteen Sermons Preached at the Rolls Chapel and A Dissertation upon the Nature of Virtue*, W.R. Matthews (ed.) (London: G. Bell & Sons Ltd., 1949 [1726]), pp. 251–252.

47. See M. Weber, *The Protestant Ethic and the Spirit of Capitalism* (London: Unwin, 1930 [1904/1905]).

48. The philosopher C.A. Mace (1894–1971), discussing motivation, recalls Dostoevsky's remark that no one ever acts from a single motive. He rejects the suggestion that the only effective incentive is the pay packet, because this

overlooks 'the complexity of this motive'. See C.A. Mace, *Selected Papers* (London: Methuen, 1973), pp. 178–179.

49. J.J. Mansbridge notes: 'This is a sustained argument in favour of the idea that people often take account of both other individuals' interest and the common good when they decide what constitutes a "benefit" that they want to maximize', Introduction to J.J. Mansbridge (ed.), *Beyond Self-Interest* (Chicago: University of Chicago Press, 1990), p. x.

50. R. Nozick, *Anarchy, State and Utopia* (New York: Basic Books, 1975), pp. 28–33.

51. J. Elster, 'Selfishness and Altruism', in J.J. Mansbridge (ed.), *Beyond Self-Interest* (Chicago: University of Chicago Press, 1990), p. 49.

52. Butler, *Fifteen Sermons Preached at the Rolls Chapel and A Dissertation upon the Nature of Virtue*, p. 166.

53. Ibid., Sermon XI, p. 173.

54. Some commentators seem to want to read Butler in a way that renders him a proponent of the invisible hand. Private interest might well lead to public good, but it is not private vice that is at work here. See the readings in J. Mainsbridge, *Beyond Self-Interest* where he is lumped with Hume and Smith. See p. 322, fn.2. While he concedes that self-interest and benevolence can coincide he is not an advocate for self-interest as vice having good social consequences.

55. Flew, *Ethics,* p. 316.

56. Cited in ibid., p. 315.

57. Ibid., p. 316.

58. Ibid., p. 319.

59. See B. Gordon, *Economic Analysis before Adam Smith* (London: Macmillan, 1975), p. 88.

60. G. O'Brien, *An Essay on Medieval Economic Teaching* (London: A.M. Kelley, 1920), p. 154.

61. L. Jardine, *Worldly Goods* (London: Macmillan, 1996), pp. 324–325.

62. J. Wesley, 'The Use of Money', in *The Works of John Wesley*, Vol. VI (Grands Rapids, Michigan: Zondervan Publishing House, 1872), pp. 124–136.

63. Ibid., pp. 127–128.

64. Ibid., p. 126.

65. Ibid., p. 130.

66. Ibid., p. 127.

67. Ibid.

68. Ibid., p. 128.

69. Ibid., p. 129.

70. Ibid.

71. E.J. Mishan, *The Costs of Economic Growth* (Harmondsworth, Middl.: Penguin, 1967), p. 205.

72. D. Hume, 'Of the Dignity or Meanness of Human Nature', in J. Gross (ed.), *The Oxford Book of Essays* (Oxford: Oxford University Press, 1991), pp. 85–86.

73. Flew, p. 313.

74. Ibid.

75. Ibid., p. 317. Though he immediately makes a point that if we are to worry about motives then we should look to the envy which is 'much nastier' than self-interest.

76. Ibid., p. 319.

77. G. Trease, *The Condottieri: Soldiers of Fortune* (London: Thames and Hudson, 1970), p. 150. Another mercenary from the period, Federigo, once claimed that '[K]eeping faith is better still and worth more than all the gold in the world' (Trease, *The Condottieri*, p. 317).

4 Usury and the ethics of interest-taking

1. O'Callaghan's view on usury can be found in a pamphlet entitled 'Usury or Interest: Proved to be Repugnant to the Divine and Ecclesiastical Laws and Destructive to Civil Society' (1824). It is said to have inspired William Cobbett in his opposition to usury.
2. bookwritht@bogvaerker.dk. Note that usury here included the taking of interest not only in loans of money but also in loans of fungible goods, such as wine or grain.
3. As we shall see, such possibilities are realised in many contemporary Islamic banking practices.
4. See E. Kerridge, *Usury, Interest and the Reformation* (London: Ashgate, 2002), who stresses the importance of this distinction. See also C.J. Mews and I. Abraham, 'Usury and Just Compensation: Religious and Financial Ethics in Historical Perspective', *Journal of Business Ethics*, 2006, 72, no. 1, pp. 1–15.
5. E. Roll, *A History of Economic Thought* (London: Faber and Faber, 1938), p. 50.
6. Langholm notes that most scholars no longer view usury as analogical with just price. See O. Langholm, *The Aristotelian Analysis of Usury* (Oslo: Universitetsforlaget Press, 1984), p. 51.
7. Cited in K. Marx, *Capital*, Vol. 1 (Moscow: Progress Publishers, 1954), pp. 555–556.
8. Concerns over usury can be found in the Ancient World too. The Athenian political reformer Solon in 594 BC cancelled all private and public debts. The Lex Genucia (340 BC) of the Roman Republic prohibited any interest-taking whatsoever; and by the fifth century AD the Church had already forbidden clerics and the laity from loaning at interest.
9. Dante, *The Inferno: A New Verse Translation*, trans. R. Pinsky (New York: Farrar, Straus and Giroux, 1994), Canto xi.
10. K. Lindskoog, *Dante's Divine Comedy* (Mercer: Mercer University Press, 1997), pp. 111–112.
11. Concern with the fate of their souls was a continual source of anxiety for businessmen of the period. Many on their deathbeds would order restitution to those from whom they had collected interest. See R. Heilbroner, *The Making of Economic Society*, 4th edition (New Jersey: Prentice Hall, 1972), p. 48.
12. Cato, 'On Agriculture', cited in T. Divine, *Interest: An Historical and Analytical Study in Economics and Modern Ethics* (Milwaukee: Marquette University Press, 1959), p. 21.
13. See B. Nelson, *The Idea of Usury: From Tribal Brotherhood to Universal Otherhood* (Chicago: University of Chicago Press, 1969).
14. O'Brien, *An Essay on Medieval Economic Teachings* (London: A.M. Kelley, 1920), p. 175.
15. Ibid.

16. R. De Roover, 1955, pp. 175–176. De Roover adds: 'With this decision, scholastic economics, which had emphasized usury so much, received its death blow' (p. 176). Well, perhaps. But it is interesting that when Father O'Callaghan repudiated such directions on the basis of fundamental Church Doctrine, the Church refused to make explicit the grounds for this directive.

17. Saint Ambrose writes: 'He fights without force of arms who demands usury: he wreaks vengeance on the enemy who is an exactor of usury from the foe. Therefore where there be a right of war, there also is a right of usury.' See Kerridge, *Usury, Interest and the Reformation*, p. 17.

18. Aristotle, *The Politics of Aristotle*, trans. E. Barker (Oxford: Clarendon Press, 1946), Bk. 1, [1258b], pp. 28–29.

19. Ibid., p. 29.

20. Aquinas, *Summa Theologica* (London: Blackfriars, 1963), 2a 2ae, 78, 1 ad.5.

21. O'Brien (*An Essay on Medieval Economic Teachings*, pp. 176–177) even suggests that Aquinas' account was universally accepted by all the theologians of the fourteenth and fifteenth centuries and thus '[t]o quote later writings is imply to repeat in different words the conclusions at which Aquinas arrived'.

22. W. Shakespeare, 'The Merchant of Venice', in S. Barnet (ed.), *The Complete Signet Classic Shakespeare* (New York: Harcourt, Brace Jovanovich). Act 1, Scene 3, line 133.

23. O. Langholm, *The Legacy of Scholasticism: Antecedents of Choice and Power* (Cambridge: Cambridge University Press, 1998), pp. 62–63.

24. As Langholm makes the point, money is consumed in use and therefore has no use separate from its substance and hence no use-value. Langholm, *The Legacy of Scholasticism*, p. 63.

25. The term 'fungible', which is fundamentally a legal notion, comes from the Latin *fungi vice* 'to take the place of'. So in jurisprudence it refers to cases where a thing which is the subject of an obligation need not be satisfied by that very thing, but simply by another thing of the same class. To this fundamental sense we have added the ideas of being consumed in use and being estimated by weight, number or measure, examples being wine, corn and money. See J. Burke (ed.), *Jowitt's Dictionary of English law*, Vol. 1 A–K (London: Sweet and Maxwell, 1977), p. 841.

26. A. Gray, *The Development of Economic Doctrine* (London: Longmans, 1931), pp. 55–57. It is worth noting that Catholic thinkers were still using the distinction in the twentieth century. In Canon 1543 promulgated by Benedict XV in 1917, it was argued that fungible goods should not be subject to any increase. See A. Birnie, *The History and Ethics of Interest* (London: William Hodge & Company, 1952), pp. 10–11.

27. From the Medieval morality play *Dives and Pauper*. See D. Wood, *Medieval Economic Theory* (Cambridge: Cambridge University Press, 2002), pp. 75–76.

28. Marx, *Capital*, pp. 555–556.

29. Langholm, *The Legacy of Scholasticism*, p. 65.

30. See T. Negishi, *History of Economic Theory* (Amsterdam: North-Holland, 1989), pp. 6–7. There were in fact many more concerns. For a comprehensive discussion, see J.T. Noonan, *The Scholastic Analysis of Usury* (Cambridge, Mass.: Harvard University Press, 1957).

31. For Giles of Rome's discussion of this argument, see O. Langholm, *Economics in the Medieval Schools: Wealth, Exchange, Value, Money, and Usury According to the Paris Theological Tradition, 1200–1350* (Leiden: EJ Brill, 1992), pp. 310–311.
32. Cited in G. Clark, 'Commerce, Culture and the Rise of English Power', *The Historical Journal*, 2006, 49, no. 4, p. 1241.
33. See J.W. Baldwin, *Masters, Princes and Merchants: The Social Views of Peter the Chanter and His Circle* (Princeton, N.J.: Princeton University Press, 1970), p. 301.
34. Langholm, *Economics in the Medieval Schools*, p. 56.
35. Birnie, *The History and Ethics of Interest*, p. 25.
36. Neither did the twentieth-century Catholic philosopher Jacques Maritain who saw it as a reprehensible collusion with evil, since the personnel of the Church had ignored completely what the Church has taught for centuries. See J. Maritain, 'A Society without Money', *Review of Social Economy*, 1985, 43, no. 1, pp. 73–83.
37. See Noonan, *The Scholastic Analysis of Usury*, pp. 209–210.
38. See R. De Roover, *San Bernardino of Siena and Sant'antonino of Florence: The Two Great Economic Thinkers of the Middle Ages* (Boston: Baker Library, 1967), p. 31.
39. H. Grotius, *The Law of War and Peace* (New York: Bobbs-Merrill, 1962), p. 367.
40. Roll, *A History of Economic Thought*, p. 61.
41. Our discussion of the metaphysical basis of the Islamic position on interest draws on N.A. Saleh's work, *Unlawful Gain and Legitimate Profit in Islamic Law: Riba, Gharar and Islamic Banking* (Cambridge: Cambridge University Press, 1986).
42. Ibid., p. 13.
43. Ibid., p. 14.
44. Ibid., pp. 35–36.
45. See J.B. Sauer, 'Metaphysics and Economy – The Problem of Interest. A Comparison of the Practice and Ethics of Interest in Islamic and Christian Cultures', *International Journal of Social Economics*, 2002, 29, no. 1/2, p. 99. Sauer's reference is J.K. Sundaram, 'Riba: Interest, Usury or Surplus?', *Journal of Alternative Political Economy*, January 1999, 1, no. 1, p. 44.
46. A.R. Jonsen and S. Toulmin, *The Abuse of Casuistry: A History of Moral Reasoning* (Berkeley: University of California Press, 1988).
47. De Roover, *San Bernardino of Siena and Sant'antonino of Florence*, p. 34.
48. For a detailed discussion of the *Mohatra*, see M.G. Hutchison, 'Contribution of the School of Salamanca to Monetary Theory as a Result of the Discovery of the New World', in L.S. Moss and C.K. Ryan (eds), *Economic Thought in Spain* (Aldershot, Hants: Edward Elgar, 1993). Hutchison has an extensive discussion of usury in M.G. Hutchison, *Early Economic Thought in Spain 1177–1740* (London: Allen and Unwin, 1978).
49. From A.E. Monroe (ed.), *Early Economic Thought* (Cambridge, Mass.: Harvard University Press, 1930), p. 105.
50. J. Bentham, 'A Defence of Usury' [1787], in W. Stark (ed.), *Jeremy Bentham's Economic Writings* (London: George Allen and Unwin, 1952), p. 158.
51. G. Harkness, *John Calvin: The Man and his Ethics* (New York: Abingdon Press, 1958), p. 206. Calvin continues: 'The reasoning of St Ambrose and of Chrysotom, that money does not beget money, is in my judgement too superficial.

What does the sea beget? What does the land? I receive income from the rental of a house. Is it because money grows there? The earth produces things from which money is made, and the use of a house can be bought for money. And is not money more fruitful in trade than in any other form of possession one can mention? Is it lawful to let a farm, requiring a payment in return, and unlawful to receive any profit from the use of money?' Harkness, *John Calvin*, p. 206. O'Brien (*An Essay on Medieval Economic Teachings*, p. 181) suggests that both San Bernardino of Sienna and San Antonino of Florence had made similar claims about the productivity of capital.

52. Roll, *A History of Economic Thought*, p. 53. See also Tawney, *Religion and the Rise of Capitalism* (London: John Murray, 1926), p. 106.
53. A.R.J. Turgot, 'Reflexions sur la Formation et la Distribution des Richesses', in Monroe (ed.), *Early Economic Thought*, p. 367.
54. Bentham, *Jeremy Bentham's Economic Writings*, p. 132.
55. Cf. H.J. Davenport, *The Economics of Alfred Marshall* (New York: A.M. Kelley, 1965 [1935]), p. 439.
56. See Sauer, *International Journal of Social Economics*, pp. 97–118.
57. A. Smith, *An Inquiry into the Nature and Causes of Wealth*, Vol. 1, R.H. Campbell and A.S. Skinner (General Editors), A. Todd (Textual Editor) (Oxford: Clarendon Press, 1976), p. 113.
58. Mews and Abraham, *Journal of Business Ethics*, p. 5.
59. 'On the question of the justification of interest, the trumpet of the economist gives forth an uncertain sound. The average textbook tends to ignore this aspect of the subject. It takes the rightness of interest for granted. But surely we are entitled to ask for some proof of this. Has the capitalist a claim to his interest on the same ground that the labourer has a claim to his wages?', Birnie, *The History and Ethics of Interest*, p. 20.
60. Karl Pribram, in his *History of Economic Reasoning*, cites only three that were of interest to the neo-classical marginalist tradition. He writes: 'Three partly conflicting theories of interest were of primary importance within the framework of marginalism: the productivity theory, which reflected the scholastic substance concept of capital; the "abstinence" theory, which conceived of interest as a reward for deferred consumption and was a heritage of utilitarianism; and the *agio* theory, which was based on the idea of time preference in favor of present, as opposed to future goods. The last theory was the most refined outcome of hypothetical reasoning.' K. Pribram, *A History of Economic Reasoning* (Baltimore: The Johns Hopkins University Press, 1983), p. 326.
61. Birnie, *The History and Ethics of Interest*, p. 20.
62. J.A. Schumpeter, *History of Economic Analysis* (London: Routledge, 1994), p. 656.
63. Cf. ibid., p. 660.
64. Marshall writes: 'The sacrifice of present pleasure for the sake of future, has been labelled *abstinence* by economists . . . . Since, however, the term is liable to be misunderstood, we may with advantage avoid its us, and say that the accumulation of wealth is generally the result of postponement of enjoyment or a *waiting* for it . . .' (cited Davenport, *The Economics of Alfred Marshall*, p. 451).

65. One explanation for the shift might be that time is now viewed as being owned by the lender rather than God.
66. Birnie, *The History and Ethics of Interest*, p. 16.
67. These figures are drawn from the United States Consumers Union Fact Sheet on Payday Loans, <http://www.consumersunion.org.finance/paydayfact.htm>
68. Cf. M.A. Stegman and R. Faris, 'Payday Lending: A Business Model that Encourages Chronic Borrowing', *Economic Development Quarterly*, February 2003, 17, no. 1, pp. 8–32.
69. This moral distinction between consumption and investment loans has been invoked by a number of writers. For instance, in Sir Sayeed's School of Islam *riba* was interpreted as 'the primitive form of money-lending when money was advanced by Marx in *Capital*, volume three draws a related distinction between usurer's capital and interest-bearing capital.
70. H. Belloc, 'On Usury', *Essays of a Catholic* (Rockford, I.L.: Tan Books & Publishers, Inc., 1992), p. 15.
71. R. Ruston, 'Does it Matter What We Do with Our Money?', *Priests and People*, May 1993, pp. 171–177.
72. Cited in Langholm, *Economics in the Medieval Schools*, p. 197.
73. See Sauer, *International Journal of Social Economics*, p. 111.
74. S.A. Ahmad, *Economics of Islam (A Comparative Study)* (Lahore: Muhammed Ashraf, 1958), p. 21. See the discussion in W.A.M. Visser and A. MacIntosh, 'A Short Review of the Historical Critique of Usury', *Accounting, Business and Financial History*, 1998, 8, no. 2, pp. 175–189.
75. Saleh, *Unlawful Gain and Legitimate Profit in Islamic Law*, pp. 36–37.
76. Marx writes: 'The mere death of his cow may render the small peasant incapable of renewing his reproduction on its former scale. He then falls into the clutches of the usurer, and once in the usurer's power he can never extricate himself.' *Capital*, Vol. 3 (Moscow: Progress Publishers, 1959), p. 599.
77. The economist Eugen Bohm-Bawerk (1851–1914) ascribed original productivity only to nature and labour and defined the reward for these factors in terms of their contribution to the discounted value of the future production. His theory attributed the existence of interest as a general category to the combined effects of time preferences and the productivity of investments. See Pribram, *A History of Economic Reasoning*, p. 328.
78. Plato, 'Republic', in *The Dialogues of Plato Vol. II*, 4th edition, trans. B. Jowett (Oxford: Clarendon Press, 1953), [555e–556a], pp. 422–423.
79. We find similar sentiments expressed in the colloquial term for handcuffs or manacles, 'darbies', in honour of a well-known sixteenth-century usurer by the name of Derby, or in the Italian term for predatory lenders, *strozzini*, which literally means stranglers.
80. In addition to these distinctive harms that can be sheeted home to the interest – taking itself, there are also *generic* harms that are associated with any commercial activity. For instance, the borrower might find him or herself in financial trouble because of poor decision-making or miscalculation. But this applies to any commercial contract, not just those that apply to the sale of money.
81. Bentham, *Jeremy Bentham's Economic Writings*, p. 159.
82. For the full list, see Harkness, *John Calvin*, p. 207.
83. See, for instance, Ruston, *Priests and People*, p. 179.

84. Calvin writes: 'For if we wholly condemn usury, we impose tighter fetters on the conscience than God himself.' Harkness, *John Calvin*, p. 20.
85. Birnie, *The History and Ethics of Interest*, p. 13.
86. K. Marx, *Grundrisse: Foundations of the Critique of Political Economy*, trans. M. Nicolaus (Harmondsworth, Middl.: Pelican Books, 1973), pp. 850–851.
87. Bentham writes: 'Among the Romans, till the time of Justinian, we find it as high as 12 per cent: in England, so late as the time of Hen. VIII, we find it at 10 per cent: succeeding statutes reduced it to 8, then to 6, and lastly to 5, where it stands at present. Even at present in Ireland it is at 6 per cent; and in the West-Indies at 8 per cent; and in Hindostan, where there is no rate limited by law, the lowest customary rate is 10 or 12. At Constantinople, in certain cases, as I have been well informed, thirty per cent is a common rate. Now, of all these widely different rates, what one is there, that is intrinsically more proper than another?' Bentham, *Jeremy Bentham's Economic Writings*, p. 132.
88. M.J. Radin, *Contested Commodities* (Cambridge, Mass.: Harvard University Press, 1996), pp. 123–130.
89. See Mews and Abraham, *Journal of Business Ethics*, pp. 1–15.
90. M. Yunus, 'Is Grameen Bank Different From Conventional Banks?', August, 2006, <http://www.grameen-info.org/bank/Gbdifferent.htm>
91. The Grameen Bank's approach emphasises the creation of enabling conditions in which every human being may have the opportunity to carve out dignified ways of living for herself/himself. The Grameen Bank views its loans as a means to gain command over resources. United Nations Educational, Scientific and Cultural Organisation, *Education and Poverty Eradication – Grameen Bank*, <http://www.unesco.org/education/poverty/grameen.shtml>
92. For a sense of the contemporary relevance of this, see a recent report in the Boston Globe on medical loans. Christopher Rowland, *Boston Globe*, 'Patients piling medical costs on cards', 22 January 2007: 'Peggy Sherry, 50…Patients who "max out" their credit cards because of medical debt "shouldn't be treated the same as someone who buys big-screen TVs," Sherry said. "We're not out buying fur coats on Mastercard and Visa. We're trying to live."'
93. B. Williams, 'Practical Necessity', in *Moral Luck: Philosophical Papers 1973–1980* (Cambridge: Cambridge University Press, 1981), pp. 126–127.
94. Henry Sidgwick writes in *The Methods of Ethics* on just this topic:…where an individual or combination of individuals, has the monopoly of a certain kind of services, the market-price of the aggregate of such services can under certain conditions be increased by diminishing their total amount; but it would seem absurd to say that the social Desert of those rendering the services is thereby increased, and a plain man has grave doubts whether the price thus attained is fair. Still less is it thought fair to take advantage of the transient monopoly produced by emergency: thus, if I saw Croesus drowning and no one near, it would not be held fair in me to refuse to save him except at the price of half his wealth. But if so, can it be fair for any class of persons to gain competitively by the unfavourable economic situation of another class with which they deal?' See H. Sidgwick, *The Methods of Ethics* (New York: Dover, 1966 [1907]), p. 288.

5 The morality of pricing: just prices and moral traders

1. R.G. Collingwood, 'Economics as a Philosophical Science', *Ethics*, 1926, 36, no. 2, p. 174.
2. See also J. Buchanan and G. Tullock, *Calculus of Consent: The Logical Foundations of Constitutional Democracy* (Ann Arbor: University of Michigan, 1963), pp. 267–270.
3. St. Augustine, 'On the Holy Trinity', in P. Schaff (ed.), *Nicene and Post-Nicene Fathers*, Vol. 3 (Peabody, Mass.: Hendrickson Publishers, 1995), p. 169.
4. J. Baldwin, 'The Medieval Theories of Just Price: Romanists, Canonists, and Theologians in the Twelfth and Thirteenth Centuries', *Transactions of the American Philosophical Society*, 1959, 49, no. 4, pp. 18–21, 43, 55.
5. E.P. Thompson, 'The Moral Economy of the English Crowd in the Eighteenth Century', *Past and Present*, 1971, no. 50, pp. 94–140.
6. R. Wells, 'E.P. Thompson, Customs in Common and Moral Economy', *Journal of Peasant Studies*, 1994, p. 278.
7. Quoted in R. Malcolmson, *Life and Labour in England 1700–1780* (London: Hutchinson, 1981), p. 118.
8. G. Rudé, *The Crowd in History: A Study of Popular Disturbances in France England 1730–1848* (New York: John Wiley & Sons, 1964), p. 226.
9. K. Nelson, 'GSK and Boehringer Agree to Generic AIDS Drugs Deal', *The Lancet*, 2003, 362, no. 9401, p. 2074.
10. B. Frey, *Not Just for the Money* (Brookfield, Vt.: Edward Elgar, 1997), pp. 1–2.
11. R. Nozick, *Anarchy State and Utopia* (New York: Basic Books, 1975) and M. Friedman and R.D. Friedman, *Free to Choose: A Personal Statement* (London: Secker and Warburg, 1980).
12. See H.R. Sewall, *The Theory of Value Before Adam Smith* (New York: A.M. Kelley, 1971), p. 19; R. Kaulla, *Theory of the Just Price* (London: George Allen and Unwin, 1940), p. 44; K. Polanyi, 'Aristotle Discovers the Economy', in G. Dalton (ed.), *Primitive, Archaic and Modern Economics: Essays of Karl Polanyi* (Boston: Beacon Press, 1968), pp. 78–115 and G.W. Wilson, 'Economics of the Just Price', *History of Political Economy*, 1975, 7, no. 2, p. 68.
13. See B. Gordon, *Economic Analysis Before Adam Smith: Hesiod to Lessius* (London: Macmillan, 1975), p. 229.
14. Ibid., p. 228.
15. See ibid., p. 158.
16. See ibid., pp. 228–229.
17. Robbins suggests that this interpretation is of recent provenance, beginning with the nineteenth-century German economic historian Roscher. Subsequently, it was picked up by a great many writers. See L. Robbins, *A History of Economic Thought* (Princeton, N.J.: Princeton University Press, 1998), p. 28.
18. H.R. Sewall, *The Theory of Value Before Adam Smith* (New York: A.M. Kelley, 1971), p. 1.
19. In the works of San Bernardino of Siena a distinction is drawn between *virtuositas* (usefulness) and *complacibilitas* (desirability). De Roover suggests that these can be read as objective and subjective utility respectively. He also believes that although the distinction probably originated in the works of the Franciscan Olivi, it was Bernardino's work that popularised the notion. See De Roover Raymond, 'The Concept of the Just

Price: Theory and Economic Policy', *Journal of Economic History*, 1958, 18, pp. 418–438, 18.

20. According to marginal utility theory it is not the total satisfaction from the possession and use of a product that gives it value, it is the satisfaction or enjoyment from the last and least wanted addition to one's consumption that does so.

21. N.S.B. Gras, 'Economic Rationalism in the Late Middle Ages', *Speculum*, 3 July 1933, 8, p. 305.

22. K. Marx, *Capital*, Vol. 1. (Moscow: Progress Publishers, 1954), pp. 48–53, 164–165, 477–478.

23. R.H. Tawney, *Religion and the Rise of Capitalism* (London: John Murray, 1926), p. 36.

24. See for instance, De Roover, *Journal of Economic History*, pp. 418–438; D. Barath, 'The Just Price and the Costs of Production According to St. Thomas Aquinas', *The New Scholasticism*, 1960, 34, pp. 413–430; D. Friedman, 'In Defence of Thomas Aquinas and the Just Price', *History of Political Economy*, 1980, 12, pp. 234–242.

25. See Baldwin, *Transactions of the American Philosophical Society*, p. 58 and B.W. Dempsey, 'Just Price in a Functional Economy', *American Economic Review*, September 1935, 25, pp. 471–486.

26. J.L. Mackie, *Ethics: Inventing Right and Wrong* (Harmondsworth, Middl.: Penguin, 1977), pp. 38–42.

27. This, of course, does not rule out the possibility of ranking goods 'ordinally' in terms of their value to us and for one to view that ordinal ranking as being somehow objective.

28. Whilst those Medieval thinkers committed to the cost-of-production view must, by implication, have been committed to the idea of just price as a unique magnitude, explicit rejections of the notion of a unique magnitude can be found in various Medieval texts. San Bernardino, for instance, explicitly disavows it. See Gordon, *Economic Analysis Before Adam Smith: Hesiod to Lessiu*, p. 234.

29. It is important to note that this is not a convention in the sense that economic agents consciously sit down to work out the correct price by conventional agreement. It is a convention arrived at unintentionally through the market activities of a series of agents.

30. T. Hobbes, *Leviathan* (Harmondsworth, Middl.: Penguin, 1968 [1651]), pp. 198, 207.

31. Baldwin, *Transactions of the American Philosophical Society*, pp. 18–21, 43, 55.

32. J.W. Baldwin, *Masters, Princes and Merchants: The Social Views of Peter the Chanter and His Circle* (Princeton: Princeton University press, 1970), pp. 262–263

33. Baldwin, *Transactions of the American Philosophical Society*, p. 58.

34. The Medieval writers, in the main, accepted the pursuit of wealth as a morally licit activity only when it was undertaken at the service of other ends, such as raising a family. Moneymaking could not be an end-in-itself, for it feeds the 'acquisitive urge which knows no limit but tends to increase to infinity'. See T. Aquinas, *Summa Theologica* (London: Blackfriars, 1963), Vol. 38, 2a 2ae, 77, art. 4. On our model the pursuit of wealth as an end-in-itself can be a morally permissible activity. For a general discussion of the Medieval view, see Baldwin, *Transactions of the American Philosophical Society*, p. 41.

35. It is also worth noting that often one will only be able to distinguish between various action-types *counterfactually*.
36. A. Sen, *Poverty and Famines: An Essay on Entitlement and Deprivation* (Oxford: Clarendon Press, 1981).
37. B. Frey, *Economics as a Science of Human Behaviour*, extended 2nd edition (Kluwer, 1999), p. 172.
38. Of course, this does not exclude the stipendiaries (for whom money is not a primary goal) from the realm of the morally acceptable. Thus the admirable work of those in most non-profit organisations is endorsed alongside that of the accumulator.
39. During the Second World War, the United States imposed a complete price control system on virtually all goods and services. For an account, see J.K. Galbraith, *A Theory of Price Control* (Cambridge, Mass.: Harvard University Press, 1980).
40. J. Bentham, 'Defence of Maximum', in W. Stark (ed.), *Jeremy Bentham's Economic Writings*, Vol. 3 (London: George Allen and Unwin, 1954 [1801]).
41. W. Stark (ed.), 'Introduction', *Jeremy Bentham's Economic Writings*, Vol. 3 (London: George Allen and Unwin, 1954 [1801]), p. 33.
42. 'Governor Announces Toll-free Hot Line to Report on Price Gouging', 19 August 2003, <http://www.govtech.com/gt/articles/64608>.
43. *Price Gouging During Emergencies or Natural Disasters*, Partnership for Civil Justice, Inc. http://www.justiceonline.org/consum/gouging. html, p. 1.
44. Press Release, Office of the Governor, 12 August 1998.
45. Press Release, 6 August 2004. http://ncdoj.com/DocumentStreamerClient? directory=PressReleases/&file-pricegrouge.pdf.
46. 'Profiting from Pain: Where Prescription Drug Dollars Go: A Report by Families USA, July 2002, http://www.familiesusa.org/assets/pdf/PPreport 89.a5.pdf.
47. R. Lee, 'Critics decry escalating HIV/AIDS drug prices', *Washington Blade*, Friday, 16 January 2004, http://www.wahsblade.com/2004.1-16/news/healthnews.critics.cfm.
48. Ibid.

6 Money, commodification and the corrosion of value: an examination of the sacred and intrinsic value

1. S.T. Coleridge, in *Collected Works*, Vol. 6, R.J. White (ed.) (London: Routledge and Kegan Paul, 1972), p. 218, fn. 1.
2. K. Marx, *Capital*, Vol. 1 (Moscow: Progress Publishers, 1954), pp. 132–133.
3. The Catechism of the Catholic Church defines simony as 'the buying and selling of spiritual things'. It suggests that it is 'impossible to appropriate to oneself spiritual goods and behave towards them as their owner or master, for they have their source in God'. The idea is that one can only receive these goods from God without payment. See *The Catechism of the Catholic Church* (Liguori, Missouri: Liguori Publications, 1994), p. 514.
4. 'A Practical Dictionary of Biblical and General Catholic Information', in Rev. P.P. O'Connell (ed.), *The Holy Bible* (London: Virtue & Company, 1956), p. 116.
5. For a discussion of supererogation, see D. Heyd, *Supererogation: Its Status in Ethical Theory* (Cambridge: Cambridge University Press, 1982).

6. Very roughly, this was, in dollar terms, over $1,50,000 – a sum equal in purchasing power to near $4 million today.
7. That this was no idle threat Luther knew already, for his compatriot, John Hus (1369–1415), had been executed for denying the spiritual potency of such indulgence.
8. P. Smith, *The Life and Letters of Martin Luther* (Boston and New York: Houghton Mifflin Co., 1911), p. 92.
9. Ibid., p. 179.
10. In a sense what they have done here is embed the pursuit of money within a framework that would satisfy Aristotle's view on meaningful activities having an end point or *telos*.
11. O. Goldsmith, 'The Traveller', in A. Freidman (ed.), *Collected Works*, Vol. IV (Oxford: Oxford University Press, 1966 [1764]), p. 252.
12. R. Dworkin, *Life's Dominion: An Argument about Abortion and Euthanasia* (London: Harper Collins, 1993), pp. 73–74.
13. For a more detailed account of Kant's views on price and dignity, see A. Walsh, 'Are Market Norms and Intrinsic Valuation Mutually Exclusive?', *Australasian Journal of Philosophy*, December 2001, 79, no. 4, pp. 525–543.
14. Paton suggests that dignity is a technical term that Kant borrowed from the Stoics. See H.J. Paton, *The Categorical Imperative: A Study in Kant's Moral Philosophy* (London: Hutchinson's University Library, 1953), p. 188.
15. In *The Metaphysics of Moral*, Kant explores the thought in terms of his distinction between the noumenal and phenomenal realms. See I. Kant, 'The Doctrine of Virtue', in M. Gregor (ed.), *The Metaphysics of Morals* (Cambridge: Cambridge University Press, 1996), [434], p. 186.
16. Kant subsequently distinguishes between two kinds of price; 'market price' and 'fancy price' (*Affectionspreis*). Market price, he defines as being determined by the universal inclinations and needs of human beings, whereas fancy price is determined by taste and not on any previous need. See Paton, *The Categorical Imperative*, pp. 189–190.
17. I. Kant, *The Metaphysics of Morals*, trans. M. Gregor (Cambridge: Cambridge University Press, 1991), p. 177.
18. Ibid., p. 177.
19. A. Walsh and R. Giulianotti, *Ethics, Money and Sport: This Sporting Mammon* (Oxford: Routledge, 2007), p. 26.
20. K. Marx, 'On the Jewish Question', in D. McLellan (ed.), *Karl Marx: Selected Writings* (Oxford: Oxford University Press, 1977), p. 60.
21. H. Arendt, *The Human Condition* (Chicago: University of Chicago Press, 1958), pp. 165–166.
22. D. Erasmus, *Praise of Folly* (Harmondsworth, Middl.: Penguin, 1971), pp. 127–128.
23. A useful distinction might be drawn at this point between *recognising-as* and *appreciating-as* a commodity: the latter would involve regarding an object's worth as being encapsulated in its price.
24. *Pace* Anderson, who in describing the commodity form, claims that it involves mere use and '[t]o merely use something is to subordinate it to one's own ends without regard for its intrinsic value'. E. Anderson, *Value in Ethics and Economics* (Cambridge, Mass.: Harvard University Press, 1993), p. 144.

25. M.J. Radin, *Contested Commodities* (Cambridge, Mass.: Harvard University Press, 1996), p. 105. Radin describes 'work' (as opposed to 'labour') as being 'incompletely commodified'.
26. See, for instance, B. Brecher, 'Organs for Transplant: Donation or Payment', in R. Gillon (ed.), *Principles of Health Care Ethics* (New York: John Wiley and Sons, 1994), p. 993; R. Chadwick, 'The Market for Bodily Parts: Kant and Duties to Oneself', *Journal of Applied Philosophy*, 1989, 6, no. 2, p. 132; N. Gerrand, 'The Misuse of Kant in the Debate About a Market for Human Body Parts', *Journal of Applied Philosophy*, 1999, 16, no. 1, pp. 59–67.
27. H.J. Paton, *The Moral Law or Kant's Groundwork of the Metaphysics of Morals* (London: Hutchison, 1946), p. 96.
28. I. Kant, *Lectures on Ethics*, trans. L. Infield (New York: Harper & Row, 1963), p. 165.
29. Ibid., p. 165.
30. Cf. J. Andre, 'Blocked Exchanges: A Taxonomy', in D. Miller and M. Walzer (eds), *Pluralism, Justice and Equality* (New York: Oxford University Press, 1995), p. 190.
31. Anderson, *Value in Ethics and Economics*, p. 10.
32. Ibid., p. 143.
33. Ibid., p. 146.
34. Ibid., p. 146.
35. Ibid., p. 151.
36. Ibid., p. 154.
37. Ibid., p. 141.
38. For this non-market menu to be necessary, Anderson must assume that market modes of valuation exclude other modes of valuing.
39. Anderson, *Value in Ethics and Economics*, p. 150.
40. For instance, see J. Burgess, J. Clark and C. Harrison, *Valuing Nature: What Lies Behind Responses to Contingent Valuation Surveys* (London: University College London, 1995). For a useful philosophical discussion of such reactions, see J. O'Neill, 'King Darius and the Environmental Economist', in T. Hayward and J. O'Neill (eds), *Justice, Property and the Environment* (Aldershot, Hants: Avebury Series in Philosophy, 1997), pp. 114–130.
41. Nor do logically possible, but physically impossible, counter-examples disprove the Corrosion Thesis any more than they would in the medical case.
42. M. Walzer, *Spheres of Justice* (New York: Basic Books, 1983), p. 296.

7 Money-measurement as the moral problem

1. O. Wilde, 'Lady Windermere's Fan', in *Oscar Wilde's Plays, Writings and Poems* (London: Dent, 1970), Act III, p. 329. This line is spoken by the alleged cynic Cecil Graham.
2. See D.M. Hausman and M.S. McPherson, *Economic Analysis and Moral Philosophy* (Cambridge: Cambridge University Press, 1996), pp. 9–10.
3. For a useful critical discussion, see E. Anderson, 'Cost–Benefit Analysis, Safety and Environmental Quality', *Value in Ethics and Economics* (Cambridge, Mass.: Harvard University Press, 1993).

4. See G. Becker, *A Treatise on the Family* (Cambridge, Mass.: Harvard University Press, 1981); and R. Posner, *Economic Analysis of Law*, 2nd edition (Boston: Little, Brown, 1977).

5. See E.J. Mishan, *Cost–Benefit Analysis: An Informal Introduction* (London: George Allen and Unwin, 1971), pp. 6–8.

6. O. Wilde, *Oscar Wilde's Plays, Writings and Poems*, p. 329.

7. See, for instance, J. Burgess, J. Clark and C. Harrison, *Valuing Nature: What Lies Behind Responses to Contingent Valuations* (London: University College London, 1995).

8. See E. Anderson, *Value in Ethics and Economics* (Cambridge, Mass.: Harvard University Press, 1993), pp. 190–195.

9. A. Smith, *An Inquiry into the Nature and Causes of the Wealth of Nations*, Vol. 1, R.H. Campbell and A.S. Skinner (General Editors), A. Todd (Textual Editor) (Oxford: Clarendon Press, 1976), pp. 44–45.

10. St. Augustine, *City of God*, Bk. XI, Ch. 16, trans. H. Bettenson (Harmondsworth, Middl.: Penguin Books, 1972), pp. 447–448.

11. See O. Langholm, *Price and Value in the Aristotelian Tradition* (Bergen: Universitetsforlaget, 1979), pp. 86–87.

12. Michael Fogarty notes: 'The Scholastic Writers borrow freely from one another, including the examples which they use to drive their points home. A Worthy Mouse scuttles through several hundred years of chapters on Value: the mouse who is worth in terms of "natural" value than an inanimate thing such as a loaf of bread, but does not have the "use" value that is relevant to justice in the market. The coarser early scholastics talked instead about a louse', 'Appendix: The Scholastic Theory of the Just Wage', M. Fogarty, *The Just Wage* (London: Geoffrey Chapman, 1961), p. 257.

13. See J. Eatwell, M. Milgate and P. Newman (eds), *The New Palgrave: A Dictionary of Economics*, Vol. 3 (London: Macmillan, 1987), pp. 107–113. For a more detailed discussion, see R.L. Meek, *Studies in the Labour Theory of Value*, 2nd edition (London: Lawrence and Wishart, 1973).

14. H. Landreth, *History of Economic Theory: Scope, Method and Content* (Boston: Houghton Mifflin, 1976), pp. 53–54.

15. J.E. Stiglitz, *Economics*, 2nd edition (New York: W.W. Norton and Co, 1993).

16. R. Cooter and P. Rappaport, 'Were the Ordinalists Wrong about Welfare Economics?', *Journal of Economic Literature*, June 1984, XXII, pp. 507–530.

17. Cooter and Rappaport note that '[a] concept that described mental impulses (marginal utility) was replaced by a behaviourist concept (marginal rate of substitution)', Ibid., p. 523.

18. John Broome argues that the things we rank are options rather than values or goods. He may well be correct, but there are times where it seems more natural, from the point of view of ordinary language, to talk of either values or goods and so we shall persist with the use of all of the three (where appropriate) in our discussion. For our purposes herein little hangs on it. See J. Broome, *Ethics out of Economics* (Cambridge: Cambridge University Press, 1999), p. 146.

19. See J. Aldred, 'Cost–Benefit Analysis, Incommensurability and Rough Equality', *Environmental Values*, 2002, 11, pp. 27–47.

20. J. Raz, *The Morality of Freedom* (Oxford: Clarendon Press, 1986), pp. 346–347.

21. J. O'Neill, 'Cost–Benefit Analysis, Rationality and the Plurality of Values', *The Ecologist*, 1996, 26, no. 3, pp. 98–103. It seems that James Griffin was the

first to coin the phrase: in *Well-Being: Its Meaning, Measurement, and Moral Importance* (Oxford: Clarendon Press, 1986), he writes that '[T]here is no single substantive supervalue' (p. 89). Griffin makes the further point that we do not need a supervalue in order to have a scale.

22. For a useful critical discussion, see E. Anderson, *Value in Ethics and Economics.*

23. C.R. Sunstein, 'Incommensurability and Valuation in Law', *Michigan Law Review*, February 1994, 92, no. 4, p. 779. See also M. Adler, 'Incommensurability and Cost–Benefit Analysis', *University of Pennsylvania Law Review*, June 1998, 146, no. 5, p. 1371.

24. See J. Burke (ed.), *Jowitt's Dictionary of English Law*, Vol. 2, 2nd edition (London: Sweet and Maxwell, 1977), p. 1683.

25. Sunstein, *Michigan Law Review*, p. 779.

26. See, for instance, Burgess *et al.*, *Valuing Nature?*

27. It is interesting to note the extent to which the peculiarities of money are employed in defence of the claim that there are incommensurable values. For instance, much of Joseph Raz's discussion of 'constitutive incommensurability' revolves around the problem of whether one should even contemplate the price that one's child will bring. Money-measurement is the datum if you like that is used to convince us that incommensurable values exist. It thus functions at different times as both the evidence for the theory and the *explanandum* to be explained by the theory.

28. For useful surveys of these issues, see John Broome, 'Incommensurable Values', *Ethics out of Economics*, pp. 145–161; and R. Chang (ed.), *Incommensurability, Incomparability and Practical Reason* (Cambridge, Mass.: Harvard University Press, 1997).

29. See R. Chang, 'Introduction', in Chang (ed.), *Incommensurability, Incomparability and Practical Reason.*

30. Ibid., p. 21. In a related manner, some talk of 'pricelessness' involves cases where it is not that the good cannot be given a price but that the price would be a very high one. This we might call, following Chang's example, 'emphatic pricelessness'.

31. James Griffin refers to this as 'trumping': '... any amount of A no matter how small is more valuable than any amount of B, no matter how large'. See Griffin, *Well-being*, p. 83.

32. Here the idea of lexical priority is modelled on the relationship that Rawls ascribes to his two principles of justice. See J. Rawls, *A Theory of Justice*, revised edition (Oxford: Oxford University Press, 1999), pp. 37–38, 53–54.

33. See Chang, *Incommensurability, Incomparability and Practical Reason*, pp. 14–15.

34. K. Marx, *Capital*, Vol. 1 (Moscow: Progress Publishers, 1954), p. 97.

35. Ibid., pp. 163–164.

36. Ibid., p. 180.

37. Aristotle, *Nicomachean Ethics*, trans. Sir D. Ross (London: Oxford University Press, 1969), Bk. V, 5, [1133b3–1133b20], p. 120.

38. Ibid., Bk. V, 5 [1133b20–1134a11], p. 121.

39. Contrast this with the orthodox economic use of the term: 'Moral hazard is defined as actions of economic agents in maximising their own utility to the detriment of others in situations where they do not bear the full consequences

or equivalently do not enjoy the full benefits of their actions due to uncertainty and incomplete or restricted constraints which prevent the assignment of full damages to the agent responsible.' Eatwell *et al.* (eds), *The New Palgrave* pp. 549–551.

40. See S. Freud, *The Interpretation of Dreams,* trans. J. Strachey (New York: Avon Books, 1965), Section IV. See also J. Church, 'Morality and Its Internalized Other', in J. Neu (ed.), *The Cambridge Companion to Freud* (Cambridge: Cambridge University Press, 1991), pp. 209–223.

41. For useful discussions of the difficulties of determining the grounds of irreplaceability claims, see J.N. Martin, 'The Concept of the Irreplaceable', *Environmental Ethics*, Spring, 1979, 1, no. 1, pp. 31–48; and R. Goodin, 'The Ethics of Destroying Irreplaceable Assets', *International Journal of Environmental Studies*, 1983, 21, pp. 55–66.

42. C. Sunstein, 'Incommensurability and Kinds of Valuation', in Chang (ed.), *Incommensurability, Incomparability and Practical Reason*, p. 251.

43. For another example, consider John Foster's discussion of cost–benefit analysis of environmental goods. J. Foster (ed.), 'Environment and Creative Value', *Valuing Nature? Economics, Ethics and Environment* (London: Routledge, 1997). Foster notes (pp. 233–234) that single-axis cost–benefit analysis, as commonly employed, cannot appropriately represent the different values we bring to choice. Although we do engage in weightings of different values in everyday choice, the existence of this practice only provides grounds for what he calls 'weak commensurability' rather than 'strong commensurability' (which involves a single-axis of value). But significantly, he notes of this weak commensurability that it does not mean that the different values so arrayed are substitutable for one another. Again, although the case is described using the language of incommensurability, it is the notion of non-substitutability that does the moral work.

44. C. Fell, *Women in Anglo-Saxon England* (Oxford: Basil Blackwell, 1984), p. 83.

45. W.S. Jevons, *The Theory of Political Economy* (London: Macmillan, 1871), p. 157.

46. See, for instance, P. Samuelson, *Economics*, 10th edition (New York: McGraw-Hill, 1976), pp. 437–438.

47. Cf. M. Sagoff, *Price, Principle and the Environment* (Cambridge: Cambridge University press, 2004). Sagoff argues that economic theory cannot measure the value of environmental goods. The intrinsic value of environmental goods is distinct from the value provided by the market.

48. G. Simmel, *The Philosophy of Money*, 2nd edition (London: Routledge and Kegan Paul, 1990), p. 256.

49. See Sagoff, *Price, Principle and the Environment*.

50. F.H. Knight, *The Ethics of Competition and Other Essays* (New York: Harper, 1935), p. 56.

51. See A. Walsh and T. Lynch, 'The Development of Price Formation Theory and Subjectivism about Ultimate Values', *Journal of Applied Philosophy*, 2003, 20, no. 3, p. 275.

52. See Eatwell *et al.*, *The New Palgrave*, pp. 263–265.

8 The charge of 'economic moralism': might the invisible hand eliminate the need for a morality of money?

1. R. Fullinwider, 'On Moralism', *Journal of Applied Philosophy*, 2005, 22, no. 2, p. 106.
2. B. Brecht, *The Threepenny Opera*, trans. R. Manheim and J. Willet (London: Methuen, 2000), p. 55.
3. Cited in E.R. Canterbury, *The Making of Economics*, 2nd edition (Belmont, CA: Wadsworth, 1980), p. 120.
4. R. Nozick, *Anarchy, State and Utopia* (New York: Basic Books, 1975), p. 19. For further discussions of invisible hand explanations, see C. McMahon, 'Morality and the Invisible Hand', *Philosophy and Public Affairs*, Summer 1981, 10, pp. 247–272; and E. Ullmann-Margalit, 'Invisible Hand Explanations', *Synthese*, October 1978, 39, pp. 263–292.
5. A. Smith, *Theory of the Moral Sentiments*, in D.D. Raphael and A.L. Macfie (eds) (Oxford: Clarendon, 1976), p. 234.
6. It might be argued – as M. Friedman has argued in his 'The Social Responsibility of Business is to Increase its Profits', in *New York Times Magazine*, september 13, 2007 (Reprinted in S. Donaldson and P. Warhane, *Ethical Issues in Business* (New Jersey: Prentice Hall, 1999), pp. 154–159.) – that business managers do have one crucial other-regarding obligation, *viz* that to their shareholders or owners, as they seek to maximise their returns. Such an argument fails to acknowledge that such managers are (i) often (part)owners themselves, and (ii) can hardly be assumed to have such altruistic concerns when they are typically more than ready to abandon such owners for others who promise them higher returns. Further, if in fact such managers are genuinely altruistically concerned with the well-being of others, why only some others (owners)? And if they are altruistic, why not others (such as the owners themselves)? Friedman has got himself into an awful mess. His real ambition would appear to be to morally justify *non*-altruistic market behaviour, though he cannot find a way of doing this without appealing to (some) agents' altruistic concern for others. We suggest that Friedman's case can be better understood, and better explicated, through what we discuss herein as the Mandevillean Conceit.
7. To object that to honour such concerns involves pursuing activities which *aim at* such outcomes is simply to miss the point of the Invisible Hand explanation.
8. We find similar ideas expressed by Samuel Brittan. See S. Brittan, *Capitalism with a Human Face* (Cheltenham: Edward Elgar, 1995), p. 32.
9. This point is not, of course, entirely novel. For a good example of earlier discussions (though not one we eventually endorse), see J.N. Keynes, *The Scope and Method of Political Economy* (London: Macmillan, 1890), pp. 118–135.
10. C.J. Berry, *The Idea of Luxury: A Conceptual and Historical Investigation* (Cambridge: Cambridge University Press, 1994), is an exception.
11. This is where we diverge from Keynes' analysis, for while he allows for multifarious forms of the profit-motive, he contends that for the purposes of abstraction in 'economic science' the purified conception we object to is perfectly sufficient. However, it is not sufficient because the abstracted 'economic science', as Keynes admits, presupposes certain given conditions ('certain limits [set] by law, morality, and public opinion,' p. 125) which can only be

sustained by a profit-motive that *necessarily* includes more than a commitment to maximising personal advantage. We take this point up further when
we discuss (and criticise) *ad hocery* in economic theorising.

12. We mention later Roger Scruton and Nathan Rosenberg as instances of this
claim. For earlier versions of the same thesis, see F.B. Kaye, 'Commentary',
in his edited, B. Mandeville, *The Fable of the Bees*, Vol. 1 (Oxford: Clarendon,
1957); and E. Connan's 'Introduction' to Adam Smith, *An Inquiry into the
Nature and Causes of the Wealth of Nations* (New York: Modern Library Edition, 1937). S. Hollander, *The Economics of Adam Smith* (Toronto: University
of Toronto Press, 1973), p. 35, suggests that Nicolas Barbon better fits the
characterisation than Mandeville.

13. M.M. Goldsmith, *Private Vices, Public Benefits: Bernard Mandeville's Social and
Political Thought* (Cambridge: Cambridge University Press, 1985), p. 124.

14. R.I. Cook, ' "The Great Leviathan of Lechery": Mandeville's Modest Defence
of Public Stews', in I. Primer (ed.), *Mandeville Studies* (The Hague: Martinus
Nijhoff, 1975), p. 29.

15. Kaye, 'Commentary', p. lxix.

16. R. Scruton, *A Dictionary of Political Thought* (London: Pan Books, 1983), p. 234.

17. N. Rosenberg, 'Mandeville', in J. Eatwell, M. Milgate and P. Newman (eds), *The
New Palgrave: A Dictionary of Economics* (London: Macmillan, 1987), p. 298.

18. Mandeville, *The Fable of the Bees*, pp. 36–37.

19. Ibid., p. 369.

20. Kaye goes so far as to suggest that Smith simply *pretended*, for reasons of pro-
priety that his account differed from Mandeville's. Kaye, *The Fable of the Bees*,
fn. 3, p. cxlii.

21. A. Smith, *An Inquiry into the Nature and Causes of the Wealth of Nations*, Vol. 1,
R.H. Campbell and A.S. Skinner (General Editors), A. Todd (Textual Editor)
(Oxford: Clarendon Press, 1976), p. 540.

22. Ibid., pp. 26–27.

23. Ibid., p. 456.

24. Smith, *Theory of the Moral Sentiments*, pp. 184–185.

25. And in place in essentially Rawlsian terms, rather than in the utilitarian terms
to which Mandeville tends to appeal.

26. Smith also defends the idea that immersion in commerce improves at least
some of our virtues. A. Smith, *Lectures on Jurisprudence* (Cambridge: Cambridge
University Press, 1978), pp. 538–539. For an interesting discussion of the
idea that commerce softens our natures (the *'doux commerce'* thesis), see
A. Hirschmann, *The Passions and the Interests: Political Arguments for Capitalism
before Its Triumph* (Princeton: Princeton University Press, 1977).

27. Samuel Johnson, *The Adventurer*, no. 67, quoted in D. Winch, *Riches and
Poverty: An Intellectual History of Political Economy in Britain, 1750–1834*
(Cambridge: Cambridge University Press, 1996), p. 57.

28. Perhaps, as Emma Rothschild has recently argued in her *Economic Sentiments:
Adam Smith, Condorcet, and the Enlightenment* (Cambridge, Mass.: Harvard
University Press, 2001), this reading does Smith an injustice. That may be
so, but what cannot be denied is that he gives more than adequate material
for the avarice-only reading of the profit-motive and for the Mandevillean
Conceit with which it naturally associates; and that he has been taken by
many influential figures – for example, those associated with the Adam Smith

Institute in Britain, and The Leadership Institute in the United States – to be doing precisely this.

29. F. Hutcheson, in D. Gauthier (ed.) *Inquiry into the Original of our Ideas of Beauty and Virtue* (New Jersey: Prentice Hall, 1970), Section III, 'Concerning the immediate motive to virtuous action'. For a useful, if brief, discussion of the relationship between self-interest and selfishness, see A. Flew, 'The Profit Motive', *Ethics*, July 1976, Vol. 86, pp. 312–322.

30. H.J. Paton (ed.), *The Moral Law or Kant's Groundwork of the Metaphysics of Morals* (London: Hutchinson, 1946), p. 102. Cf. Adrian Walsh, 'Are Market Norms and Intrinsic Valuation Mutually Exclusive?', *Australasian Journal of Philosophy*, December 2001, 79, no. 4, pp. 523–543.

31. Mandeville, *The Fable of the Bees*, p. 10.

32. Smith, *Wealth of Nations*, V.i.b.1.

33. Ibid., p. 710.

34. Smith, *The Theory of Moral Sentiments*, pp. 231, 318.

35. Cf. T. Lynch, 'Legitimating Market Egoism: The Availability Problem', *Journal of Business Ethics*, 2008, 83, no. 4, pp. 256–268.

36. Berry, *The Idea of Luxury*, p. 169.

37. Ibid.

38. Smith, *An Inquiry into the Nature and Causes of the Wealth of Nations*, pp. 26–27.

39. K. Marx, *Capital*, Vol. 1 (Moscow: Progress Publishers, 1954), p. 238.

40. Smith, *Wealth of Nations*, Vol. 1, p. 422.

41. Smith, *Theory of the Moral Sentiments*, p. 86.

42. In a related point, the economist Alfred Marshall suggests that although the 'opportunities for knavery' are certainly more numerous than they were in the past, 'there is no reason fro thinking that men avail themselves of a larger proportion of such opportunities than they used to'. He suggests that modern methods of trade require habits of trustfulness and the power to resist temptations to dishonesty. See A. Marshall, *Principles of Economics*, 8th edition (London: Macmillan, 1920), p. 7.

43. It is also, interestingly, the place for corporations, whose existence is, otherwise, somewhat of a mystery given the standard economists' assumption that the price of goods as determined by the market is the most efficient way of adjusting supply to demand. But while market transactions may aim to allocate resources efficiently, they have their own costs in an environment that is not entirely free of lucrepathic temptations. It is to minimise the transaction costs associated with such temptations that firms vertically integrate, thereby removing whole swathes of economic activity from the competitive marketplace. See R.H. Coase, 'The Nature of the Firm', *Economica*, 1937, 6, pp. 386–405.

Bibliography

Addis, W., *A Catholic Dictionary Containing Some Account of the Doctrine, Discipline, Rites, Ceremonies, Councils and Religious Orders of the Catholic Church* (London: Virtue, 1916).

Adler, M., 'Incommensurability and Cost-benefit Analysis', *University of Pennsylvania Law Review*, June 1998, 146, no. 5, pp. 1371–1418.

Ahmad, S.A., *Economics of Islam (A Comparative Study)* (Lahore: Muhammed Ashraf, 1958).

Aldred, J., 'Cost-benefit Analysis, Incommensurability and Rough Equality', *Environmental Values*, 2002, 11, pp. 27–47.

Anderson, E., 'The Ethical Limitations of the Market', *Economics and Philosophy*, 1990, 6, pp. 179–205.

Anderson, E., *Value in Ethics and Economics* (Cambridge, Mass.: Harvard University Press, 1993).

Anderson, W.S. (ed.), *Ballentine's Law Dictionary*, 3rd edition (Rochester, N.Y.: Lawyers Cooperative Publishing, 1969).

Andre, J., 'Blocked Exchanges: A Taxonomy', in D. Miller and M. Walzer (eds), *Pluralism, Justice and Equality* (New York: Oxford University Press, 1995).

Aquinas, T., *Summa Theologica* (London: Blackfriars, 1963).

Arendt, H., *The Human Condition* (Chicago: University of Chicago Press, 1958).

Aristotle, *Nicomachean Ethics*, trans. Sir D. Ross (London: Oxford University Press, 1969).

Aristotle, *Nicomachean Ethics*, trans. R. Crisp (Cambridge: Cambridge University Press, 2000),

Aristotle, *The Politics of Aristotle*, trans. E. Barker (Oxford: Clarendon Press, 1946).

Augustine, S., *City of God*, trans. H. Bettenson (Harmondsworth, Middl.: Penguin Books, 1972).

Augustine, S., 'On the Holy Trinity', in P. Schaff (ed.), *Nicene and Post-Nicene Fathers*, Vol. 3 (Peabody, Mass.: Hendrickson Publishers, 1995), pp. 1–228.

Austin, M.M. and Vidal-Naquet, P., *Economic and Social History of Ancient Greece; An Introduction* (London: B.T. Batsford, 1977).

Baldwin, J., 'The Medieval Theories of Just Price: Romanists, Canonists, and Theologians in the Twelfth and Thirteenth Centuries', Transactions of the *American Philosophical Society*, 1959, 49, no. 4, pp. 5–92.

Baldwin, J.W., *Masters, Princes and Merchants: The Social Views of Peter the Chanter and His Circle* (Princeton: Princeton University Press, 1970).

Barath, D., 'The Just Price and the Costs of Production According to St. Thomas Aquinas', *The New Scholasticism*, 1960, 34, pp. 413–430.

Barnet, S. (ed.), *The Complete Works of William Shakespeare* (New York: Harcourt, Brace, Jovanovich, 1972).

Becker, G., *A Treatise on the Family* (Cambridge, Mass.: Harvard University Press, 1981).

Belloc, H., 'On Usury', in *Essays of a Catholic* (Rockford, I.L.: Tan Books & Publishers, Inc., 1992).

Bentham, J., 'A Defence of Usury' [1787], in W. Stark (ed.), *Economic Writings* (London: George Allen and Unwin, 1952).

Berry, C.J., *The Idea of Luxury: A Conceptual and Historical Investigation* (Cambridge: Cambridge University Press, 1994).

Birnie, A., *The History and Ethics of Interest* (London: William Hodge & Company, 1952).

Brecher, B., 'Organs for Transplant: Donation or Payment', in R. Gillon (ed.), *Principles of Health Care Ethics* (New York: John Wiley & Sons, 1994), pp. 993–1002.

Brecht, B., *The Threepenny Opera*, trans. R. Manheim and J. Willet (London: Methuen, 2000).

Brittan, S., *Capitalism with a Human Face* (Cheltenham: Edward Elgar, 1995).

Broome, J., *Ethics out of Economics* (Cambridge: Cambridge University Press, 1999).

Buchanan, J. and Tullock, G. *Calculus of Consent: The Logical Foundations of Constitutional Democracy* (Ann Arbor: University of Michigan, 1963).

Bunyan, J., *Grace Abounding; and The Life and Death of Mr. Badman* (London: Dent, 1968).

Burgess, J., Clark, J. and Harrison, C., *Valuing Nature: What Lies Behind Responses to Contingent Valuations* (London: University College London, 1995).

Burke, J. (ed.), *Jowitt's Dictionary of English Law*, 2nd edition (London: Sweet and Maxwell, 1977).

Butler, B. 'A Dissertation upon the Nature of Virtue', in W.R. Matthews (ed.), *Fifteen Sermons Preached at the Rolls Chapel and A Dissertation upon the Nature of Virtue* (London: G. Bell & Sons Ltd., 1949 [1726]).

Canterbury, E.R., *The Making of Economics*, 2nd edition (Belmont, C.A.: Wadsworth, 1980).

Carlyle, T., 'The Gospel of Mammonism', in *Past and Present* (London: Champan and Hall, 1843).

Chadwick, R., 'The Market for Bodily Parts: Kant and Duties to Oneself', *Journal of Applied Philosophy*, 1989, 6, no. 2, pp. 129–139.

Chandler, R., 'The Long Good-bye', in *The Chandler Collection,* Vol. 2 (London: Picador 1983).

Ruth, C. (ed.), *Incommensurability, Incomparability and Practical Reason* (Cambridge, Mass.: Harvard University Press, 1997).

Church, J., 'Morality and its Internalized Other', in J. Neu (ed.), *The Cambridge Companion to Freud* (Cambridge: Cambridge University Press, 1991), pp. 209–223.

Cicero, *Cicero on Moral Obligation: A New Translation of Cicero's 'De Officiis'*, trans. J. Higginbotham (Berkeley: University of California Press, 1967).

Cicero, 'On Duties' III, in *Cicero, Selected Works* (Harmondsworth: Penguin, 1974).

Clark, G., 'Commerce, Culture and the Rise of English Power', *The Historical Journal*, 2006, 49, no. 4, pp. 1–13.

Coase, R.H., 'The Nature of the Firm', *Economica*, 1937, 6, pp. 386–405.

Coleman, J., 'Property and Poverty', in J.H. Burns (ed.), *The Cambridge History of Medieval Political Thought* (Cambridge: Cambridge University Press, 1988).

Coleridge, S.T., *Collected Works,* Vol. 6 edited by R.J. White (London: Routledge and Kegan Paul, 1972).

Collingwood, R.G., 'Economics as a Philosophical Science', *Ethics*, 1926, 36, no. 2, pp. 162–185.

Connan, E., ' "Introduction" to Adam Smith', in *An Inquiry into the Nature and Causes of the Wealth of Nations* (New York: Modern Library Edition, 1937).

Cook, R.I., ' "The Great Leviathan of Lechery": Mandeville's Modest Defence of Public Stews', in I. Primer (ed.), *Mandeville Studies* (The Hague: Martinus Nijhoff, 1975).

Cooper, D., *The Death of the Family* (London: Allen Lane, 1971).

Cooter, R. and Rappaport, P., 'Were the Ordinalists Wrong about Welfare Economics?', *Journal of Economic Literature*, June 1984, XXII, pp. 507–530.

Cowley, A., 'Of Avarice' [1665], in J. Gross (ed.), *The Oxford Book Of Essays* (Oxford: Oxford University Press, 1991), pp. 27–28.

Dante, *The Inferno: A new Verse Translation*, trans. R. Pinsky (New York: Farrar, Straus and Giroux, 1994).

Davenport, H.J., *The Economics of Alfred Marshall* (New York: Augustus M. Kelley 1935 [1965]).

Defoe, D., *Moll Flanders* (London: J.M. Dent and Sons, 1930).

Degler, C.L., *Out Of Our Past* (New York: Harper & Row, 1984).

Dempsey, B.W., 'Just Price in a Functional Economy', *American Economic Review*, 1935, 25, pp. 471–486.

De Roover, R., 'The Concept of the Just Price: Theory and Economic Policy', *Journal of Economic History*, 1958, 18, 4, pp. 418–438.

De Roover, R., *San Bernardino of Siena and Sant'anonino of Florence: The Two Great Economic Thinkers of the Middle Ages* (Boston: Baker Library, 1967).

Laertius, D., *The Lives and Opinions of Eminent Philosophers*, trans. C.D. Yonge (London: Henry G. Bone, 1853).

Divine, T.F., *Interest: An Historical and Analytical Study in Economics and Modern Ethics* (Milwaukee: Marquette University Press, 1959).

Dorsch, T.S. (ed.), *Classical Literary Criticism*: Aristotle; *On the Art of Poetry*. Horace; *On the Art of Poetry* (Harmmondsworth: Penguin Books, 1965).

Dostaler, G. and Maris, B., 'Dr. Freud and Mr. Keynes on Money and Capitalism', in J. Smithin (ed.), *What is Money?* (London: Routledge, 2000), pp. 235–256.

Dworkin, R., *Life's Dominion: An argument about Abortion and Euthanasia* (London: Harper Collins, 1993).

Eatwell, J., Milgaten, M. and Newman, P. (ed.), *The New Palgrave Dictionary of Economics* (London: Macmillan, 1987).

Elster, J., 'Selfishness and Altruism', in J.J. Mansbridge (ed.), *Beyond Self-Interest* (Chicago: University of Chicago Press, 1990).

Erasmus, D., *Praise of Folly* (Harmondsworth, Middl.: Penguin, 1971).

Everson, S., *Aristotle on Perception* (Oxford: Clarendon Press, 1997).

Fell, C., *Women in Anglo-Saxon England* (Oxford: Basil Blackwell, 1984).

Flew, A., 'The Profit Motive', *Ethics*, 1976, 86, pp. 312–322.

Fogarty, M., *The Just Wage* (London: Geoffrey Chapman, 1961).

Foster, J., 'Environment and Creative Value', in J. Foster (ed.), *Valuing Nature? Economics, Ethics and Environment* (London: Routledge, 1997), pp. 232–246.

Fourier, C., *Harmonian Man: Selected Writings of Charles Fourier*, edited with an Introduction by M. Poster (New York: Anchor Books, 1971).

Franklin, B., *The Means and Manner of Obtaining Virtue*, Penguin 60s Classics (Harmondsworth: Penguin, 1986).

Freud, S., *The Interpretation of Dreams,* trans. J. Strachey (ed.) (New York: Avon Books, 1965).

Frey, B., *Not Just for the Money* (Brookfield, Vt.: Edward Elgar, 1997).

Frey, B., *Economics as a Science of Human Behaviour*, extended 2nd edition (Dordrecht: Kluwer, 1999).

Friedman, D., 'In Defence of Thomas Aquinas and the Just Price', *History of Political Economy*, 1980, 12, pp. 234–242.

Friedman, M., 'The Social Responsibility of Business is to Increase its Profits', *New York Times Magazine*, 13/09/'70: reprinted in S. Donaldson and P. Warhane, *Ethical Issues in Business* (New Jersey: Prentice Hall, 1999), pp. 154–159.

Friedman, M. and Rose, D., *Free to Choose: A Personal Statement* (London: Secker and Warburg, 1980).

Fullinwider, R., 'On Moralism', *Journal of Applied Philosophy*, 2005, 22, no. 2, pp. 105–120.

Galbraith, J.K., *A Theory of Price Control* (Cambridge, Mass.: Harvard University Press, 1980).

Galbraith, J.K., *Economics in Perspective: A Critical History* (Boston: Houghton Miflin Co., 1987).

Galbraith, J.K., 'A Perfect Crime: Global Inequality', *Daedelus, Journal of the American Academy of Arts and Sciences*, 2002, 131, no. 1, Winter, pp. 11–25.

George, S., *The Debt Boomerang* (London: Pluto Press, 1991).

Gerrand, N., 'The Misuse of Kant in the Debate about a Market for Human Body Parts', *Journal of Applied Philosophy*, 1999, 16, no. 1, pp. 59–67.

Goldsmith, M.M., *Private Vices, Public Benefits: Bernard Mandeville's Social and Political Thought* (Cambridge: Cambridge University Press, 1985).

Goldsmith, O., 'The Traveller' in A. Freidman (ed.), *Collected Works*, Vol. IV (Oxford: Oxford University Press, 1966 [1764]).

Goodin, R., 'The Ethics of Destroying Irreplaceable Assets', *International Journal of Environmental Studies*, 1983, 21, pp. 55–66.

Gordon, B., *Economic Analysis Before Adam Smith* (London: Macmillan 1975).

Gras, N.S.B., 'Economic Rationalism in the Late Middle Ages', *Speculum*, July 1933, 8, 3, pp. 304–312.

Gray, A., *The Development of Economic Doctrine* (London: Longmans, 1931).

Gray, J., *False Dawn: The Delusions of Global Capitalism* (London: Granta, 1998).

Griffin, J. *Well-being: Its Meaning, Measurement, and Moral Importance* (Oxford: Clarendon Press, 1986).

Grotius, H., *The Law of War and Peace* (New York: Bobbs-Merrill, 1962).

Harkness, G., *John Calvin: The Man and His Ethics* (New York: Abingdon Press, 1958).

Haug, W.F., *Critique of Commodity Aesthetics: Appearance, Sexuality and Advertising in Capitalist Society*, trans. R. Bock (Cambridge: Polity, 1986).

Hausman, D.M. and McPherson, M.S., *Economic Analysis and Moral Philosophy* (Cambridge: Cambridge University Press, 1996).

Heilbroner, R., *The Making of Economic Society*, 4th edition (New Jersey: Prentice Hall, 1972).

Heyd, D., *Supererogation: Its Status in Ethical Theory* (Cambridge: Cambridge University Press, 1982).

Hill, G.B. (ed.), *Boswell's Life of Johnson* (Oxford: Clarendon Press, 1934).

Hirschmann, A., *The Passions and the Interests: Political Arguments for Capitalism before Its Triumph* (Princeton: Princeton University Press, 1977).

Hobbes, T., *Leviathan* (Harmondsworth, Middl.: Penguin, 1968 [1651]).

Hobbes, T., *Leviathan*, edited by R. Tuck (Cambridge: Cambridge University Press, 1996 [1651]).

Hollander, S., *The Economics of Adam Smith* (Toronto: University of Toronto Press, 1973).

Hume, D., *Enquiries Concerning the Human Understanding and Concerning the Principles of Morals*, 2nd edition edited by L.A. Selby-Begge (Oxford: Clarendon Press, 1902).

Hume, D., 'Of Money', in E. Rotwein (ed.), *David Hume: Writings on Economics* (Edinburgh: Nelson, 1955).

Hume, D., 'Of the Dignity or Meanness of Human Nature', in J. Gross (ed.), *The Oxford Book of Essays* (Oxford: Oxford University Press, 1991).

Humphreys, A.R., *The Augustan World: Society, Thought, and Letters in Eighteenth Century England* (New York: Harper & Row, 1963).

Hutcheson, F., *Inquiry into the Original of our Ideas of Beauty and Virtue*, edited by D. Gauthier (New Jersey: Prentice Hall, 1970).

Hutchison, M.G., *Early Economic Thought in Spain 1177–1740* (London: Allen and Unwin, 1978).

Hutchison, M.G., 'Contribution of the School of Salamanca to Monetary Theory as a Result of the Discovery of the New World', in L.S. Moss and C.K. Ryan (eds), *Economic Thought in Spain* (Aldershot, Hants: Edward Elgar, 1993), pp. 1–22.

Irwin, T., *Aristotle's First Principles* (Oxford: Clarendon, 1980).

Jardine, L., *Worldly Goods* (London: Macmillan, 1996).

Jevons, W.S., *The Theory of Political Economy* (London: Macmillan, 1871).

Johnson, S., *Poetry and Prose*, edited by M. Wilson (London: Rupert Hart-Davis, 1969).

Jonsen, A.R. and Toulmin, S., *The Abuse of Casuistry: A History of Moral Reasoning* (Berkeley: University of California Press, 1988).

Kant, I., *Lectures on Ethics*, trans. L. Infield (New York: Harper & Row, 1963).

Kant, I., 'The Doctrine of Virtue', in M. Gregor (ed.), *The Metaphysics of Morals* (Cambridge: Cambridge University Press, 1996).

Kaulla, R., *Theory of the Just Price* (London: George Allen and Unwin, 1940).

Kaye, J., *Economy and Nature in the Fourteenth Century: Money, Market Exchange, and the Emergence of Scientific Thought* (Cambridge: Cambridge University Press, 1998).

Kerridge, E., *Usury, Interest and the Reformation* (London: Ashgate, 2002).

Keynes, J.M., *A Treatise on Money*, Vol. 1 (London: Macmillan, 1930).

Keynes, J.M., *Essays in Persuasion* (London: Macmillan, 1931).

Keynes, J.N., *The Scope and Method of Political Economy* (London: Macmillan, 1890).

Knight, F.H., *The Ethics of Competition and Other Essays* (New York: Harper, 1935).

Laing, R.D. and Esterton, A., *Sanity, Madness and the Family* (London: Penguin, 1964).

Lalor, J., *Money and Morals: A Book for Our Times* (London: John Chapman, 1852).

Landreth, H., *History of Economic Theory: Scope, Method and Content* (Boston: Houghton Mifflin, 1976).

Lane, R., *The Market Experience* (Cambridge: Cambridge University Press, 1991).

Langholm, O., *Price and Value in the Aristotelian Tradition* (Bergen: Universitetsforlaget, 1979).

Langholm, O., *The Aristotelian Analysis of Usury* (Oslo: Universitetsforlaget Press, 1984).

Langhorn, O., *Economics in the Medieval Schools: Wealth, Exchange, Value, Money, and Usury According to the Paris Theological Tradition, 1200–1350* (Leiden: EJ Brill, 1992).

Langholm, O., *The Legacy of Scholasticism: Antecedents of Choice and Power* (Cambridge: Cambridge University Press, 1998).

Larkin, P., 'Toads', in *The Less Deceived* (Hessle, Yorkshire: The Marvell Press, 1955).

Leachman, R., *A History of Economic Ideas* (New York: Harper & Row, 1959).

Leo XIII, Pope, *Rerum Novarum*, 'On the Conditions of the Working Classes' (Sydney: Pauline Books, 2000 [1891]).

Lindskoog, K., *Dante's Divine Comedy* (Mercer: Mercer University Press, 1997).

Locke, J., *Two Treatises of Civil Government* (London: J.M. Dent, 1924).

Long, A.A., *Epictetus: A Stoic and Socratic Guide to Life* (Oxford: Oxford University Press, 2002).

Longinus, 'On the Sublime', in T.S. Dorsch (ed.), *Classical Literary Criticism* (Harmondsworth: Penguin, 1965).

Lukes, S., *Marxism and Morality* (Oxford: Clarendon Press, 1985).

Lynch, T., 'Temperance, Temptation and Silence', *Philosophy*, April 2001, 76, no. 296, pp. 251–269.

Lynch, T., 'Legitimating Market Egoism: The Availability Problem', *Journal of Business Ethics*, 2008, 83, no. 4, pp. 256–268.

Mace, C.A., *Selected Papers* (London: Methuen, 1973).

Mackie, J.L., *Ethics: Inventing Right and Wrong* (Harmondsworth, Middl.: Penguin, 1977).

Mandeville, B., *The Fable of the Bees*, edited by F.B. Kaye (Oxford: Clarendon, 1957).

Mansbridge, J.J. (ed.), *Beyond Self-Interest* (Chicago: University of Chicago Press, 1990).

Manuel, F.E., *Prophets of Paris* (New York: Harper & Row, 1965).

Maritain, J., 'A Society without Money', *Review of Social Economy*, 1985, 43, no. 1, pp. 73–83.

Marshall, A., *Principles of Economics*, 8th edition (London: Macmillan, 1920).

Martin, J.N., 'The Concept of the Irreplaceable', *Environmental Ethics*, Spring 1979, 1, no. 1, pp. 31–48.

Marx, K., *Capital*, Vol. 1. (Moscow: Progress Publishers, 1954).

Marx, K, *Capital*, Vol. 3 (Moscow: Progress Publishers, 1959).

Marx, K., *Early Writings [1], Economic and Philosophical Manuscripts*, trans. T.B. Bottomore (London: Watts, 1963).

Marx, K., *Grundrisse: Foundations of the Critique of Political Economy* trans. M. Nicolaus (Harmondsworth, Middl.: Penguin, 1973).

Marx, K., 'On the Jewish Question', in D. McLellan (ed.), *Karl Marx: Selected Writings* (Oxford: Oxford University Press, 1977).

Marx, K., 'The Eighteenth Brumaire of Louis Bonaparte', in R.C. Tucker (ed.), *The Marx-Engels Reader*, 2nd edition (New York: W.W. Norton and Co, 1978).

Marx, K. and Engels, F., *The Communist Manifesto* (Peking: Foreign Languages Press, 1970).

McMahon, C., 'Morality and the Invisible Hand', *Philosophy and Public Affairs*, Summer, 1981, 10, pp. 247–272.

Meek, R.L., *Studies in the Labour Theory of Value*, 2nd edition (London: Lawrence and Wishart, 1973).

Meikle, S., 'Aristotle on Money', in J. Smithin (ed.), *What is Money?* (London: Routledge, 2000), pp. 157–173.

Meszaros, I., 'Conceptual Structure of Marx's Theory of Alienation', in E.K. Hunt and J.G. Schwartz (eds), *A Critique of Economic Theory* (Harmondsworth, Middl.: Penguin, 1971), pp. 124–171.

Mews, C.J. and Abraham, I., 'Usury and Just Compensation: Religious and Financial Ethics in Historical Perspective', *Journal of Business Ethics*, 2006, 72, no. 1, pp. 1–15.

Mill, J.S., *Principles of Political Economy: With Some of the Applications to Social Philosophy* (New York: A.M. Kelley, 1973 [1848]).

Mishan, E.J., *The Costs of Economic Growth* (Harmondsworth, Middl.: Penguin, 1967).

Mishan, E.J., *Cost-Benefit Analysis: An Informal Introduction* (London: George Allen and Unwin, 1971).

Monroe, A.E. (ed.), *Early Economic Thought* (Cambridge, Mass.: Harvard University Press, 1930).

Moss, L.S. (ed.), *Economic Thought in Spain: Selected Essays of Marjorie Grice-Hutchison* (Brookfield, Vermont.: Edward Elgar, 1993).

Negishi, T., *History of Economic Theory* (Amsterdam: North-Holland, 1989).

Nelson, B., *The Idea of Usury: From Tribal Brotherhood to Universal Otherhood* (Chicago: University of Chicago Press, 1969).

Nelson, K., 'GSK and Boehringer agree to Generic AIDS Drugs Deal', *The Lancet*, 2003, 362, no. 9401, p. 2074.

Noonan, J.T., *The Scholastic Analysis of Usury* (Cambridge, Mass.: Harvard University Press, 1957).

Nozick, R., 'Coercion', in S. Morgenbesser, P. Suppes, and M. White (eds), *Philosophy, Science and Method: Essays in Honor of Ernest Nagel* (New York: St. Martin's Press, 1969), pp. 440–472.

Nozick, R., *Anarchy, State & Utopia* (New York: Basic Books, 1975).

O'Brien, G., *An Essay on Medieval Economic Teachings* (London: A.M. Kelley, 1920).

O'Connell, Rev. P.P. (ed.), *The Holy Bible* (London: Virtue & Company, 1956).

O'Neill, J., 'Cost-Benefit Analysis, Rationality and the Plurality of Values', *The Ecologist*, 1996, 26, no. 3, pp. 98–103.

O'Neill, J., 'King Darius and the Environmental Economist', in T. Hayward and J. O'Neill (eds), *Justice, Property and the Environment* (Aldershot, Hants: Avebury Series in Philosophy, 1997), pp. 114–130.

Parks, T., *Medici Money: Banking, Metaphysics and Art in Fifteenth-Century Florence* (London: Profile books Ltd, 2006).

Paton, H.J., *The Moral Law or Kant's Groundwork of the Metaphysics of Morals* (London: Hutchinson, 1946).

Paton, H.J., *The Categorical Imperative: A Study in Kant's Moral Philosophy* (London: Hutchinson's University Library, 1953).

Plato, 'The Republic', in *The Dialogues of Plato*, Vol. II, trans. B. Jowett, 4th edition (Oxford: Clarendon Press, 1953), pp. 321–428.

Plato, 'The Sophist', in *The Dialogues of Plato*, trans. B. Jowett, 4th edition (Oxford: Clarendon Press, 1953).

Plato, *The Collected Dialogues*, edited by E. Hamilton and H. Cairns (Princeton: Princeton University Press, 1961).

Plato, *The Laws*, translated with an introduction by T.J. Saunders (Harmondsworth, Middl.: Penguin, 1970).

Polanyi, K., 'Aristotle Discovers the Economy', in G. Dalton (ed.), *Primitive, Archaic and Modern Economics: Essays of Karl Polanyi* (Boston: Beacon Press, 1968), pp. 78–115.

Posner, R., *Economic Analysis of Law*, 2nd edition (Boston: Little, Brown, 1977).

Postgate, R. (ed.), *The Conversations of Dr. Johnson* (New York: Taplinger Publishing Company, 1970).

Pribram, K., *A History of Economic Reasoning* (Baltimore: The Johns Hopkins University Press, 1983).

Radin, M.J., *Contested Commodities* (Cambridge, Mass.: Harvard University Press, 1996).

Rawls, J., *A Theory of Justice*, revised edition (Oxford: Oxford University Press, 1999).

Raz, J., *The Morality of Freedom* (Oxford: Clarendon Press, 1986).

Reid, T., *Essays on the Active Powers of Man* (New York and London: Garland Press, 1977 [1788]).

Robbins, L., *An Essay on the Nature and Significance of Economic Science* (London: Macmillan, 1935).

Robbins, L., *A History of Economic Thought* (Princeton, N.J.: Princeton University Press, 1998).

Roll, E., *A History of Economic Thought* (London: Faber and Faber, 1938).

Rosenberg, N., 'Mandeville', in J. Eatwell, M. Milgate and P. Newman (eds) *The New Palgrave: A Dictionary of Economics* (London: Macmillan, 1987), p. 298.

Rothschild, E., *Economic Sentiments: Adam Smith, Condorcet and the Enlightenment* (Cambridge, Mass.: Harvard University Press, 2001).

Rousseau, *The Social Contract and other Later Political Writings*, edited & trans. V. Gourevitch (Cambridge: Cambridge University Press, 1997).

Rudd, N. (ed.), 'Introduction', *Horace: Satires and Epistles. Persius: Satires* (Harmondsworth: Penguin, 1997).

Rudé, G., *The Crowd in History: A Study of Popular Disturbances in France England 1730–1848* (New York: John Wiley & Sons, 1964).

Ruskin, J., *Past and Present* (London: Chapman and Hall, 1847).

Russell, B., 'Impressions of Bolshevik Russia', in R.A Rempel and B. Haslam with the assistance of A. Bone and A.C. Lewis (eds) *Collected Papers of Bertrand Russell*, Vol. 15 (London: Routledge, 2000), pp. 174–198.

Ruston, R., 'Does it Matter What We Do with our Money?', *Priests and People,* May 1993, pp. 171–177.

Sagoff, M., *Price, Principle and the Environment* (Cambridge: Cambridge University Press, 2005).

Saleh, N.A., *Unlawful Gain and Legitimate Profit in Islamic Law: Riba, Gharar and Islamic Banking* (Cambridge: Cambridge University Press, 1986).

Samuelson, P., *Economics*, 10th edition (New York: McGraw-Hill, 1976).

Sauer, J.B., 'Metaphysics and Economy – the Problem of Interest: A comparison of the Practice and Ethics of Interest in Islamic and Christian Cultures', *International Journal of Social Economics*, 2002, 29, no. 1/2, pp. 97–118.

Schofield, M., 'Aristotle on the Imagination', in J. Barnes, M. Schofield and R. Sorabji (eds), *Articles on Aristotle. 4: Psychology and Aesthetics* (London: Duckworth, 1979), pp. 103–132.

Schopenhauer, A., *The Essential Schopenhauer* (London: Unwin Books, 1962).

Schopenhauer, A., 'Human Nature', in *The Essays of Arthur Schopenhauer*, trans. T.B. Saunders (Mila, U.S.A.: Kessing Press, 2004).

Schumpeter, J.A., *History of Economic Analysis*, with a new introduction by M. Perlman (London: Routledge, 1994).

Scruton, R., *A Dictionary of Political Thought* (London: Pan Books, 1983).

Seaford, R., *Money and the Early Greek Mind: Homer, Philosophy and Tragedy* (Cambridge: Cambridge University Press, 2004).

Sen, A., 'Rational Fools: A Critique of the Behavioural Foundations of Economic Theory', *Philosophy and Public Affairs*, 1977, 6, pp. 317–144.

Sen, A., *Poverty and Famines: An Essay on Entitlement and Deprivation* (Oxford: Clarendon Press, 1981).

Sewall, H.R., *The Theory of Value Before Adam Smith* (New York: A.M. Kelley, 1971).

Shakespeare, W., 'The Merchant of Venice', in S. Barnet (ed.), *The Complete Signet Classic Shaksepeare* (New York: Harcourt, Brace Jovanovich), pp. 607–642.

Sidgwick, H., *The Methods of Ethics* (New York: Dover, 1966 [1907]).

Simmel, G., *The Philosophy of Money*, 2nd enlarged edition, D. Frisby (ed.) (London: Routledge, 1990).

Smith, A., *An Inquiry into the Nature and Causes of the Wealth of Nations*, R.H. Campbell and A.S. Skinner (General Editors), A. Todd (Textual Editor) (Oxford: Clarendon Press, 1976).

Smith, A., *Theory of the Moral Sentiments*, edited by D.D. Raphael and A.L. Macfie (Oxford: Clarendon, 1976).

Smith, A., *Lectures on Jurisprudence* (Cambridge: Cambridge University Press, 1978).

Smith, P., *The Life and Letters of Martin Luther* (Boston & New York: Houghton Mifflin Co., 1911).

Solomon, R.C., 'Business Ethics', in P. Singer (ed.), *A Companion to Ethics* (Cambridge: Blackwell, 1991), pp. 354–365.

Sorenson, R., *Blindspots* (Oxford: Clarendon Press, 1988).

Stegman, M.A., and Faris, R., 'Payday Lending: A Business Model that Encourages Chronic Borrowing', *Economic Development Quarterly*, February, 2003, 17, no. 1, pp. 8–32.

Stehr, N., Henning, C. and Weiler, B., W. (eds), *The Moralization of the Markets* (New Brunswick, N.J.: Transaction Publishers, 2006).

Stiglitz, J.E., *Economics*, 2nd edition (New York: W.W. Norton and Co, 1993).

Suetonius, *The Lives of the Twelve Caesars, Caius Caesar Caligula* (Harvard: Loeb Classical Library, 1913 [121AD]).

Sunstein, C.R., 'Incommensurability and Valuation in Law', *Michigan Law Review,* February 1994, 92, no. 4, pp. 779–861.

Tawney, R.H., *Religion and the Rise of Capitalism* (London: John Murray, 1926).

Thaler, R., *The Winner's Curse: Paradoxes and Anomalies of Economic Life* (Princeton, N.J.: Princeton University Press, 1994).

The Catechism of the Catholic Church (Liguori, Missouri: Liguori Publications, 1994), p. 514.

Thompson, E.P., 'The Moral Economy of the English Crowd in the Eighteenth Century', *Past and Present*, February 1971, 50, pp. 94–140.

Titmuss, R., *The Gift Relationship: From Human Blood to Social Policy* (London: George Allen and Unwin, 1970).

Trease, G., *The Condottieri: Soldiers of Fortune* (London: Thames and Hudson, 1970).

Tucker, R. (ed.), *The Marx-Engels Reader*, 2nd edition (New York: W.W. Norton and Co, 1972).

Turgot, A.R.J., 'Reflexions sur la Formation et la Distribution des Richesses', in A.E. Monroe (ed.), *Early Economic Thought* (Cambridge, Mass.: Harvard University Press, 1930), pp. 349–376.

Ullmann-Margalit, E., 'Invisible Hand Explanations', *Synthese*, October 1978, 39, pp. 263–292.

Usher, B.J., *The Annals of the World* (Green Forest AR: Master Books, 2003).

Varro, M.T., *Roman Farm Management: The Treatises of Cato and Varro* (Mila, U.S.A.: Kessinger Publishing, 2004).

Veblen, T., 'The Limitations of Marginal Utility Theory', in D.M. Hausman (ed.), *The Philosophy of Economics* (Cambridge: Cambridge University Press, 1984), pp. 129–142.

Velasquez, M.G., 'Some Lessons and Nonlessons of Casuist History', in T.J. Donaldson and R.E. Freeman (eds), *Business as a Humanity* (New York: Oxford University Press, 1994), pp.184–195.

Visser, W.A.M. and Macintosh, A., 'A Short Review of the Historical Critique of Usury', *Accounting, Business and Financial History*, 1998, 8, no. 2, pp. 175–189.

Walsh, A., 'Are Market Norms and Intrinsic Valuation Mutually Exclusive?', *Australasian Journal of Philosophy*, December 2001, 79, no. 4, pp. 525–543.

Walsh, A., 'The Morality of the Market and the Medieval Schoolmen', *Politics, Philosophy and Economics*, 2004, 3, no. 2, pp. 241–259.

Walsh, A. and Lynch, T., 'The Development of Price Formation Theory and Subjectivism about Ultimate Values', *Journal of Applied Philosophy*, 2003, 20, no. 3, pp. 262–278.

Walsh, A. and Giulianotti, R., *Ethics, Money and Sport* (Oxford: Routledge, 2007).

Walzer, M., *Spheres of Justice* (New York: Basic Books, 1983).

Weber, M., *The Protestant Ethic and the Spirit of Capitalism* (London: Unwin, 1930 [1904/1905]).

Wells, R., 'E.P. Thompson, Customs in Common and Moral Economy', *Journal of Peasant Studies*, 1994, 21, no. 2, 263–307.

Wesley, J., 'The Use of Money', in T. Jackson (ed.), *The Works of John Wesley*, Vol. VI (Grands Rapids, Michigan: Zondervan Publishing House, 1872), pp. 124–136.

Whitehead, A.N., *Process and Reality* (New York: Free Press, 1979).

Wiggins, D., 'Truth Invention and the Meaning of Life', in *Needs, Values, Truth: Essays in the Philosophy of Value*, 3rd edition (Oxford: Clarendon Press, 1998), pp. 87–138.

Wilde, O., 'Lady Windermere's Fan', in H. Pearson (ed.), *Oscar Wilde's Plays, Writings and Poems* (London: Dent, 1970).

Wilde, O., 'The Soul of Man Under Socialism', in H. Pearson (ed.), *De Profundis and Other Writings* (Harmondsworth: Penguin, 1986).

Williams, B., 'Practical Necessity', in *Moral Luck: Philosophical Papers 1973–1980* (Cambridge: Cambridge University Press, 1981).

Wilson, G.W., 'Economics of the Just Price', *History of Political Economy*, 1975, 7, no. 2, pp. 56–74.

Winch, D., 'Adam Smith: Scottish Moral Philosopher as Political Economist', in H. Mizuta and C. Sugiyama (eds), *Adam Smith: International Perspectives* (New York: St. Martin's Press, 1993).

Winch, D., *Riches and Poverty: An Intellectual History of Political Economy in Britain, 1750–1834* (Cambridge: Cambridge University Press, 1996).

Wolff, J., *Robert Nozick: Property, Justice and the Minimal State* (Cambridge: Polity, 1991).

Wood, D., *Medieval Economic Thought* (New York: Cambridge University Press, 2002).

Wood, E.M., *Democracy against Capitalism* (Cambridge: Cambridge University Press, 1995).

Yunus, M., 'Is Grameen Bank Different From Conventional Banks?', August, 2006, http://www.grameen-info.org/bank/Gbdifferent.htm.

Web Addresses:

The United States Consumers Union Fact Sheet on Payday Loans, http://www.consumersunion.org.finance/paydayfact.htm

Muhammad Yunus, *Is Grameen Bank Different From Conventional Banks?*, August 2006, http://www.grameen-info.org/bank/Gbdifferent.htm

United Nations Educational, Scientific and Cultural Organisation, *Education and Poverty Eradication – Grameen Bank*, http://www.unesco.org/education/poverty/grameen.shtml

Governor Announces Toll-free Hot Line to Report on Price Gouging', August 19, 2003, <http://www.govtech.com/gt/articles/64608>

Press Release, August 6, 2004. http://ncdoj.com/DocumentStreamerClient?directory=PressReleases/&file-pricegrouge.pdf

Price Gouging During Emergencies or Natural Disasters, Partnership for Civil Justice, Inc. http://www.justiceonline.org/consum/gouging.html

'Profiting from Pain: Where Prescription Drug Dollars Go: A Report by Families USA, July 2002, http://www.familiesusa.org/assets/pdf/PPreport89.a5.pdf

Ryan Lee, 'Critics decry escalating HIV/AIDS drug prices', *Washington Blade*, Friday, January 16, 2004, http://www.wahsblade.com/2004.1-16/news/healthnews.critics.cfm

Index

In this index notes are indicated in italics, enclosed in parenthesis, following the page number; E.g. abstinence, 223(*n.64*). Works are entered in italics.